McCall's
new book of
NEEDLE
CRAFTS

McCall's
new book of
NEEDLE
CRAFTS

quilting appliqué
patchwork needlepoint
embroidery

The Editors of McCall's
Needlework & Crafts Magazines

W. H. ALLEN · LONDON
A Howard & Wyndham Company
1983

CONTENTS

CONTENTS

PREFACE

Welcome to the world of needle arts, a world where beauty can be created with a needle, a bit of material, some thread—plus the magical element of imagination.

We have gathered together a tempting array of projects in quilting, patchwork, applique, embroidery and needlepoint, with step-by-step instructions for each color illustration. In addition, handsome examples of work by many, many, creative people are shown to illustrate the endless variety of needle arts. Many of our projects are just right for beginners: a bright butterfly pillow, all in cross-stitch; another pillow in easy patchwork; a nostalgic motto pictured on open-mesh needlepoint; a handsome appliqued wall hanging; a whimsical quilt for a lucky child.

And for everyone—beginner and expert—we offer a wealth of technical information in each chapter. We tell you what materials and equipment you'll need and how to get started. There are pages and pages of fascinating stitches, patterns and ideas to kindle your imagination and help you design personal works of art. We also give you a glimpse of needlework history and show traditional forms you may not have seen before. So learn, create, enjoy!

THE BIG
QUILTING

REVIVAL

Revival? Quilting has been around ever since the Crusaders wore padded quilting under their armor — and even long before that. A craft born of necessity, it has blossomed through many periods of popularity, often for very practical reasons. But today, quilting seems to satisfy the craving for a decorative handicraft that is also a personal form of expression. It can be applied to almost anything made of fabric. It is, after all, just two or more layers stitched together in a decorative fashion. The techniques are easy to master; if you can propel a needle through fabric or do straight machine stitching, you can quilt. And the satisfaction of choosing colors and fabrics, of creating your own design or adding your individual touch to a time-honored one, far outweigh the amount of effort involved.

QUILTING

THE HISTORY OF

The origins of quilting, like those of most needlework, are vague and indistinct, obscured by the veil of centuries of time. The basic construction of layers of fabric, with or without some form of padding between them, has been used as protection and insulation for the human body, and as covering for both beds and floors, for thousands of years. The oldest example known to exist is a carpet found on the floor of a tomb, which was probably made during the first century B.C. Curiously enough, the quilted pattern in the center of that carpet consists of rows of spirals joined by smaller scrolls between the large circles—a very familiar type of pattern still in extensive use today.

From there the record skips to the Early Middle Ages, when two heavy outer fabrics, quilted with layers of soft padding between them, were worn as body armor by the armies of William the Conqueror and the Crusaders. Even when armor of chain or plate was introduced, quilted armor was still worn underneath it, as protection against cold weather and chafing as well.

Quilted armor probably inspired the use of quilted bedcovers, which are mentioned in inventories and household accounts of the eleventh, twelfth and thirteenth centuries. And when, in the fourteenth century, a drastic change in the climate of Western Europe resulted in winters of unprecedented, lacerating coldness, the quilted bedcover became, quite literally, a necessity of life. The first quilting frames were invented, and anything that would add warmth to the bedcovers made on them was employed for padding; moss, feathers and even grass were used as well as lambs' wool. Quilted clothing for everyday use, also inspired by the armor, must have appeared about this time; evidence exists that quilted garments were worn at least as early as the beginning of the fifteenth century.

The outer layers of sturdy linen or canvas and the various materials used as padding for quilted armor were simply stitched together with strong thread in straight lines. Protection was the prime concern, and there was no need or desire for any kind of decorative stitching. But as quilting came to be used for clothing and household articles, it was seen that the stitching made a kind of surface decoration, and quilting stitches were soon designed to be more decorative. Scrolls and ornamental motifs were stitched on caps and gloves and shoes as well as on bedcovers, and by the end of the fourteenth century, bedcovers—or quilts—were being decorated with elaborate stitched designs depicting knights and kings and castles, as well as horses, ships and flowers.

In Southern Europe, where winters were less rigorous, quilting was regarded solely as a means of embellishment. Here trapunto, or corded quilting, came into use because the added warmth of padding wasn't needed. A cord inserted in a channel between two stitched layers of fabric served to outline or emphasize part of a design. In another version, the second layer of fabric was dispensed with, and the cord simply stitched to the wrong side of a single layer of fabric, giving the same raised effect.

This was all very well for the sunny South of Europe, but in the North quilting was serious business, depended upon as vital protection against the inclement weather. And in Britain and Holland it became a kind of business, developing into something akin to a cottage industry. The quilting became more intricate, and as the level of craftsmanship rose, quilts—or "bed furniture" as they were called—became the most-prized possessions of many families. As such, they were passed down from generation to generation, gaining status with every change of ownership. Many were embroidered with pious mottoes and some were decorated with appliques, but they all differed from later American versions in that the top was always a single piece of fabric—and so, usually, was the backing.

Thus, born of necessity but gradually developing into a folk art, quilts became so important that a kind of mystique grew up around them. The female members of a family started quilt-making at an early age, and thereafter spent a major portion of their time at the quilting frame. Every young girl was intent on having a

A typical Bridal Quilt, always the showpiece of a betrothed girl's dower chest. Here, printed cotton fabrics are appliqued on white blocks. No two prints are identical, but all have a similar soft red background. A block in the bottom row is embroidered with the words "Priscilla Halton's Work, 1849."

full quota of intricate quilts in her dowry. When she became formally engaged, her Bridal Quilt was begun, with appropriate ceremony. This would be the most elaborate quilt in her collection, and friends and relatives would be invited over to help her finish it.

Like so many other customs, this one crossed the ocean with the pilgrim families who emigrated to America. They often could bring very little, but bed furniture was always included in anticipation of the hard winters ahead. The hard winters came, and were—somehow— survived; the unwelcoming land was eventually conquered. But the settlers were bone-poor, and had no way of replacing even essential possessions when they wore out. Everything was repaired as well as possible, and re-used again and again—"recycled" as we say today. This was certainly true of the family quilts, which were patched up with scraps of fabric from old clothing as long as they held together. After many repairs, the quilt top looked more like patchwork than solid fabric. So again, necessity was the mother of handsome invention, because these worn-out and patched-up quilts were the forerunners of the beautiful and inventive patchwork patterns of the eighteenth and nineteenth centuries.

More and more settlers arrived, and the bitter struggle for survival in the New World gradually gave way to economic prosperity. Commerce between Europe and America was brisk, and trade routes to the Near East and the Orient were established. Imported fabrics became available, at least on the Atlantic seaboard, but the thrifty Colonial housewife still made use of every scrap of fabric. The idea of making bedcovers of patchwork instead of solid pieces of fabric took hold, and now, having at least a little more choice, the industrious quiltmakers began to aspire to attractive color combinations and arrangements.

As the New England colonies and parts of the South became more populated, the more adventurous spirits of the day continued their pioneering push westward. Once again, the family quilts went with them, and in barren new homes became even more firmly entrenched as basic furnishing. Exposure to new lands, new experiences and new emotions gave the women new ideas, which found expression in their continued quiltmaking. A patchwork top became a kind of chronicle, reflecting what was happening to a family. And since these hard-working pioneer women had to spin and weave their own fabrics, old garments became the major source of patchwork materials. Cut up and used for patches only after years of service and being "handed down," the well-used fabrics were also a kind of history of family life.

In addition to recording family history, quilts became an important part of social life. The custom of friends and relatives gathering to help make a marriage quilt developed into the quilting bee, which was a major social event in the life of the small communities. They were often engagement parties, but no special occasion was needed for friends and relatives to gather for a day of stitching and gossip followed by an evening of eating and socializing after the men joined the party.

As imported fabrics became more plentiful back in the Colonies, they also became more expensive, and a textile industry began to evolve. Before long, cloth was being produced in a wide selection of colors at lower prices than the bolts that came by sailing ship commanded. Coincidentally or not, applique work became popular about this time, and the practice of applying decorative pieces of one fabric over another gave a new dimension to quilts. True, it was considered an extravagant waste of fabric by many still-thrifty settlers, but gained in popularity none the less. The appliqued quilts were kept for "best", and brought out for display and limited use only on special occasions. Thus, many beautiful examples still exist, while antique patchwork quilts, which were used day after day for generations, are rare.

Quilt-making remained a household art as well as a popular pastime until fabrics manufactured by machine became widely available. Except for a few brief spurts of popularity after that, quilt-making was largely forgotten until the renaissance of interest in all needlework and crafts swept the country in the 1960's. Since then, some crafts have risen and fallen in favor, but the challenge and satisfaction of quilting—and by association, of patchwork and applique—continue to increase. As more and more people feel impelled to create something of lasting value with their own hands, quilt-making seems more and more the answer.

Distinctive Hawaiian quilts were created when the
wives of New England missionaries taught Hawaiian women
how to sew. Since their attire had consisted of grass
skirts and flower leis, they had no stockpile of patches
and cut large, single-color designs from new fabric.

QUILTING EQUIPMENT

Since quilting is simply the stitching that holds two or more layers of material together, it can be done with a few very basic tools. The basic necessities are pins, needles, thread and scissors. The other tools and aids listed below are necessary or useful for making patterns and templates, preparing and finishing fabric, and the sewing involved in quilt-making.

PINS must be fine and sharp for accurate pinning of seams and small pieces of fabric. Some quilters prefer glass-headed pins for anchoring layers of fabric and padding together because they're easy to see and don't get "lost" in puffy quilting. T-pins, upholstery pins or safety pins are also useful for this purpose.

NEEDLES for hand-quilting should be short, strong and sharp, between No. 7 and No. 10. A No. 8 or No. 9 needle, specifically, is often recommended for beginners; experienced quilters may prefer a longer one. Have a good supply of the size you prefer on hand so several can be threaded at one time and waiting; this avoids interrupting your work at frequent intervals to re-thread a single needle. Fine needles can also be used to pin delicate fabrics which may be marred or damaged by regular pins. When quilting by machine, use a new, medium-size needle such as No. 14; needles which have been used for any length of time may be blunted.

THREAD coated with silicone, specifically made for quilting, is best because it's strong and rather stiff; however, it is not available everywhere and comes in a comparatively limited range of colors. Heavy-duty threads are easy to work with because they're strong and durable. No. 5 mercerized cotton thread has traditionally been used for quilting, but many people now prefer cotton-wrapped polyester core thread because of its strength and stretchability, although it sometimes has a tendency to knot.

SCISSORS should be sharp and have slender points for accurate cutting. In addition to cutting shears, it is convenient to have a pair of small embroidery scissors handy for fine work and clipping into seam allowances around curves.

PENCILS: Lead pencils must be hard enough and sharply pointed to trace cleanly and accurately. When marking dark fabrics for appliques, use a light-colored pencil. Soft lead pencils should not be used; they'll smudge your fabric and the lead will come off on hands and paper.

DRY BALL-POINT PEN: Preferred by some people for tracing patterns. The rounded point will not break or tear tracing paper.

TRACING WHEEL: Useful and fast for tracing large-scale patterns and marking seam lines or long quilting patterns.

PAPER FOR PATTERNS: Any plain paper is suitable for patterns which will be used only once or a few times. Thin, stiff cardboard should be used if the pattern will be traced repeatedly. Edges can be coated with clear nail polish to prevent fraying. Rolls of newsprint (not newspaper) and shelf paper are good for planning, laying out or copying long quilting patterns. If these are not readily available, tape sheets of plain paper together to obtain the necessary length.

TRACING PAPER: Thin, transparent paper used by commercial artists; needed for copying and transferring patterns.

DRESSMAKER'S TRACING PAPER: Actually carbon paper which comes in a range of colors; used with a tracing wheel or other marker for transferring patterns to fabric. Usually sold in packs which include a selection of colors suitable for use on both light and dark fabrics.

LARGE-GRID GRAPH PAPER: Ideal for copying patterns which must be enlarged. The alternative is to rule plain paper in 1″ or 2″ squares, whichever is specified in the directions.

PLASTIC OR SANDPAPER SHEETS: Also used for making patterns and templates. Sandpaper won't slide around on fabric as cardboard sometimes does. Templates cut from plastic sheets are firm and durable; the transparent type is especially easy to use.

RULER, YARDSTICK OR TAPE MEASURE: These are all useful (and at least one is necessary) for measuring patterns and fabrics, tracing or making patterns, and laying them out.

BEESWAX: Running thread across a cake of beeswax or paraffin will both strengthen it and make it easier to pull through thick layers of material.

IRONING BOARD AND IRON: Fabrics to be quilted should be ironed thoroughly before the layers are tacked together; removing wrinkles and creases is difficult after they have been stitched. Fabric should also be ironed before being marked for cutting so that both marking and cutting will be accurate. The turning allowance on pieces to be appliqued by hand must be turned and pressed with an iron to insure a smooth, even edge. Seam allowances should be pressed open or flat. So having an iron and ironing board set up and ready to use will make all the steps involved in quilting and quilt-making go faster.

QUILTING FRAMES AND HOOPS: A quilting frame was once considered indispensable for keeping the layers of material stretched evenly together and fairly taut while the quilting stitches were being taken through them. Frames large enough for full-size quilts traditionally rested on the backs of four low-backed "quilting chairs" which were standard equipment in Early American kitchens. Such frames went the way of rooms large enough to accommodate them easily for long periods of time, and adjustable embroidery frames small enough to be used on a table and even smaller double-ring frames known as quilting hoops took their place. The back of a smoothly-finished picture frame can also be used for smaller pieces. Today quilting is often done a section at a time with the work resting in one's lap. If using a hoop, start in the center of the piece, pulling it taut between the rings. As you work toward the edges, smaller embroidery hoops can be used to keep the layers taut. A frame or hoop not only makes quilting easier and better, it also saves time, because when working without a frame, the layers must be basted together much more closely.

FABRICS USED FOR QUILTING

Linen was originally used more than any other fabric for quilted bedcovers, and for quilted clothing as well. Later, silk fabrics, including satin, and various types of woolen material were used for bed quilts until they were largely replaced by cotton prints around the end of the eighteenth century. Sturdy, economical cottons have been used ever since for everyday quilts of the padded variety, with silks and satins being reserved for "best."

Fabrics used for either quilting or patchwork should be smooth, soft and firmly woven. For making serviceable, everyday quilts, they should also be washable, wrinkle-resistant and colorfast. Many expert quilters feel that only fabrics made of natural fibers, notably cotton, meet all these specifications. Broadcloth, calico, medium-weight gingham, percale and poplin are just a few of the cotton weaves which are suitable for quilting. All-synthetic fabrics are generally considered hard to quilt, especially by hand, but cotton-and-polyester blends, which combine cotton's softness with polyester's easy-care characteristics, are a good solution. Fabrics made of rayon are also considered unsuitable for quilting, as is heavy satin or any stiff, thick fabric which is difficult to pierce with a needle.

The top and backing of padded quilts, which are often reversible, are frequently of the same fabric, or at least of similar quality. If economy is an important factor, inexpensive muslin sheeting, challis or flannel makes a sturdy backing. Sheer or loosely-woven fabric is not a good choice for the quilt top, but a loosely-woven fabric which has a little "give" is sometimes best for the backing of corded or stuffed quilts. Silk fabrics in soft, smooth weaves, if affordable, make luxurious tops for padded or stuffed quilts, but should not be used for corded quilting; the cord tends to make the silk wear poorly.

An amazing variety of materials has been used for padding down through the centuries, including paper. Wool in many forms, including old blankets, was used when warmth was still the major consideration. Layers of thin flannel were a popular choice until comparatively recently, because they lie flat and are easy to stitch through. Cotton batting came next and was the traditional choice for American quilts until polyester batting appeared. Considered by most contemporary quilters to be the best material available for padding, polyester batting is inexpensive to buy by the yard, easy to quilt, and washes and dries quickly without bunching up or wadding. It's light and fluffy (although surprisingly warm) and gives quilts a desirable puffiness without the weight of former fillers. The layers can also be pulled and stretched to a thinner consistency if less puffiness is desired.

QUILTING BY HAND

The two basic hand-quilting stitches are a short running stitch and the backstitch; the running stitch is the one most frequently used, especially for anything quilted with a fairly thick layer of padding. The running stitch is always used if the work is reversible or will be seen from the wrong side. Each stitch, as well as the space between it and the next, should be the same on both sides, so the pattern will be identical on both sides. Using a No. 9 quilting needle threaded with an 18″ length of quilting or heavy-duty thread, knotted at one end, start in the center of the piece or section to be worked. Bring the needle up from the backing through the padding and quilt top; tug on the thread gently so the knot passes through the backing and lies buried in the padding. Stitching along the marked line, push the needle straight down through all layers with one hand; take the needle in the other hand, which is held beneath the work, pull the thread through the layers and push the needle back up through the top close to the point where it was first inserted, thus taking a small stitch. This is called a "stab" stitch, and is the method of stitching recommended for beginners. An experienced quilter may be able to take two, three or four stitches before pulling the needle all the way through by holding the needle at a slant in one hand while holding the work in place with the thumb of the other hand. This usually can be done successfully only if the work is held taut in a frame.

The backstitch is practical only when a thin layer of padding is used between the top and backing, and the back of the work isn't likely to be seen. The stitches should be short and very even. Starting with a single running stitch, insert the needle where the thread was brought through for the preceding stitch, and bring it out again two stitch lengths ahead.

Whichever stitch is used, make sure the needle goes completely through to the back of the quilt at every stitch and that the thread is pulled tight. Make the stitches as small as possible, between eight and twelve to an inch; remember, the longer the stitch, the less durable the quilting. Using heavy or stiff fabrics will make it harder to take small stitches; if this is the case, take only one stitch at a time, with the needle going through the layers in a vertical position. To fasten an end of thread, backstitch for several stitches through all layers, then take a long stitch through the top and padding only; take another backstitch and clip the thread off at the surface. The end of the thread will sink back into the padding.

Machine quilting has come to be considered quite acceptable, especially for utilitarian household articles, and can be quite charming in spite of its regularity. One definite advantage is that it is possible to use thicker batting when quilting by machine than by hand. Dacron batting as thick as one inch can be used, resulting in a deeper, more sculptured effect, which is often desirable. It is very important that the top, batting and backing be tacked together securely when quilting so the layers will not move or shift while being quilted. If they do, bubbling and wrinkling will be the result. Starting at the center, and taking stitches two to three inches long, baste the layers together horizontally and vertically, diagonally from corner to corner in both directions, and around the edges. On a very large piece of work, tacking in horizontal and vertical rows across the entire piece is recommended. If using cotton batting, it's advisable to tack more closely than is necessary when using polyester batting.

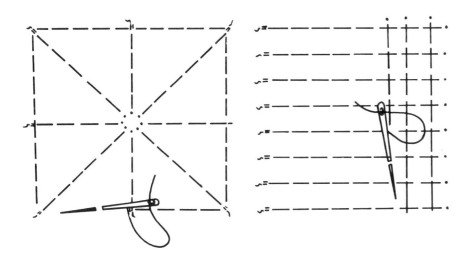

Most machine quilting is done with a straight stitch, with the machine set for a stitch length of 8 to 12 stitches per inch. If your machine does not have a numbered dial setting, count the number of stitches in an inch. Release the pressure on the presser foot slightly so the layers of fabric being quilted will pass under it easily. Upper and lower tensions must be balanced so the stitching locks in the center of the thickness of the layers. Be sure to use the throat plate with the smaller hole if your machine is equipped with more than one. The smaller opening will help keep the work from pulling against the needle.

To guide the work under the presser foot, spread the fingers of the left hand flat on the work in front of the foot; hold the work behind the presser foot with the right hand to maintain a steady tension, without pulling the fabric. Keep your eye on the edge of the presser foot, using it as a guide. Don't look at the needle; concentrate on the work about half an inch ahead as it feeds under the presser foot. When pivoting the work, do so with the needle fully inserted; release the presser foot, move the work into position, and replace the presser foot to stitch in the new direction.

If the piece you are working on is large, such as a quilt, the weight of it should not be allowed to pull on the part being stitched as it feeds under the presser foot. Place a small table, a lowered ironing board or several chairs close to the machine to support the rest of the piece. Whenever possible, try to keep the bulk of the piece to the left of the presser foot. When this is not possible, roll the work tightly from one end toward the center and pin the roll securely so you can work with the roll to the right of the presser foot. You may find it easier to work with the piece rolled from both sides, leaving about 18 inches of flat surface to work on in the center.

Patterns which are stitched on the bias in diagonal lines are the easiest to quilt on a machine. It is not necessary to use a quilting foot and the fabric "gives" a little when on the bias, so it's easier to keep the work flat. In addition, regularly-spaced straight lines do not have to be marked; the gauge or edge marker on the machine can be used after the first line is stitched. If using cotton batting as padding, stitching lines should be no farther than two inches apart; the spacing between lines can be increased to three inches when Dacron batting is used.

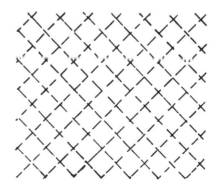

Diagonal quilting does not have to be done only in straight lines across the entire piece. In addition to the simple diamond pattern thus produced, many geometric designs can be worked out. Two easy variations, which can be used for blocks or borders, are shown here.

It is possible, of course, to quilt other types of patterns on a machine. If the pattern is scrolled or cursive, use the short, open toe of a quilting foot, which makes it easy to follow curved lines easily and accurately.

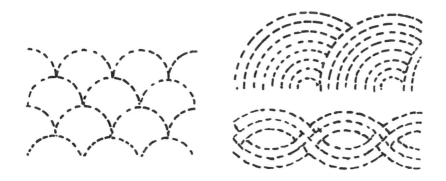

With experience, an entire quilt can be successfully quilted on a sewing machine in about twelve to fifteen hours. It's easier, of course, to quilt one being made in blocks or sections which are joined after the quilting is completed. If making a quilt in one piece, be sure to remove it from the machine occasionally and place it on a bed as it will eventually be used. It's far easier to judge how the work is progressing when standing a few feet away from it and seeing it as a whole.

TYPES OF QUILTING

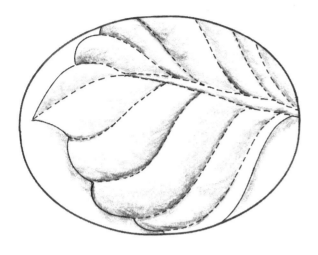

FLAT QUILTING: Two layers of fabric quilted together without any padding between them. Used primarily for decoration, this technique also adds substance to lightweight fabrics and increases the wearing qualities of articles which will be handled extensively. Small household furnishings such as pot holders and place mats are often quilted in this manner. Flat quilting is also used for pillow covers, bed covers, upholstery, wall hangings and apparel—both for trimming and for complete garments, particularly vests, skirts and jackets.

PADDED QUILTING: The oldest form of quilting, in which two outer layers of fabric are quilted together with one or more layers of padding between them. Originally devised as protective body armor, padded quilting was a "natural" for adding warmth to bed covers and clothing during the inclement winters of the Middle Ages in northern Europe. Batting is now commonly used for padding, and the three layers referred to as the top, batting and backing. Most widely used where warmth combined with a decorative surface treatment is desired, as in bedcovers, housecoats, bedjackets, children's snowsuits and other cold-weather apparel, it is also employed solely to enhance the design of such things as pillow covers and headboards by giving the design depth and definition. Equally effective in all-over geometric patterns and outlining individual motifs. Called "wadded" quilting in England, it is sometimes referred to as "American" quilting.

STUFFED QUILTING: An interesting variation of quilting in which only certain areas or motifs are padded—or "stuffed"—to make them stand out from the background in bas-relief. This technique is very much in vogue right now because of the sculptural quality it gives to pillows and other decorative furnishings. A design for stuffed quilting must be made up of small, separated sections such as the petals and center of a flower.

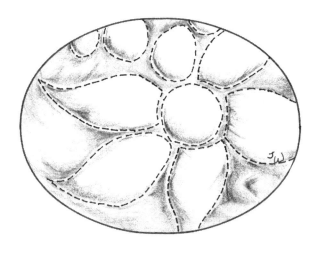

Two fabrics are used, the top one preferably smooth and closely woven, the backing a loosely-woven muslin or similar material. The design is marked on the backing; then the two layers must be tacked together thoroughly, but over the background areas only, not over the design. After marking and tacking, the design is stitched through both fabrics, by hand or by machine, using a running stitch or backstitch.

Then comes the fun part. Working from the backing side, the sections or motifs are individually stuffed with fiberfill or pulled-apart pieces of batting, using a knitting needle or a crochet hook and being careful to stuff every corner or point. If the areas are small, a few threads of the backing can be pulled to one side so the motif can be stuffed. Then the parted threads are drawn back together and held with a few lacing stitches so the stuffing can't escape. For larger areas, a slit is made in the backing at the center of the motif. After stuffing, the slit can be closed with a few overcasting stitches. Stuffed quilting should be lined.

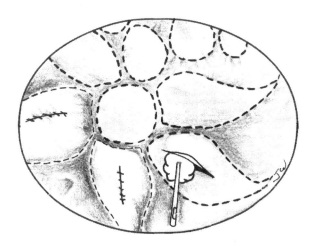

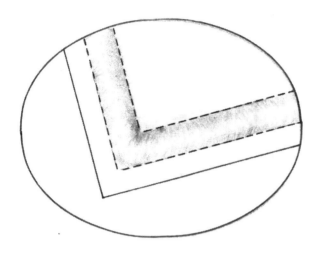

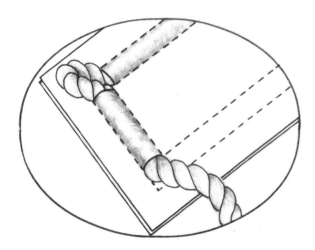

CORDED QUILTING: Believed to have originated in Italy, and also known as "trapunto" quilting, corded quilting is used primarily for decoration. Two layers of fabric are stitched together in parallel lines that form a channel, the lines spaced slightly farther apart than the width of the cord which is inserted between them and between the two fabrics. The cording adds weight and "body" to the fabrics and is sometimes used around necklines, sleeves and hemlines of women's clothing.

Appreciable warmth is added only when an article is solidly corded, but solid cording is sometimes used as a decorative background for other types of quilting, giving an effect of deeply textured stripes. It is important to space the distance between the two lines accurately for the cord being used. If they're too close, the cord will be too tight and pull the design out of shape; if they're too far apart, the raised effect will be lost.

The cord is usually cotton, inserted by threading in a rug or tapestry needle which is pushed along between the lines of stitching without piercing either fabric. When a sharp angle or bend occurs in the quilting pattern, the needle is brought out on the backing side and reinserted at the same point, leaving a small amount of cord projecting; this prevents puckering and distortion of the top fabric.

The same effect can be achieved using only one fabric by attaching the cord to the wrong side of the single layer. Two rows of backstitch, one on each side of the cord, are worked simultaneously, with the thread criss-crossing over the cord on the wrong side to hold it in place. Only the two rows of backstitching appear on the right side of the fabric. Corded quilting must be lined unless used for something such as a pillow cover, where the backing is not exposed.

PILLOW QUILTING: The four traditional types of quilting described earlier are likely to take considerable time and patience, especially if the quilting is done by hand. "Pillow quilting" is one of several techniques that simulate quilting but can be done at a much faster clip. It actually is more like patchwork than quilting, but whatever you choose to call it, it has a certain bouncy, spontaneous charm that blends well with the decorating mood of today. It's used almost exclusively for quilts and throws, and is especially well-suited to crib or carriage quilts.

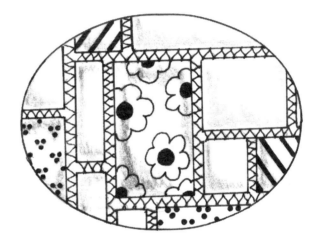

Pillow quilting consists of stuffed geometric patches joined together in one of several ways. Each patch — or miniature pillow — is made just like a real pillow, by cutting top and backing the same size and machine-stitching them together with right sides facing around three sides. After the seam allowances are trimmed at the corners, the patch is turned right side out and stuffed with fiberfill or batting. The raw edges of fabric along the fourth side are turned in and the opening slip-stitched closed. It's a good idea to make the patches squares and rectangles in a few modular sizes so

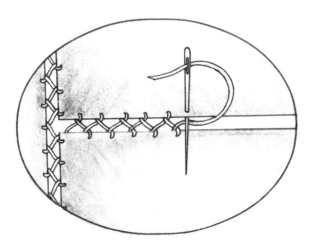

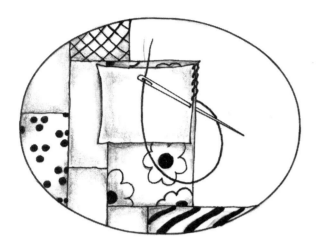

they'll fit together evenly, even though the arrangement is random.

Use fabrics of the same weight in related solid colors, or in a harmonious mixture of small patterns interspersed with solid colors. When you've made enough miniature pillows, lay them out in a pleasing arrangement and join them together with plain or fancy faggoting. Or place adjoining pillows with right sides facing and overcast the edges on the wrong side.

TIED QUILTING: A variation of padded quilting in which the three basic layers of top, batting and backing are held together by separate stitches which are tied and knotted instead of by continuous stitching which forms a design. The three layers must be tacked securely together, and this type of quilting is difficult to do unless the layers are held taut in a frame.

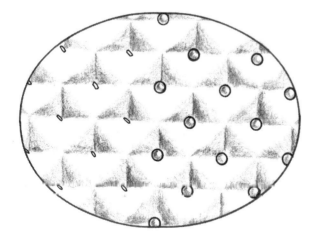

The knots are usually lined up in a simple geometric pattern, but they could follow a cursive course just as well, provided they were spaced at regular intervals and covered the area evenly. Starting at the back and leaving an end of thread about two inches long, the needle is brought through to the top and two small stitches taken in the same place, ending at the back just one small stitch away from the end left hanging. The two ends are then tied securely with two or three firm knots and the excess thread trimmed away. A small bead, such as a make-believe pearl, or a button can be added for decoration while taking the second small stitch. In any case, a strong thread, such as buttonhole twist or pearl cotton should be used.

For a different effect, the stitching can be reversed and the ends tied in little bows on the right side of the quilt. This is often done in contrasting color, using a thick, fluffy yarn.

CABLE QUILTING: This is a method of machine stitching which can be used for flat or padded quilting and gives either one a distinctive look because the stitching is bolder and more emphatic than the usual running stitch.

First, fill the bobbin of your machine with unstranded embroidery thread such as pearl cotton. Loosen the tension screw on the bobbin case so the thread is released evenly and smoothly. Thread the top of the machine with regular sewing thread, preferably of the polyester-wrapped cotton variety, and tighten the upper tension slightly. Work with the backing of the piece uppermost, so the pearl cotton will be on the right side of the top fabric. The resulting stitching will have the look of a neatly couched line.

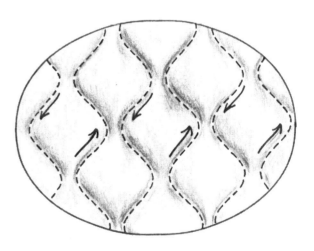

The stitch is even more outstanding when used for a cable pattern. Try varying the length of the stitch for different effects. When stitching a cable pattern in this manner, stitch alternate rows in opposite directions.

QUILTING PATTERNS

*Feather and cable patterns make stunning borders
and are extremely versatile. Here are some variations
you can easily enlarge to any size desired.*

PATCHWORK

is a saga of rags to riches—from the hoarded bits and pieces of long-used clothing saved by early settlers until they had enough to make a bedcover, to the beautiful patchwork patterns that later evolved. The richness of patchwork lies in the color, variety, and vitality it can add to the simplest things—from pillows and hangings to game boards and clothes. Just turn the pages and see!

QUILTING

is truly a double-purpose craft. It has been used to make everything from baby clothes to coverlets more functional and/or more beautiful. It can be as basic as straight stitching or as elaborate as intricate embroidery. Explore with us the possibilities of quilting. In this section, you'll see such simple items as pot holders and eyeglass cases easily made into little treasures by the addition of quilting. Or, start with a quilted tablecloth such as the one opposite. Choose any print, add batting and backing, and begin. Outlining simple motifs with straight stitching is easy. See page 52.

COLORFUL CASES *for today's big, bold eyeglasses are quilted with simple stitching. Just outline the motifs of a printed fabric or trace a perky posy in running stitch.* **Page 52.**

DECORATIVE LEAVES

are really handy pot holders, quickly quilted along the "veins" by hand or machine. Embroider a bright orange beetle on one, a colorful dragonfly on another. Any one or all three make an ideal first project. **See Page 53.**

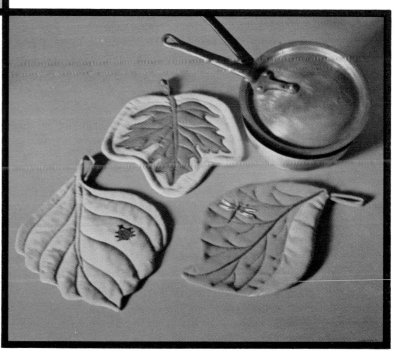

FANTASYLAND EXPRESS *is a bus that's touring an imaginative terrain—complete with a rather spooky castle. The child-like quality of the design makes it ideal for a youngster's quilt or wall hanging. Appliqueing and quilting are both done the easy way—on a sewing machine. Directions for the 34" x 43½" quilt are on Page 55.*

PUFFED DELICACIES, *below, look as airy as cream puffs.*

But they're very usable pillows, and the effect of trapunto quilting is prettily faked. Simple stitching through the pastel fabric and a double layer of batting gives them that bas-relief look. Directions, with full-size patterns, Page 56.

BLUE DENIM PATCHES *lend a brand-new look to traditional*
patchwork designs. Recognize the old favorites used in the four pillows above? Their
names are included in the directions that start on Page 56. How-to's for the hen plaque
and pot holder are included too.

PORTABLE GAMES

adults play and a fun gift for baby all employ patchwork in clever ways. Backgammon and checkerboards made of fabric are easy to pack up and take along to faraway beach or nearby back yard. Both are easy to quilt because all the stitching is done in straight lines.

One-of-a-kind gift for proud new parents: a patchwork-covered baby album that's a cinch to make. Colorful scraps will do nicely for both patches and appliques—and you can make the present more personal by substituting a name and some special motifs. Directions for this trio of charmers begin on Page 64.

"STILL LIFE" PATCHWORK
starts out with square patches in traditional fashion—but the way they're put together and the final result are far from usual. Piecing and quilting are done in sections, working from a chart. Stuff the bowl and fruit sections of this "painting" if this king-size quilt is to be used as a wall hanging. Directions, Page 71.

VESTS *are top-layer fashion—for the man in your life, too. If he's the romantic type, make him a luxurious vest to wear at home or for holiday parties. Patchwork can be a "crazy quilt" of festive fabrics or made mostly from squares, as shown above. See Page 72 for directions.*

Invest a little time in making a vest that's different from any other vest in the world! How? By creating your own material from strips of fabric you simply stitch together and quilt. The vest is then cut from this quilted patchwork—and because you did it all, the result is really unique. Directions on Page 73.

PATCHWORK

*If you can sew a short, straight seam,
you can do patchwork! All you need are
some interesting bits of fabric—
treasured scraps or bright new pieces—
plus a few helpful hints to make
the job go smoothly. In the following
pages, we touch on the history of patchwork
in America, giving diagrams for 24
classic patterns. We then show you
ways to design a patchwork block of
your own—from the old folding-a-square
method to using more modern tools.
There are how-to's for cutting and sewing,
with step-by-step illustrations for
joining patches into blocks. You'll even
find actual-size patterns to trace for
clamshell, diamond, and hexagon patches,
with advice on how to handle these
more challenging pieces. It's not hard to
become an expert—with a little help!*

HOW PATCHWORK EVOLVED

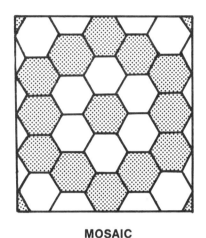

MOSAIC

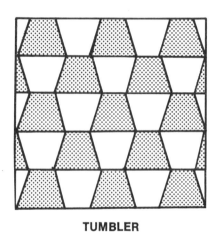

TUMBLER

CLAMSHELL

"Patchwork," as we use it, is another word for piecing—that is, the joining of two or more bits of fabric along their edges to make a larger fabric. It's impossible to say when the craft first began—certainly it is not an American invention, as is sometimes claimed. There are references in French and English literature to pieced coverings as far back as the 12th or 13th centuries. Few of the earliest American pieced quilts survive; those that remain were the little-used "best" quilts, which are very like their English counterparts: a central medallion, usually of printed fabric, is surrounded by appliquéd or pieced borders. Gradually the style in America changed; the central figure tended to disappear and the patchwork border sections grew in importance until they became the whole design.

The early quilts that have not survived were the everyday bed coverings made for warmth rather than show. Many were simply two plain pieces of fabric enclosing a filling. Others might have a top layer pieced with random-shaped scraps for a "crazy quilt." More often the scraps were probably trimmed into a regular shape such as a square or a triangle that could be fitted together in an overall pattern. Hexagons made especially beautiful one-patch quilts, as we see from the early honeycomb Mosaics; a later version was Grandma's Garden, in which the hexagons fall into flower blocks.

Another one-patch was Tumbler, whose name reflects the homey nature of these quilts. The lovely Clamshell pattern, still a one-patch, was nonetheless difficult to piece because of its curving shape. The same effect can be obtained by overlapping circles, but traditionally the pattern was made with shell-shaped patches in light and dark rows.

As the bordered "best" quilt and the everyday one-patch evolved, they tended to influence each other's style. Eventually there developed a distinctly American idiom of piecework: This was the block-style quilt, in which geometric patches were sewn into identical square blocks; the blocks were then joined together to make up the entire surface of the quilt. Thus the first one-patch designs were succeeded by two-patch blocks, then four-patch and nine-patch blocks. (Some of the patterns discussed are shown here and on the next two pages.) The simplest two-patch, two triangles joined for a square, had a number of variations. One popular block was Birds in the Air, which combines two triangles to make a square, one triangle being already pieced with nine smaller triangles. Appliqué a handle to the plain triangle and you have another pattern, Basket. Flock of Geese is a four-patch version of Birds in the Air. Broken Dishes is all small triangles arranged in four four-patch blocks, which are four-patched again for the final block.

The fundamental Nine-Patch is simply one block divided into nine equal squares. For variety, the dark and light squares can be arranged in a number of different schemes or they can be divided into smaller squares or triangles. The old Shoofly pattern is a good illustration, while even more intricate variations can be seen in Duck and Ducklings (also known as Hen and Chicks).

Squares and diamonds are combined for an interesting stepped effect in Pandora's Box; another version of this pattern, Baby Blocks, is pieced entirely with diamonds.

One of the most fascinating patchwork patterns is the Log Cabin block, wherein strips of fabric, half light and half dark, are arranged around a central square. The blocks can then be joined in different ways to create several overall quilt designs, such as Courthouse Steps, Barn Raising, and Straight Furrow.

Another popular group of patterns uses variations on the lend-and-borrow theme, in which light and dark curving pieces seem to change places in alternate squares. See Rob Peter to Pay Paul, Drunkard's Path, and Steeplechase. Like Clamshell, these are all difficult to piece because of the curves. Perhaps the most intricate of all curving blocks is Double Wedding Ring, which nevertheless achieved great popularity in the 1920's; here, tiny wedge-shaped patches are pieced together to make up the curving ring segments.

Today, patchwork continues to fascinate us with its endless variety of geometric forms. We love to copy the old patterns, and some of us are inspired to design new ones. Whichever you prefer, please turn to page 46 for some ideas on how to go about it.

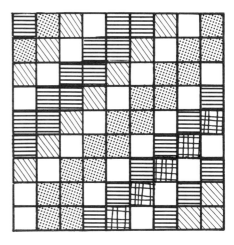

DIAGONAL STRIPES

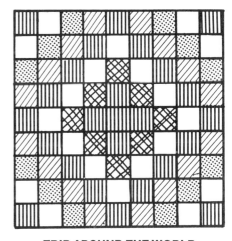

TRIP AROUND THE WORLD

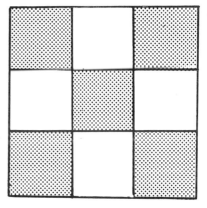

NINE-PATCH

PATCHWORK PATTERNS

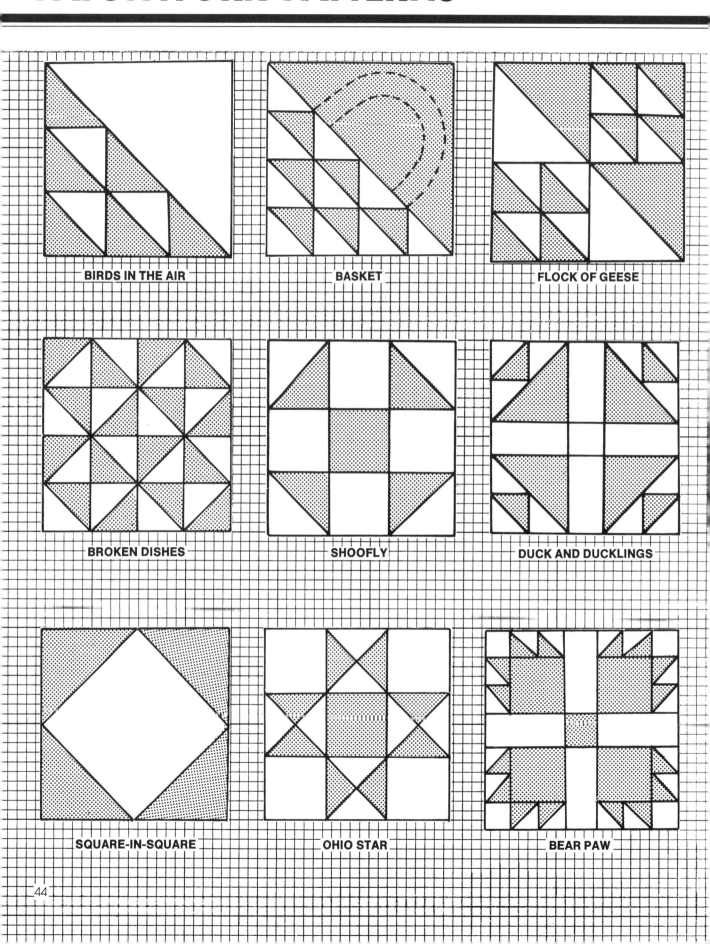

BIRDS IN THE AIR

BASKET

FLOCK OF GEESE

BROKEN DISHES

SHOOFLY

DUCK AND DUCKLINGS

SQUARE-IN-SQUARE

OHIO STAR

BEAR PAW

AUNT SUKEY'S CHOICE

LOG CABIN

PINEAPPLE

PANDORA'S BOX

ROB PETER AND PAY PAUL

DRUNKARD'S PATH

SCHOOLHOUSE

STEEPLECHASE

DOUBLE WEDDING RING

45

MAKING PATTERNS
FOR PATCHWORK

Anyone at all can make patch patterns, whether by copying a traditional motif or designing a new one. A good way to begin is to do as our pioneer ancestors did: experiment by folding a square of paper in a variety of ways. For a two-patch block of triangles, fold it in half diagonally. Fold it again the other way for a block of four triangles. Fold it in half on its side, then in half again, for a simple four-patch of squares. For the basic nine-patch, fold it twice one way, then twice the other way. And so on! These are the simplest shapes, but the possibilities are there for five and seven-patch blocks as well. Early patch quilters simply cut along the folds for their individual patch patterns or used them to make heavier patterns (or templates), perhaps of metal. While the paper-folding method is useful for an understanding of how to divide a square (and it's doubtful whether many of our ancestors had formal training in geometry), the modern method described below will give you more accurate patterns.

To start, you will need a few good tools: sharp pencils, a ruler with a perfect edge, a compass if you plan curves in your design, and graph paper. Available at art supply stores, graph paper is printed all over with a grid design of 1″ squares, which are subdivided into smaller squares of 8, 10, or 12 to the inch. It won't matter which size you buy.

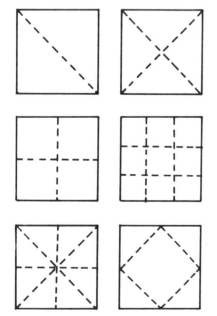

FOLDING A SQUARE OF PAPER

Using your tools, draw a square of any size on the graph paper, then experiment by dividing the square into components until you are pleased with your design. The printed lines will help you make perfect rectangles and triangles. Then shade in some areas for a light-dark contrast. Better yet, fill in the sections with colored pencils. Draw identical squares all around the first one drawn and color them too, to get an idea of how the blocks will interact together. You will probably want to start by coloring each block the same. Then as an experiment you may want to reverse the colors in alternate blocks. If you've already chosen your fabrics, you could even cut out patches to fit and paste them down on your drawing.

The final step is to decide on scale. Your blocks can be any size you choose; the larger the block, the fewer blocks you will need; the smaller the block, the more intricate and textured your design will appear. Will you be piecing by hand or by machine? If the edges in your design are all straight, you may safely decide on machine sewing, provided none of the patches within the block are smaller than 2″ square. If your block contains curving patches, you are advised to stick to hand piecing, so the blocks can be smaller.

When you have arrived at a convenient size for your block, draw the final version carefully on graph paper. Letter each separate piece of the design in sequence and write in the number of patches you will need for the quilt. (Multiply the patch by the total number of blocks needed, allowing for identical patches in one block.) Paste the graph paper design to a thin but firm cardboard such as shirt lining; let dry. Or trace it onto a transparent plastic sheet, using your ruler to draw the lines. Carefully cut the design along the lines with sharp scissors to make templates for individual patch pieces. If each template will be used for many patches, make duplicates and discard each as the edges become frayed from repeated use.

Before cutting any patches from fabric, test the accuracy of your templates by reassembling them into the original design. The edges should meet each other neatly, without any gaps or overlapping. If they don't, your patches will be equally imperfect, making it difficult to join them

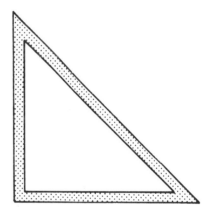

The method described above for making templates will give you a pattern the size of the finished patch, that is, what shows when the patchwork is assembled. The seam allowance is not included in the pattern, but is added when patches are cut (see page 48). If you wish to cut your seam allowance with perfectly even edges, you may want to make a window template. Make template as described above. Draw around it on cardboard; then draw another line exactly ¼″ away. Cut on both lines, creating a frame. The window is more difficult and time consuming to make, but it will make patches easier to cut. It is also advisable for using with certain prints, when placement of motifs is important.

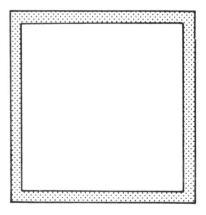

WINDOW TEMPLATES

CUTTING AND SEWING PATCHES

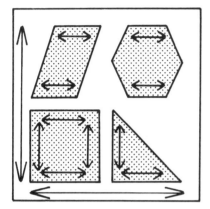

PLACING TEMPLATES ON FABRIC

CUTTING PATCH PIECES: Use fabrics that are closely woven, so seams will hold and edges will not fray. Cotton is best, if you can find it. The fabric should be fairly soft, but should not be so thin that seam allowances will show through. Before cutting patches, wash new fabrics to pre-shrink and remove sizing. Wash scraps in a net bag. Press all fabrics smooth. Lay fabric out flat, wrong side up and one layer at a time. Lay template (pattern) wrong side up on fabric, placing it so as many straight sides of template as possible are with the crosswise and lengthwise grain of fabric. If necessary, pull threads in both directions to determine grain. Using a sharp, hard pencil (light-colored for dark fabrics, dark-colored for light fabrics), draw around template; hold pencil at an outward angle, so that point is firmly against edge of template. Reposition pattern ½" away and draw around as before. Continue marking patches ½" apart; do not cut fabric until all the patches of one color are marked. (Note: If large border pieces for quilts are to be cut later from the same fabric, be sure to consider their approximate dimensions when marking smaller pieces; you may wish to mark your patches in vertical rows. Do not, however, cut out the border pieces before cutting and piecing patches.)

When all patches of one color have been marked, cut out each patch, ¼" away from marked line, which will be the stitching line. Cut the ¼" seam allowance as accurately as you can, to make piecing easier. To keep patches of same shape and color together, put them in a pile and run a thread through center with a knot in one end; lift off each patch as needed.

PIECING: Several patch pieces will be joined to create a new unit, such as a larger patch or a block. Before sewing, lay out all pieces needed for the block. Begin by joining smallest pieces first, then join the larger pieces you have made into rows, then join rows for completed block.

By Hand: If your patch pieces are small, if they have curves or sharp angles, or if your fabrics are delicate, you will find it easier to join pieces by hand.

To join two patch pieces, place them together, right sides facing. If pieces are very small, hold firmly to sew. Larger pieces can be pin-basted, matching angles first, then the marked lines between. Pin curved pieces together from center out to each corner. For piecing, use #7 to #10 sharp

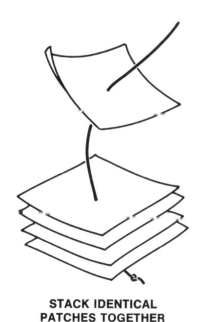

**STACK IDENTICAL
PATCHES TOGETHER**

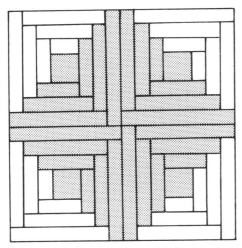

**FOUR LOG CABIN BLOCKS JOIN
FOR COURTHOUSE STEPS PATTERN**

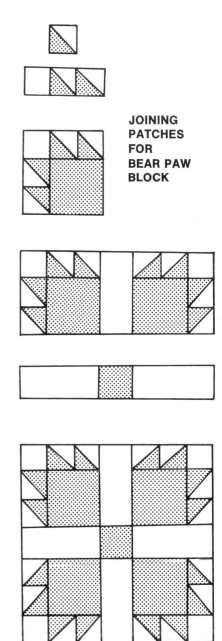

**JOINING
PATCHES
FOR
BEAR PAW
BLOCK**

needle, threaded with an 18″ length of mercerized cotton or cotton-wrapped polyester thread. Begin with a small knot, then stitch along marked seam line with tiny running stitches, ending with a few backstitches; if seam is long, take a tiny backstitch every few stitches. Try to make 8 to 10 running stitches per inch, evenly spaced. If thread tends to knot or fray as you sew, run it over a cake of beeswax. If sewing two bias edges together, keep thread just taut enough to prevent fabric from stretching. As you join pieces, press seams to one side, unless otherwise indicated; open seams tend to weaken construction. Try to press seams all in the same direction, although darker fabrics should not fall under lighter ones, lest they show through. As you piece and press, clip into seams of curves and other pieces where necessary, so they will lie flat. Clip away excess fabric, to avoid bunching. Be sure a seam is pressed flat before you cross it with another; take a small backstitch over the crossing.

By Machine: If your patchwork will have large pieces and simple shapes, you might wish to piece them by machine. Set machine for 10 stitches to the inch, unless working with very heavy fabrics, and use needle #14. Use mercerized cotton thread #50 or cotton-wrapped polyester. Follow the same procedure as for hand piecing: Pin-baste, stitch, clip seams, and press. You need not, however, begin and end your thread with each patch; let thread run on for a continuous chain of patches. Patches will be snipped apart and their seams anchored by cross-seams.

CLAMSHELLS, DIAMONDS, HEXAGONS

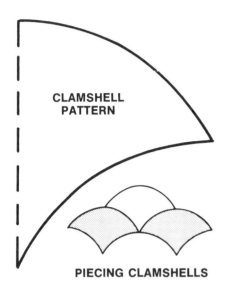

CLAMSHELL PATTERN

PIECING CLAMSHELLS

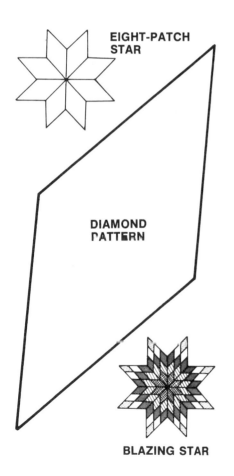

EIGHT-PATCH STAR

DIAMOND PATTERN

BLAZING STAR

Clamshells, diamonds, and hexagons are favorite shapes for one-patch patterns; nevertheless, they are not easy to piece. Unlike most patchwork, the shapes have no right angles, so the templates must be made with extreme care if the patches are to fit together properly. We give actual-size patterns for all three. To use in size given, just trace. To enlarge or reduce either the diamond or hexagon pattern, trace angles only, then lengthen or shorten the edges between. After making template and before cutting patches from fabric, test the pattern's accuracy, following individual directions. Cut patches. Since you will be sewing some edges (or, in the case of Clamshell, all edges) on the bias, you will probably find it easier to join the patches by hand, unless they are very large.

PAPER LINER: When doing diamond or hexagon patchwork, you may find paper liners will help to keep angles sharp and seams precise. Prepare a liner for each patch as follows, referring to details opposite for piecing Hexagons: Cut a firm paper pattern from wrapping paper the exact size of your cardboard template. Fit paper liner within pencil outline on wrong side of patch (Fig. 1). Fold seam allowance over edges and finger-press; tack to paper with one stitch on each side, allowing thread to cross corners (Fig. 2); finish by taking an extra stitch on first side. Cut thread, leaving about ¼". To make removal of tacking easier, do not knot thread or make backstitches. Press lightly. Hold prepared patches right sides together, matching edges to be seamed. Whip together with fine, even stitches (about 16 to the inch), avoiding paper as much as possible (Fig. 3); backstitch when crossing one seam with another. Liners may stay in place until patchwork is completed; to remove, snip tacking thread once on each patch and withdraw thread.

CLAMSHELLS: Trace shell pattern; complete half-pattern indicated by dash lines. Make cardboard template. Test pattern's accuracy as follows: Draw a horizontal line on paper; marking around pattern, draw a row of clamshells across paper, with lower points touching line and upper points of adjacent shells touching at sides. Draw a second row above first, as in piecing detail; curves should match perfectly. Cut patches, marking template on right side of fabric, but otherwise following directions on page 48, place template in same position for each patch. On each shell, mark midpoint of top curve on seam line. Starting at midpoint and working out to both sides, clip top curve just to seam line every ³/₈". Fold clipped edge on seam line to wrong side of piece; press fold carefully without stretching fabric. With right sides up, join two dark shells and one light shell, placing half of upper folded edge of each dark shell on a lower seam line of light shell; at each side point of light shell, seam line should match midpoint of a dark shell; see piecing detail. Pin shells in place. Continue pinning shells until two rows have been joined; add a half-shell to ends of rows. Slip-stitch pieces together on folded seam line of dark shells. Using first two rows as top of work, continue to add shells a row at a time, alternating light and dark.

DIAMONDS: Make diamond template. Pattern may be used for a simple star of eight patches or for a multi-patch blazing star. For either, test template's accuracy: Draw eight diamonds together with points meeting in center, to create an eight-pointed star; there should be no gaps between or overlapping of diamond segments. Cut patches as directed on page 48, placing template on fabric with two opposite sides parallel with straight of goods. When joining patches for an eight-patch star, stitch from the wide-angled corner to center. For a multi-patch star, stitch diamonds together in rows, using staggered color sequence for each; then stitch rows together, matching corners carefully, for eight diamond-shaped sections; stitch sections together for completed star. When joining diamonds, always try to stitch a bias edge to a straight-of-goods edge.

HEXAGONS: Make hexagon template. Test accuracy of pattern by drawing design in Fig. 4, with no gaps or overlaps. Cut patches as directed on page 48, placing template on fabric with two opposite sides parallel with straight of goods. For hand piecing, follow sequence shown in Figs. 1-4: Make paper liner, baste, and slip-stitch patches together; join in clusters as shown. For machine piecing, see Figs. 5 and 6: Omitting paper liners, join patches in rows as for regular piecing, then join rows as shown.

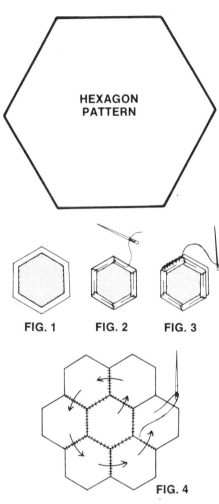

HEXAGON PATTERN

FIG. 1   FIG. 2   FIG. 3

FIG. 4

PIECING HEXAGONS BY HAND

FIG. 5

FIG. 6

PIECING HEXAGONS BY MACHINE

QUILTED ROUND TABLECLOTH
ON PAGE 33

SIZE: 87″ diameter.

EQUIPMENT: Tape measure. Scissors. Pencil. String. Thumbtack.

MATERIALS: Brown paper. Fabric with two-way design, 45″ wide, 5 yards. Lining fabric, 45″ wide, 5 yards. Batting.

DIRECTIONS: Cut fabric into two 90″ lengths. Cut one full width of fabric lengthwise into two half-widths. With right sides together, stitch one half-width to each long edge of the full width of fabric, making ½″ seams. Press seam allowances open.

Fold fabric in half, matching seams and raw edges, then in half again to form a square four layers thick. Pin layers together. To make a compass, tie a knot at one end of a length of string and place knot at center fold of fabric; stretch string taut and tie a second knot 44½″ from the first knot to indicate the bottom edge. Scribe an arc by moving the second knot from one folded edge of fabric to the other. Mark bottom edge by pinning through four layers of fabric. Mark positions of pins with tailor's chalk and connect to make a smooth, curved line.

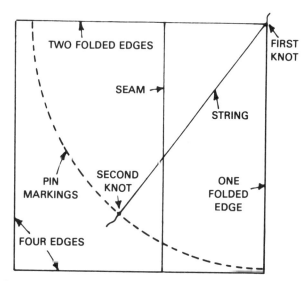

CUTTING CIRCLE FOR ROUND TABLECLOTH

Cut along marked line through all four layers and stay-stitch edges, easing fabric in slightly so there will be less fullness when hem is turned. Piece should measure 89″ in diameter.

To make lining, cut fabric into two 90″ lengths. Seam two long edges together, then fold into quarters and cut a circle as before, using a 43½″ radius instead of 44½″. Lining should measure 87″ in diameter. Cut batting same size as lining, seaming if necessary.

Center lining and batting on wrong side of outer fabric; pin in place. Baste the three layers together horizontally and vertically through the center and around the edges. Machine or hand quilt around outlines of large motifs on drop of tablecloth. To finish edge, turn under ¼″ and press. Turn ¾″ to wrong side and baste to lining, then machine stitch all around.

OUTLINE-QUILTED GLASS CASE
ON PAGE 34

EQUIPMENT: Pencil. Ruler. Scissors. Sewing needle. Straight pins.

MATERIALS: Tightly woven fabric with printed pattern that can be used as a quilting design: one piece 8½″ x 9¾″ (make sure this piece includes complete motif): one piece for boxing, 1½″ x 12″. Smoothly-finished fabric for lining, ¼ yard. Sewing thread to match fabric; black thread for quilting. Polyester fiberfill for padding.

DIRECTIONS: Cut 7½″ x 8¼″ piece of fiberfill; center on wrong side of outer fabric 1″ below top edge, and ½″ away from other three sides; baste in place. Using black thread, outline printed pattern motifs with ⅛″-long running stitches through both thicknesses. Fold quilted piece in half lengthwise, marking 1″ from the top edge to be folded inside later, and press. With right sides together, pin one long edge of boxing strip to one lower edge of folded piece and up one side edge to top of piece. Stitch together ½″ from raw edges, with stitching tapering to center of boxing strip at the fold. Pin other side of boxing strip to remaining lower and side edges of folded piece, and stitch together in same manner. Trim seam allowances; turn to right side. Turn top edge 1″ to inside as marked, and press.

To make lining, cut an 8¼″ x 8¾″ piece of fabric and a 1½″ x 12″ piece for boxing. Fold and stitch in same manner as outer fabric; do not turn right side out. Insert lining into quilted piece with wrong sides facing. Turn top edge of lining ½″ to the wrong side and slip-stitch to inside of case.

FLOWER-QUILTED GLASS CASE
ON PAGE 34

EQUIPMENT: Pencil. Ruler. Scissors. Tracing paper. Dressmaker's carbon paper. Sewing needle. Straight pins.

MATERIALS: Tightly woven fabric: striped design, ¼ yard; solid color for boxing, to match or contrast with striped fabric, 1½" wide, 20" long. Smoothly-finished fabric for lining, ¼ yard. Polyester fiberfill for padding. Sewing thread to match fabric; black thread for quilting.

DIRECTIONS: Trace pattern for flower design; complete half pattern indicated by broken line. Mark straight line in center of top center petal as on other petals. Cut two 5" x 8½" pieces of striped fabric on the bias to create diagonal stripes. Place tracing lengthwise on right side of one piece of fabric with carbon paper between them; center pattern with lower edge of stem ½" above lower edge of fabric; this will be bottom of case. Transfer pattern to fabric by tracing with pencil. Repeat on other piece of fabric.

Cut two 4" x 7" pieces of fiberfill and center on wrong sides of outer fabrics 1" below top edge and ½" away from other three sides; baste in place. Using black thread, quilt along all lines of flower with ⅛"-long running stitches through both thicknesses. With right sides together, pin one long edge of the solid-color strip of fabric around lower and side edges of one striped piece; stitch together ½" from raw edges. Pin and stitch remaining piece of striped fabric to other edge of boxing strip in same manner. Trim seam allowances; turn right side out. Turn top edge of outer fabric 1" to inside and press.

To make lining, cut two 5" x 7½" pieces, and one 1½" x 19" strip for boxing. With right sides facing, stitch the three pieces together in the same manner as for case; do not turn right side out. Insert lining into quilted case with wrong sides facing. Turn top edge of lining in ½" and slip-stitch to inside of case around top edge.

ACTUAL-SIZE HALF-PATTERN

LEAF-SHAPED POT HOLDERS
ON PAGE 34

EQUIPMENT: Pencil. Ruler. Scissors. Straight pins. Sewing and embroidery needles. Tracing paper. Dressmaker's carbon paper. Zigzag sewing machine (for Maple Leaf only). Knitting needle (optional).

MATERIALS: Paper for patterns. Closely-woven fabric: light green, 45" wide, ¼ yard for Maple Leaf and Leaf with Beetle; dark green, 45" wide, ¼ yard for Dragonfly Leaf; brown, 7" square, for Maple Leaf. Dark green sewing thread. Six-strand embroidery floss in orange, gray, yellow, black, white, orchid and magenta.

DIRECTIONS: Enlarge patterns on paper ruled in 1" squares. Broken lines indicate quilting. Make separate patterns for inner section of Maple Leaf and flap of Dragonfly Leaf.

Using patterns, cut one complete shape for each leaf in the color indicated, adding ½" seam allowance all around each one. Cut batting from same patterns, omitting seam allowances and stems. Using carbon paper, transfer insect patterns to right sides of leaf shapes as indicated;

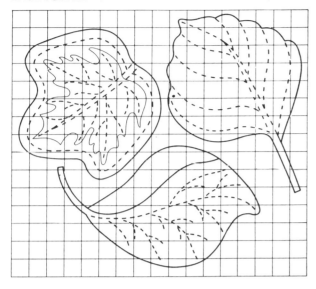

**PATTERNS FOR
LEAF-SHAPED POT HOLDERS**

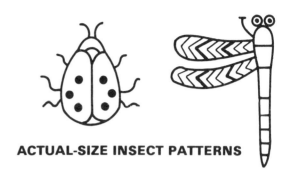

ACTUAL-SIZE INSECT PATTERNS

complete dragonfly by adding another set of wings and a leg.

Using gray floss, satin-stitch head and body of dragonfly on dark green leaf shape as indicated. Embroider two legs in gray outline stitch. Couch gray tail with twelve strands of black floss. Make French knots for eyes with white floss. Outline-stitch around wings with magenta. Using magenta and orchid, fill in wing sections in satin stitch worked in a herringbone pattern. To make leaf flap, use pattern to cut two pieces of light green fabric, adding ½" seam allowance all around each one. With right sides together, stitch ½" from one edge only. Trim seam allowance; clip to stitching line at curves; turn right side out and press. Cut batting from same pattern, omitting seam allowance, and insert into flap. Baste opening closed ¼" from raw edges. Place flap on right side of leaf shape with raw edges even; pin, then stitch in place ¼" from raw edge.

Center batting cut previously on wrong side of leaf shape; baste in place. Cut second dark green leaf shape from Dragonfly Leaf pattern, reversing the pattern and adding ½" seam allowance all around. With right sides facing, pin leaf shapes together and stitch all around ½" from raw edges. Leave a 3" opening along side opposite flap. Trim seam allowances; clip to stitching line at curves. Turn right side out, using knitting needle to turn stem. Slip-stitch opening closed.

To quilt, machine-stitch along marked lines through all thicknesses; stitch over vein lines twice. For loop, fold stem to back of leaf and stitch end to leaf.

To make Leaf with Beetle, use orange floss to satin-stitch body of beetle. Using black floss, satin-stitch head and line on back of body; outline-stitch legs and antennae, and make dots on body with French knots. Satin-stitch small section between head and body with yellow floss. Center batting cut previously on wrong side of leaf shape; baste in place. Cut second light green leaf shape from Leaf with Beetle pattern, reversing the pattern and adding ½" seam allowances all around. With right sides facing, pin leaf shapes together and stitch all around ½" from raw edges, leaving a 3" opening along one side. Trim seam allowances; clip to stitching line at curves; turn right side out, using knitting needle to turn stem. Slip-stitch opening closed. Quilt and make loop as directed for Dragonfly Leaf.

To make Maple Leaf, cut piece for inner leaf from brown fabric. Zigzag-stitch edges of brown leaf to right side of light green leaf as indicated. Center batting cut previously on wrong side of leaf shape and baste in place. Cut second light green leaf shape from Maple Leaf pattern, reversing pattern and adding ½" seam allowance all around. With right sides facing, pin leaf shapes together and stitch all around ½" from raw edges, leaving a 3" opening along one side. Trim seam allowances; clip to stitching line at curves. Turn right side out; slip-stitch opening closed. Quilt as directed for Dragonfly Leaf; stitch around outline of inner leaf also. For loop, cut a 1" x 5" bias strip of brown fabric. Fold in half lengthwise; stitch long edges together with ¼" seam. Turn to right side; turn in ends, slip-stitch closed. Fold strip in half to form loop and stitch to base of quilted stem on leaf shape.

CRIB QUILT

ON PAGE 35

SIZE: 43½" x 34"

EQUIPMENT: Pencil. Ruler. Scissors. Paper for pattern. Dressmaker's carbon paper. Tracing wheel or dry ball-point pen. Zigzag sewing machine.

MATERIALS: Cotton or cotton-blend fabric, 44" wide: green, 2¼ yards (includes lining); blue, ⅓ yard. Small pieces of purple, orange, olive drab, yellow, navy, red, brown, medium blue, and cream. Sewing thread to match fabrics. Polyester or cotton batting.

DIRECTIONS: To make background, cut 33" x 35" piece of green fabric for foreground; cut 12" x 35" piece of blue fabric for sky. Overlap long edges of sky and foreground ½" and baste together to make background 44½" x 35"; do not turn edges under.

Enlarge pattern on paper ruled in 2" squares. Using dressmaker's carbon and tracing wheel or dry ball-point pen, transfer main outlines of complete pattern, including lines in sky, to pieced background.

Cut 44½" x 35" piece of green fabric for lining. Cut batting same size as lining. Center batting on wrong side of background; pin and baste together lengthwise, crosswise, diagonally in two directions, and around perimeter. With right sides together, pin background to lining; baste together around edges, then straight-stitch ½" from raw edges around all sides, leaving a 10" opening in center of bottom edge. Turn quilt right side out

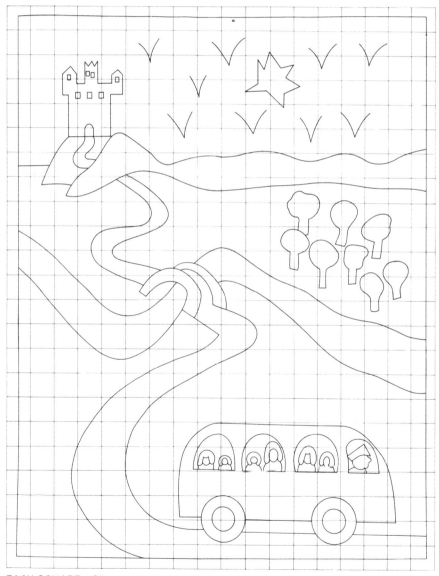

EACH SQUARE = 2"

PATTERN FOR FANTASYLAND CRIB QUILT

through opening, then slip-stitch opening closed. Baste all three layers together in same manner as for batting.

Cut paper pattern along main outlines of each piece to be appliqued. Referring to photograph, trace around each pattern on fabric of appropriate color.

Cut out appliques, adding ¼" all around each traced outline. Pin and baste door and windows to castle; do not turn under ¼" margin. Using matching thread, stitch around each applique on marked line. Trim away extra fabric to ⅛" from straight stitching. Set sewing machine for close zigzag stitch; zigzag around appliques, covering straight stitching and ⅛" margin. Pin completed castle and all other appliques in previously-marked positions on background. Applique in same manner as for castle; use green thread in bobbin and matching color thread in needle. Zigzag over seam dividing sky and foreground at left. Quilt lines in sky and around all edges of quilt, using straight stitch. Remove all basting.

tern on right side of one piece of outer fabric. Trace, using dry ball-point pen or hard-lead pencil and dressmaker's carbon paper. On pattern for square pillow, trace looped stem separately and connect to short section of stem under flower, matching asterisks.

Center double layer of batting on muslin backing, then place quilted outer fabric, right side up, on top. Pin and baste together with raw edges even.

To quilt, use medium-size stitch on sewing machine, or make small stitches with quilting needle if quilting by hand. Stitch along marked outlines of flower design through all thicknesses. When stitching is completed, bring all thread ends to wrong side and knot securely.

Pin the quilted pillow top and matching unquilted piece together with right sides facing and raw edges even. Stitch together ½" from raw edges, leaving a 6" opening in center of one side. Clip into seam allowances all around curve of round pillow; clip corners of seam allowances on other two pillows. Turn each to right side. Stuff pillows fully with fiberfill, pushing fiberfill well into corners. Turn edges of opening in ½", and slip-stitch opening closed.

PUFFED PILLOWS
ON PAGE 36

EQUIPMENT: Ruler. Compass (for round pillow only). Sharp, hard-lead pencil or dry ball-point pen. Scissors. Dressmaker's carbon paper. Sewing machine or quilting needle. Straight pins. Sewing needle.

MATERIALS: Paper for patterns. Pastel, closely-woven fabric, 36" wide, ½ yard for each pillow. Matching sewing thread. Muslin, 36" wide, ¾ yard for all three pillows. Dacron polyester batting and fiberfill

DIRECTIONS: For each pillow, mark two outlines on right side of outer fabric using hard-lead pencil. Mark two 14½"-diameter circles for round pillow; mark two 11" x 17" rectangles for rectangular pillow; mark two 14½" squares for square pillow. Cut out, adding ½" all around each outline for seam allowance. For backing, cut one piece of muslin to match each outline. Omitting seam allowance, cut two matching pieces of batting for each pillow.

Trace the three actual-size patterns shown on the following six pages. To transfer each design, center pat-

DENIM PATCHWORK PILLOWS
ON PAGE 37

SIZE: 13½" square.

EQUIPMENT: Pencil. Ruler. Scissors. Straight pins. Lightweight cardboard. Iron. Sewing needle. Clear nail polish.

MATERIALS: For each pillow: large scraps of denim in various shades of blue; number of shades for each is shown in diagrams. Harmonizing cotton or cotton-blend fabric for back, 14½" square. Blue sewing thread. For inner pillow: ½ yard of muslin, 36" wide. Polyester fiberfill for stuffing.

DIRECTIONS: Dimensions and shape of each patch are shown in the piecing diagrams. All Log Cabin pieces are ¾" wide with the exception of the center square. Use different shades of blue as indicated in the photograph. Cut each patch shape out of cardboard to use as a template. To keep template from fraying, go over the edges with clear nail polish. Place template on wrong side of fabric; mark outline, then mark ¼" beyond outline all around for seam allowance. On Log Cabin square, positioning of shades may vary from block to block, as long as the distinction between light and dark is maintained.

Diagrams are for one-quarter of design for Log Cabin, Eastern Star and Octagon Mosaic, and for one-half of design for Jacob's Ladder. With right sides facing, pin and sew pieces for each quarter or half together following diagram and stitch ¼" from edges; press seam allowances to one side. Repeat for remaining quarters or half of each pillow. For Octagon Mosaic, make two quar-

ters with dark centers and two with light centers. Stitch the quarters or halves for each pillow together, following photograph on Page 37.

With right sides facing, stitch completed pillow front and coordinated back together ½" from raw edges; leave a 10" opening in center of one side. Turn cover to right side.

To make inner pillow, cut two 15" squares from muslin. Stitch edges together on all sides, ½" from raw edges; leave a 6" opening at center of one side. Turn right side out and stuff with polyester fiberfill. Turn edges of opening in and slip-stitch opening closed. Insert muslin pillow into pillow cover; slip-stitch opening closed.

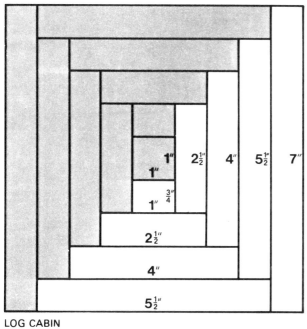

LOG CABIN

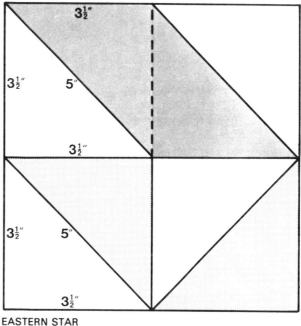

EASTERN STAR

OCTAGON MOSAIC

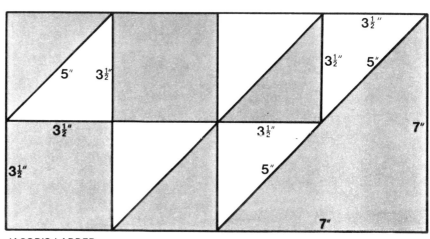

JACOB'S LADDER

ACTUAL-SIZE PATTERN
FOR SQUARE PUFFED PILLOW

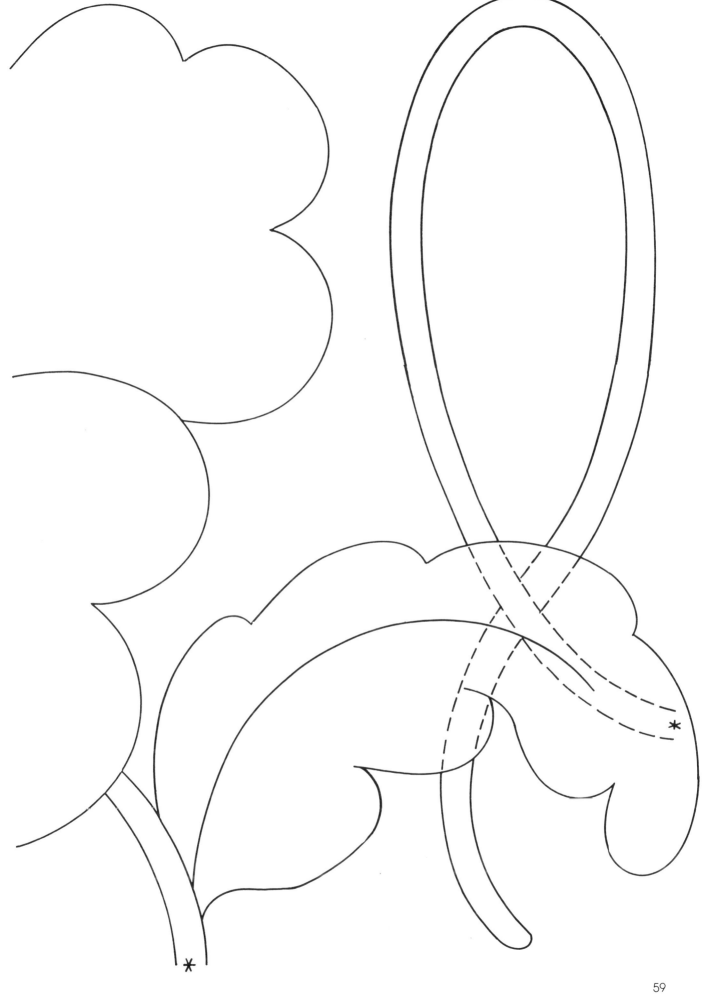

**ACTUAL-SIZE PATTERN
FOR ROUND PUFFED PILLOW**

HEN PLAQUE & POT HOLDERS
ON PAGE 37

EQUIPMENT: Pencil. Ruler. Scissors. Straight pins. Sewing needle. Sewing machine with zigzag attachment. Iron. Brush for varnishing plaque. Felt tip pen (optional).

MATERIALS: Paper for patterns. Small pieces of printed, checked, solid red, yellow, and natural-color fabrics. White sewing thread. Batting. For plaque: one 6″ x 9″ piece of unfinished wood; two small cup hooks; small can of mat-finish varnish.

DIRECTIONS: Enlarge patterns by copying on paper ruled in 1″ squares; complete half pattern for egg indicated by long broken line. Short broken line indicates completed shape of comb.

To make pot holders: Cut a 6″ square of printed fabric for each pot holder. Cut egg shape from natural-color fabric and from batting. Center egg between opposite corners on right side of square over batting; pin in place. Stitch around egg, using narrow zigzag stitch and covering edges of fabric and batting.

Cut four strips of checked fabric, each 1¼″ wide x 7½″ long, for border. Place two strips on opposite sides of square with right sides facing and raw edges flush. Stitch to square ¼″ from raw edges. Press seam allowances toward center.

Stitch remaining strips to square in same manner, overlapping ends of first strips; press allowances toward outer edges. Cut one 7½″ square of natural-color fabric for back and two 7″ squares of batting for each pot holder. Place right side of pot holder face down. Center and baste two layers of batting to wrong side. Cut a 3½″ x 1¼″ strip of printed fabric for hanging loop. Fold in half lengthwise with right sides facing; stitch along length ¼″ from raw edges, leaving both ends open. Turn right side out and press. Tack ends together and to right side of pot holder at one corner, with raw edges flush. Pin front and back of pot holder together with right sides facing. Stitch front and back together ¼″ from raw edges, enclosing loop; leave 4″ opening in center of one side. Turn pot holder to right side. Turn raw edges of opening in and slip-stitch opening closed. Stitch around egg and along inside edge of border through all thicknesses.

To make plaque: Using enlarged pattern, cut pieces for body of hen, comb, beak, wattle and eye from different fabrics as indicated by photo. Position pieces for complete hen on plaque as shown in photograph. Glue comb to wood first, then glue body of hen in place, partially overlapping comb as indicated in diagram. Glue wattle in place, then glue eye in place on wattle; glue beak to wood. If color of beak is close to color of wood, outline beak with soft pencil or felt tip pen. Screw cup hooks into bottom edge of plaque. Coat front of plaque with mat-finish varnish; let dry.

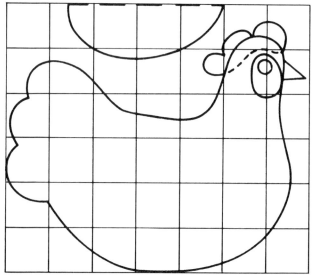

EACH SQUARE = 1″

BACKGAMMON "BOARD"
ON PAGE 38

Size: 19″ x 30″

EQUIPMENT: Ruler. Pencil. Scissors. Thin, stiff cardboard. Tailor's chalk. Sewing machine.

MATERIALS: Closely woven cotton or cotton-blend fabrics, 36″ wide: ¼ yard each green and blue; ½ yard white; ⅛ yard yellow; ⅛ yard each green and blue polka-dot fabric; ½ yard green printed fabric; ⅝ yard fabric for lining. Green singlefold bias tape, 3 yards. Dacron batting. White sewing thread. Purchased counters and dice.

DIRECTIONS: Piecing diagram is for one-quarter of board plus center strip, and shows size and placement of each section. Solid lines indicate outlines of patches; broken lines indicate quilting.

Make cardboard patterns for patches as follows: Pattern A: Mark a rectangle 2″ × 6″; draw lines from center of one 2″ side to opposite corners. Pattern B: Half of A. Pattern C: Mark rectangle 3″ × 4″. Mark center point on each of the four sides. Connect center points with four diagonal lines for diamond shape. Pattern D: Half of pattern C, cut on 4″ length. Pattern E: Half of pattern C, cut on 3″ width. Pattern F: 2″ × 3″. Pattern G: 2″ × 6″.

Mark around patterns on wrong side of fabrics. Adding ¼″ seam allowances all around, cut pieces as follows: Pattern A: 12 blue, 12 green, 20 white. Pattern B: 8 white. Pattern C: 4 yellow. Pattern D: 6 polka-dotted blue, 6 polka-dotted green. Pattern E: 4 yellow. Pattern F: 1 printed green. Pattern G: 2 yellow.

Following piecing diagram and photograph, assemble fabric pieces starting with four playing sections. Place pieces with right sides facing; stitch together ¼″ from raw edges, and press seam allowances open. Then assemble the two horizontal center strips and the center vertical strip in same manner. Join these assembled sections for main part of board. For border, cut four pieces 2½″ wide from printed green fabric, two 15½″ long and two 30½″ long. With right sides together, and raw edges flush, stitch shorter pieces of border to ends of board, then longer pieces to side, ¼″ from raw edges. Board should measure 30½″ × 19½″. Cut lining and batting same size.

Using ruler and tailor's chalk, mark quilting lines on board as shown by broken lines in piecing diagram. Pin and baste board, batting, and lining together. Using white thread and starting in center and working outward, quilt on all marked lines and along outline of each white triangle, close to all seams. Quilt along inner edge of border, and ½″ from outer edge of board.

With right sides together, stitch single-fold bias tape around edges of completed board, stitching ¼″ from edges. Fold tape around edge of board and slip-stitch to back.

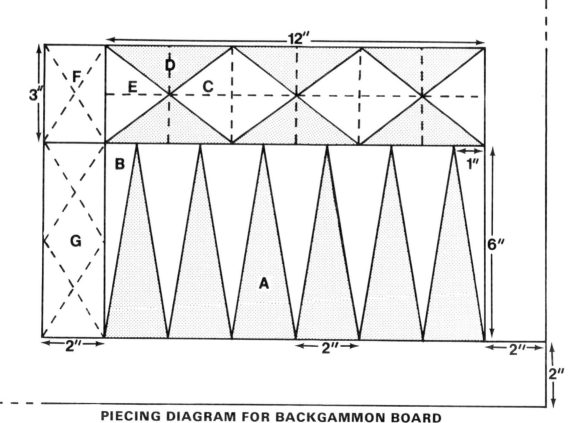

PIECING DIAGRAM FOR BACKGAMMON BOARD

PATCHWORK CHECKERBOARD

ON PAGE 38

SIZE: 17½" square.

EQUIPMENT: Pencil. Ruler. Scissors. Tracing paper. Dressmaker's tracing paper. Hard-lead pencil. Thin, stiff cardboard. Tailor's chalk. Zigzag sewing machine.

MATERIALS: Closely woven cotton or cotton-blend fabric, 36" wide, red and black, ½ yard each. Scraps of printed red fabrics. Scraps of red and black felt. Black and red sewing thread. Polyester batting. Black double-fold bias tape, ½" wide, 2 yards.

DIRECTIONS: From black fabric, cut four borders, 12" × 2¾", four corners, 2¾" square; 32 center blocks, 1½" square, adding ¼" seam allowance around all sides of each piece. From varied red print fabrics, cut 32 center blocks 1½" square; from red fabric, cut lining 17½" square, adding 1¼" seam allowance around all sides. Cut batting 17½" square.

Alternating black and printed red squares, join them to make eight rows of eight blocks each; stitch blocks together with right sides facing, ¼" from raw edges. Join rows together in same manner to make playing field as shown in photograph. Note that two corner squares of field are black and two are red.

Trace actual-size patterns on tracing paper. Transfer castle motif to four black 2¾" squares, using dressmaker's tracing paper and pencil. Embroider castle, using small zigzag stitch and red thread; fill in flags on two blocks with red satin stitch.

With right sides facing, stitch two borders to opposite sides of playing field ¼" from raw edges. Stitch embroidered corners with red flags to ends of one remaining border, and corners with black flags to ends of other border. Stitch borders to playing field, with castle flags at outside edges. Press all seam allowances away from center of "board."

With tailor's chalk, mark diagonal lines in both directions over black blocks, going through corners. Place checker "board" wrong side up. Place batting on top, making sure it is smooth. Place lining on top of batting. Baste around all sides through all thicknesses, ¼" from edges. Starting in center, stitch on marked diagonal lines and around edge of each black square, using black thread. Stitch along inner edges of black borders, close to playing field and continuing to outer edges. Bring threads to wrong side of "board" and knot.

With right sides together, stitch bias tape to edge of "board"; fold over to back enclosing raw edges, and slip-stitch to lining.

Using bottle cap, or cardboard circle with 1½" diameter, mark and cut out 24 red felt circles and 24 black felt circles. Cut 24 matching circles of batting. Transfer crown motif to 12 red circles and 12 black circles. Using zigzag stitch, embroider crown motif on red circles with black thread; embroider black circles with red thread. To make each checker, place a circle of batting between one embroidered circle and a matching plain circle; hold the three layers in place with basting stitches and stitch around the edges with zigzag stitch. Trim to edge of stitching if necessary.

PATTERNS FOR CHECKERBOARD

BABY ALBUM COVER

ON PAGE 38

SIZE: For 11¾" x 12¼" photograph album.

EQUIPMENT: Scissors. Tape measure. Pencil. Dressmaker's tracing paper. Straight pins. Sewing needle. Large-eyed needle. Embroidery scissors. Zigzag sewing machine (optional).

MATERIALS: Paper for patterns. Heavy white cotton or cotton-blend fabric, 36" wide, ⅜ yard. 25 fabric scraps for patches, each 2¾" square. Fabric scraps for appliques, including red for apple and green for leaf. Bias

66

seam tape, ½" wide, 3 yards. Lightweight white fabric for lining, 36" wide, ⅜ yard. Quilt batting, one layer, 34" x 13¾". Sewing thread to match fabrics. Pearl cotton, size 3, one small skein each of yellow and blue, or colors desired.

DIRECTIONS: If the dimensions of album to be covered are different, measure height and width of album and adjust measurements before cutting fabric. From heavy white fabric, cut piece for back 13¾" x 18" (including back inside flap); piece for front inside flap, 13¾" x 5½"; and two strips for top and bottom borders of front cover, each 1½" x 11¾". From lining fabric, cut piece 13½" x 34¼".

Arrange patches in desired order to form a square with five rows of five patches each. Since four patches along right edge will be appliqued with the word "BABY," keep colors of these appliques in mind. Other appliques can be arranged as desired. With right sides facing, stitch patches together ¼" from raw edges to make a row of five patches. Repeat for four other rows; stitch five rows together in same manner.

APPLIQUE PATTERNS FOR BABY ALBUM

Enlarge applique patterns by copying on paper ruled in 1" squares; broken lines indicate embroidery lines. Using dressmaker's tracing paper, trace outlines of appliques onto right sides of fabric scraps in various colors; trace apple on red fabric, leaf on green fabric.

To applique patches with zigzag sewing machine, baste each scrap, tracing side up, onto center of desired patch. Following photograph, place each letter of "BABY" on a patch along right edge. Place other appliques on desired squares. Using matching thread and close zigzag stitch, stitch around each traced outline. Using embroidery scissors, trim away excess fabric close to stitching; be careful when cutting around letters not to cut into patchwork. Complete flower by adding contrasting center and stitching in place. Using contrasting thread, complete butterfly and balloon with zigzag stitching along broken lines.

To applique patches by hand, cut traced patterns from scraps, adding ¼" around all edges. To turn under edges of "holes" in letters "A" and "B," make slits in center of "holes" and clip into excess fabric. Turn edges under ¼" and baste all around. Slip-stitch appliques in place.

With right sides facing and making ¼" seams, stitch strips of white fabric for top and bottom borders of front cover in place along upper and lower edges of patchwork square. In same manner, stitch piece for front inside flap along right edge of patchwork square; then stitch piece for back along left edge of patchwork square. Press all seams away from center.

Place album cover wrong side up. Place batting on top, making sure it is smooth. Place lining on top of batting. Baste all layers together. Stitch around all sides through all thicknesses, ¼" from edges.

Cut two 13¾" lengths of bias tape. With right sides together, stitch strips along right and left edges of album cover, ¼" from edges. Cut two 34¼" lengths of tape; with right sides facing, stitch one strip to upper and one strip to lower edge of cover, ¼" from each edge. Press bias tape outward, covering raw edges.

With right side up, fold each side edge of cover 4" toward center, so right sides are facing. Stitch upper and lower edges together just inside stitching line of bias tape. Trim folded corners diagonally and turn right side out. Turn bias tape along upper and lower edges to inside and slip-stitch in place between the two flaps.

Thread large-eyed needle with two strands of one color of pearl cotton. Tuft cover at each corner of each patch. To tuft, push threaded needle from right side of album cover through fabric, batting and lining to back, leaving thread end on right side. Push needle back up again to right side, about ¼" away from first stitch. Tie yarn in firm double knot. Clip ends to desired length, at least ½". Make tufts, alternating colors of pearl cotton as desired. Slip cover onto album.

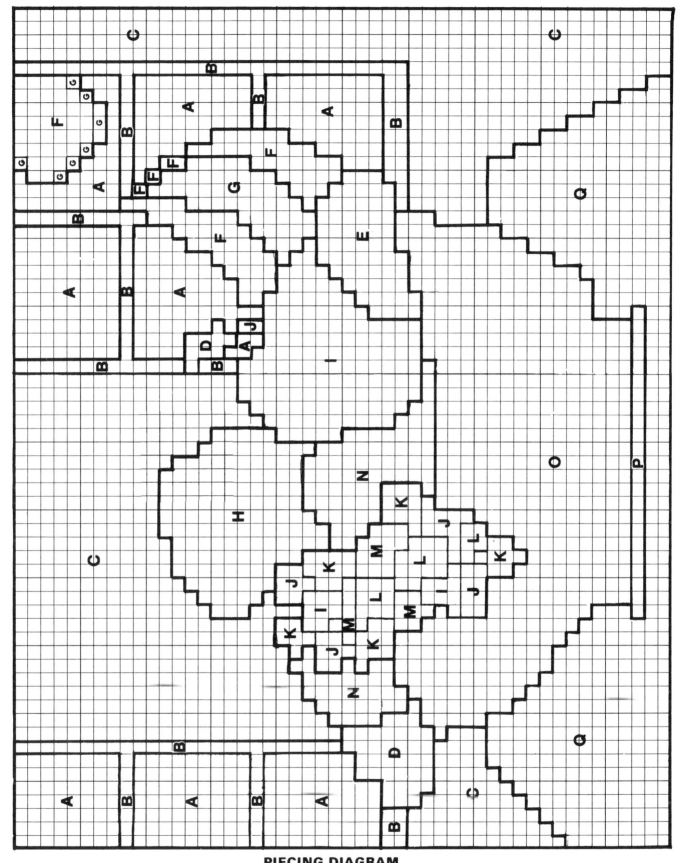

PIECING DIAGRAM

A = LIGHT BLUE	G = GOLD	L = LAVENDER
B = DARK BLUE	H = ORANGE	M = MAGENTA
C = BLUE-GREEN	I = RED	N = PEACH & PINK
D = YELLOW-GREEN	J = RED-BROWN	O = BLACK & WHITE
E = BRONZE-GREEN	K = PURPLE	P = BLACK
F = YELLOW		Q = BEIGE & TAN

"STILL LIFE" PATCHWORK

ON PAGE 39

SIZE: 106″ x 127½″

EQUIPMENT: Ruler. Scissors. Thin, stiff cardboard. Dark and light-colored pencils. Sewing needles. Sewing machine. Clear nail polish.

MATERIALS: Paper for patterns. Closely woven, printed cotton or cotton-blend fabrics, 36″ wide, in the following colors and amounts: light blue, A on piecing diagram, 1½ yards; dark blue, B, ⅝ yard; green and blue-green, C, 4¼ yards. ¼ yard each of the following: Yellow-green, D; bronze-green, E; gold, G; red-brown, J; purple, K; lavender, L; magenta, M. ½ yard each of yellow, F; orange, H; peach and pink, N. Red, I, ⅓ yard; black and white, O, 1⅞ yards; beige and tan, Q, 1⅝ yards. 45″-wide fabrics in solid colors: black, P, ⅛ yard; white, ½ yard; navy, 2 yards; medium blue for lining, 9 yards; fabric for inner lining, about 7 yards. Navy sewing thread. Polyester or cotton batting.

DIRECTIONS: Bowl of fruit design is pieced entirely of square patches; corners are appliqued. Each square on piecing diagram represents one square patch of design. To make patterns for patches, cut several 1¾″ squares from cardboard; coat edges with clear nail polish to keep them from fraying. Mark squares on wrong sides of fabrics, and add ¼″ seam allowance all around each one. Cut square patches as follows: 457 patches of light blue, A; 142 of dark blue, B; 837 green and blue-green, C; 46 yellow-green, D; 59 bronze-green, E; 120 yellow, F; 49 gold, G; 127 orange, H; 149 red, I; 34 red-brown, J; 43 purple, K; 28 lavender, L; 26 magenta, M; 99 peach and pink, N; 480 black and white, O; 23 black, P (or cut one strip 23 squares long); 401 beige and tan, Q.

Quilt is pieced and quilted in sections, starting in the center and working outward. Sections are indicated by heavy outlines on piecing diagram. Begin with bunch of grapes, left of center. Following piecing diagram, stitch I, J, K, L, and M patches together into rows, then stitch rows together to form a section. Cut batting and inner lining same size as pieced together grape section. Turn under outside seam allowance of pieced section and press to wrong side. Center lining and batting on pieced section; pin and baste all three layers together. Set sewing machine for wide, close zigzag stitch. Machine-stitch over seams dividing color areas, indicated on diagram by light lines; use navy thread. Trim lining to match folded edge of pieced section; trim batting ⅛″ smaller than pieced section all around. Make pieced sections H,

N, I, and E and join; do not turn under outside seam allowances. Cut batting and inner lining ⅛″ larger than these and all other sections; center, pin and baste all three layers together. Quilt seams indicated by heavy lines in the piecing diagram, in same manner as for grape section. To join the two completed sections, place edge of grape section on second section, overlapping edge of second section ¼″; baste together. Zigzag-stitch the pieces together, then remove basting thread. Make and join D and N sections at left of grapes and quilt on seam dividing sections. Join to left side of grapes; when joining sections, always overlap edges as before. Make and join O and P sections to make bowl, but do not quilt on seam joining O and P. Join bowl section to completed fruit section. Make and join sun, right hand window, bananas, apple stem, and leaf sections; quilt on heavy dividing lines. Join completed corner section to I, E, and O sections of fruit and bowl. Make and join remaining sections in the following order: wall section C at right to sections B and O; table section Q to O, P, and C; small wall section C at left to section D, O and Q; left hand window section to D and C; upper wall section C to window and fruit sections. Trim edges of lining and batting to match outside seam allowance of quilt.

For inner border, cut four strips of white fabric, each 2¼″ wide; cut two 88″ long and two 112½″ long; measurements include ¼″ seam allowances all around. Using straight stitch and with right sides together, sew 88″ strips to sides of quilt, ¼″ from raw edges, then sew longer strips to top and bottom of quilt. For second border, cut four strips from navy fabric, each 8¼″ wide; cut two 91½″ long and two 112½″. Cut four pieces 8¼″ square for corners. To make appliques, enlarge fruit patterns on paper ruled in 1″ squares. Make a cardboard pattern for each separate part of each design. Mark patterns on wrong side of fabric and add ¼″ seam allowances all around each piece; cut appliques out. Pin and baste each one in place on corner square and straight-stitch around marked outline. Trim excess fabric to ⅛″. Using close zigzag stitch, stitch around each applique, covering straight stitching and ⅛″ margin. Join a square to each end of the two longer navy strips by stitching ¼″ from raw edges. Stitch the 88″-long navy strips to sides of quilt, then longer strips to top and bottom, using straight stitch for all seams. Quilt should measure 106½″ x 127½″, plus outside seam allowance. Turn ¼″ seam allowance to wrong side and baste.

If using completed design for a wall hanging, fruit and bowl sections of design may be given extra dimension with padding. (If using it as a bed covering, the padding is best omitted.) To do so, turn work wrong side up. Slit inner lining only in center of each fruit and bowl section. Stuff with extra batting, then slip-stitch slits closed.

For lining, cut two pieces 107" x 43½", and one piece 107" x 43" from medium blue fabric. With raw edges flush, stitch the two 43½"-wide pieces to the 43" wide piece on long sides ½" from raw edges. Lining is 107" x 128"; turn ¼" seam allowance to wrong side of lining and baste. Cut batting 106" x 127". Place pieced quilt wrong side up; center batting on top of pieced quilt; center lining on top of batting, enclosing edges of batting between the two layers. Folded edges of pieced quilt and lining should be flush. Pin and baste all three layers together. Use zigzag stitch to quilt along inner and outer seam lines of white border, around corner squares, and ¼" in from folded edges of quilt; if using completed design as a wall hanging, do not stitch ¼" from folded top edge, this will be slip-stitched closed after inserting loops for hanging.

To make loops, cut seven 5½" x 7" pieces from blue lining fabric. With right sides facing, fold each strip in half lengthwise. Stitch ¼" from long raw edges of each strip; turn strips to right side and press. Stitch along both long edges of each strip ⅛" from edges. Fold strips in half crosswise and stitch ¼" from raw edges. Raw edges of strips are inserted ½" between front of quilt and lining, and stitched to lining. Pin one strip to lining ¼" in from each side edge; space five remaining strips evenly between them. Baste strips to lining; zigzag-stitch in place. Slip-stitch front of quilt to lining at top edge, enclosing raw edges of strips.

PATCHWORK VEST
ON PAGE 40

EQUIPMENT: Pencil. Ruler. Scissors. Lightweight cardboard. Straight pins. Sewing and embroidery needles. Sewing machine.

MATERIALS: Pattern for vest (McCall's Pattern 5838 could be used for man's vest, or Pattern 5634 for misses' vest). Fabric scraps in a variety of colors and textures, such as satin, taffeta, velvet and brocade, in solid colors and patterns. One yard lightweight fabric for lining, 44" wide. Six-strand embroidery floss to match lining fabric. Six button molds, ½" diameter. Four hooks and eyes.

DIRECTIONS: Patchwork can be a "crazy quilt" of squares, rectangles, triangles and other shapes, or made mostly of squares, as in vest shown.

Patchwork is made in sections from which pattern pieces can be cut. To make patchwork, lay out scraps of fabric on a large, flat surface and arrange adjoining colors and textures for a pleasing effect, in either a random pattern or a geometric design. Cut scraps in desired shapes, allowing ¼" seam allowance on all sides, so they can be stitched together into sections of the required size.

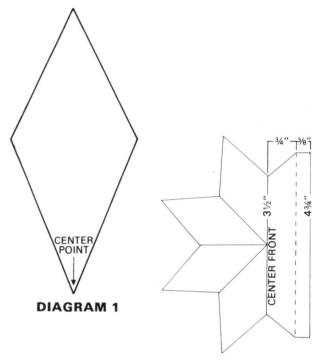

DIAGRAM 1

DIAGRAM 2

Vest shown has eight-pointed patchwork star worked into front sections of vest. Star is made of diamond-shaped patches, brown velvet on one side, brown satin on the other. To duplicate star, trace actual-size diamond pattern shown in Diagram 1 onto cardboard; add ¼" seam allowance and cut out. Cut four complete diamonds for each side of front, plus a matching strip cut to dimensions shown in Diagram 2 (plus ¼" seam allowance on all sides). Stitch pieces together by hand or machine as shown in diagram and place half-stars in patchwork layouts for front sections of vest, fitting contrasting patches between points. Stitch patchwork pieces for each section of vest together; press seams flat. With center front line of star matching center front line of pattern, pin and cut front sections of vest; then cut back sections. Stitch together following pattern directions. Trim front edge ¾" on left side for men, or right side for women. Machine-stitch ½" in from raw edges.

Four flower motifs are embroidered on front of vest shown. Any motif desired could be used, placed symmetrically or scattered at random over entire vest. Turn ⅝" seam allowance to wrong side around edges and armholes of vest, clipping ⅜" into seam allowances around curves; baste in place. Cut lining and assemble in same manner as vest. Machine-stitch ¾" in from all raw edges and clip around curves. Turn edges under on stitching line and pin lining to vest, wrong sides together, with turned edges of lining meeting stitching line on vest. Slip-stitch lining to vest. Sew on four hooks and eyes or make "eyes" by hand in matching thread. Cover buttons following directions on package. Sew to vest ½" in from edge.

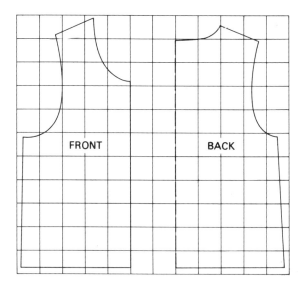

PATTERNS FOR STRIPED PATCHWORK VEST

STRIPED PATCHWORK VEST
ON PAGE 40

SIZE: Pattern is for a Misses' size 10; to make pattern larger or smaller, add ⅝" to, or subtract ⅝" from, each side seam for each one-size difference.

EQUIPMENT: Pencil. Ruler. Scissors. Paper for patterns. Pins. Sewing needle. Small crochet hook.

MATERIALS: Closely woven cotton or cotton-blend fabric, 45" wide, ⅓ yard each of nine printed fabrics in a related color scheme. Fabric for lining, 45" wide, ⅔ yard. Polyester batting. Sewing thread. Small amount of yarn or crochet cotton. Three ball buttons.

DIRECTIONS: Enlarge patterns for front and back of vest by copying on paper ruled in 1" squares; complete half pattern indicated by broken line.

To make front of vest, cut center strip 2" x 21¼". Cut 14 side strips, 1¾" x 21", cutting two each of seven different printed fabrics. Starting with center strip, place seven strips on each side of the center strip in a symmetrical arrangement of color and pattern. With right sides facing, stitch strips together ¼" from raw edges on the 21" sides. Press all seam allowances open. Pin front pattern of vest to striped "fabric," placing center of pattern in center of middle strip. Cut out vest front in one piece, then cut through center of 2" strip to separate the front into two sides.

Join fabric for back of vest in same manner as for front, using seven 1¾" strips on each side of the 2" center strip. Arrange strips in same color scheme as for front. Pin pattern for back of vest to striped "fabric," placing center of pattern in center of middle strip. Cut out back of vest in one piece.

Using paper pattern, cut lining for front in two pieces; cut lining for back in one piece. Cut two thin layers of batting a little larger than front; cut one thin layer of batting a little larger than back. Pin and baste batting to wrong sides of front and back. Pin and baste lining on top of batting, making sure raw edges of lining and striped "fabric" are even. To quilt, stitch on each strip next to seams. Trim batting to same size as each piece, then trim ¼" in from each side and shoulder seam so batting will not be caught in seams.

With right sides facing, pin front and back sections of striped "fabric" together at shoulders and side seams, leaving lining fabric free. Stitch together ¼" from raw edges; press seams open. At each seam, turn one raw edge of lining fabric under ¼"; overlap the remaining raw edge and slip-stitch in place. Stitch on finished seams to quilt.

From remaining printed fabric, cut bias strips 1¼" wide for binding. Join bias strips to make binding approximately four yards long. Stitch binding to all raw edges of vest with right sides together, stitching ¼" from raw edges. Turn binding to inside of vest, leaving a ⅜" bound edge on the right side of the vest. Turn in raw edges of binding ¼" and slip-stitch to lining.

Sew three ball buttons to front of vest, one at the top, and the remaining two spaced 3" apart. Crochet chain loops to other side of vest for fastening, using yarn or crochet cotton.

ALL ABOUT
THE ART

OF APPLIQUE

Applique means different things to different people. To the artist, it is a medium for creative expression; to a teenager, it's the quickest way to make a personal statement on her jeans; and to the homemaker, it is a rewarding needle art that can, in its simplest form, be used to brighten existing household accessories or, in its more complex, be an outlet for her own creativity. Now let the next few pages show you how to bring applique into your world. Learn about its variations, the equipment you'll need, and the steps to follow for your first project. Then, trace one of our actual-size patterns for your design, and you're on the way to discovering a fascinating "new" art that is centuries old!

THE ART OF APPLIQUE

Applique, the imaginative art of applying fabrics to other fabrics with stitches, is one of the oldest and most familiar of needlework techniques. Although we are tempted to tie its beginnings to the evolution of the American quilt, applique is, indeed, an art that is centuries old. No doubt even Cleopatra was familiar with it, as witnessed by an Egyptian funeral tent that dates back thousands of years!

Although applique is basically stitching one fabric to another, it has often been embellished with a variety of embroidery stitches, buttons, and beads. The choice of such adornments is left entirely to the discretion of the stitcher. Metallic threads of silver and gold were often embroidered onto the intricate appliques of 16th century Europe; while other textures such as leather, mohair, shells, and seed pods have been incorporated into appliques of today. The art of applique knows no bounds— it can be a simple enjoyment of color upon color, or it can be a tour de force of embroidery, constantly surprising the beholder with fascinating oddments.

Just as its creativity knows no bounds, the art of applique knows no national boundaries. The basic idea is the same, but each rendition of it is colored by local tradition, design, and mood; therefore, a basically simple needlework technique is one of the richest in looks and applications. Beautiful tapestries from fifteenth century Germany reflect the influence of the Church and the religious art of the times; brilliantly colored molas from South American Indians capture the charm and simplicity of the people who created them; intricate "reshts" from Persia duplicate the delicate bird and flower motifs so often found in Eastern art. Each is an example of applique; yet, each is an art form that is truly distinctive

It is this versatility that makes applique the vibrant art that it is. For *anyone* can applique—from the youngest child to the most accomplished needleworker. Applique can be as simple or as complicated as the stitcher desires. A simple flower shape stitched atop a well worn spot on a pair of child's overalls is just as surely applique as the finest piece of linen embellished with thousands of tiny fabric pieces. The basic materials are the same; but the individual needs, taste, and expertise are what make applique one of the most personal of all the needle arts.

APPLIQUE EQUIPMENT

As with any needle art, the proper equipment is necessary to make your work enjoyable and to assure a beautiful finished product. All equipment should be clean and in prime condition: sewing scissors should not be used for any other household chore; pins and needles should be rust free and absolutely straight; threads should be fresh from the spool. To make your maintenance job easy, keep an emery bag handy to remove rust from pins and needles—it will sharpen them too! And, when scissors seem dull, have them sharpened professionally.

NEEDLES: Embroidery needles will answer most needs for applique. Since the eye of an embroidery needle is fairly large, it can be easily threaded with floss and other fine threads. If you are planning to work with yarn, a darning needle with a sharp, pointed tip is the correct needle to use. If you are using the sewing machine, check your machine manual to determine the correct needle for the fabric you have selected.

THREADS: Before selecting colors, be sure the threads you are considering are *colorfast*. Any fine mercerized cotton thread or polyester thread may be used, but it is wise to consider how the finished piece will be used as well. Since cotton threads may shrink when washed, it is best to select a polyester thread if the item being stitched is going to be laundered. Remember, polyester thread has the ability to stretch and recover, while cotton may shrink and cause unwanted puckers in the fabric.

SCISSORS: Good, sharp scissors are a must. If applique pieces are large, use dressmaker's shears; for smaller pieces, fine embroidery scissors are needed. Pinking shears may be used for special effects and add a decorative note to felt appliques.

STRAIGHT PINS: Because all pieces are pinned in place before they are stitched, straight pins should be clean and rust free. Do not use pins that have been bent out of shape.

THIMBLE: The use of a thimble is purely personal; however, if you do not normally use a thimble when sewing, a piece of adhesive tape on the tip of your middle finger will protect it.

ALSO HELPFUL: Certain basics are needed for transferring designs to fabric; see page 80 for their description and use. Other items which might make your work easier are a steam iron, cellophane or masking tape, pen, pencils, and tailor's chalk.

APPLIQUE VARIATIONS

Although a variety of effects can be created with applique, additional interest can be added to the finished piece by including one or more of the different types of applique in your work. Or, the entire piece may be stitched in one of these variations:

RAISED OR PADDED APPLIQUE: To add dimension to your stitchery, parts of the applique can be gently padded. To create this effect, partially stitch applique pieces onto background fabric, then, using a knitting needle, gently push batting or cotton under the applique. Continue stitching and stuffing until pattern piece is contoured as you desire.

DETACHED APPLIQUE: For an unusual note in your work, make one or more of the design components detached. Butterflies, flowers, raindrops, etc., are especially effective in this technique. To make a detached applique, you must cut a front and a back for the applique piece; be sure to include ¼" seam allowance all around each piece. With right sides together, stitch around each piece; leave a small opening for turning. Turn piece right side out and sew opening closed. To attach applique to background fabric, tack at center with a small stitch or a decorative embroidery stitch.

REVERSE APPLIQUE: This technique involves sometimes as many as five or six layers of fabric, all in different colors. Parts of the top layers are cut away to reveal the color below. To try your hand at this delightful variation, follow these few simple steps: 1. After number of colors and their arrangement have been decided, baste fabrics together all around edges and diagonally across. To reveal first color under top layer, use a pair of sharp embroidery scissors to cut away design area in top layer 2. Clip the edge of fabric to be turned under on all curves or corners and turn in ⅛". Using matching sewing thread, slip-stitch edge to layer below. 3. Continue cutting out design sections, going down two or more layers so that all colors show.

SABRINA WORK: In this delightful variation of applique, complete fruits, flowers, etc., are cut from fabric and stitched onto the background with buttonhole stitches. Design areas, (such as stems) that are too delicate to be cut from fabric, are embroidered running directly from the applique fabric onto the background.

FELT APPLIQUE: This variation is perhaps the most time-saving of all. Since felt does not ravel, applique pieces are cut exactly to size and stitched, or glued to the background fabric.

CREATING YOUR OWN DESIGNS

What's the best thing about applique? The fact that there are no rules to follow! Colors can be monochromatic or borrowed from the entire spectrum; textures can be light and airy, rough and solid...or a combination of both. Best of all, the designs can be your very own. Ideas and motifs are everywhere, just waiting for you to adapt them. Not an artist? That's no problem. There's a wealth of designs at your fingertips. Following are just a few sources that are waiting to be discovered!

MAGAZINES: Almost every page in a magazine can be an inspiration for an applique design. If you are fortunate, you may see just the right subject in just the right size. If so, put a piece of tracing paper or acetate over the image and draw around it, including as much detail as you can. Then take away the tracing and carefully refine and simplify the outlines, eliminating all but the most necessary detail. Divide your image into basic sections or sub-patterns, for appliqueing with different fabrics. Later, you can add still more detailing with embroidery or quilting lines, if you need it.

COLORING BOOKS AND CHILDREN'S ART: Children's coloring books and artwork are a good source for designs already pared down to their essential outlines. Cut out shapes, move them around, combine and alter them.

COOKIE CUTTERS: Don't overlook your household utensils—starting in the kitchen with cookie cutters.

PHOTOGRAPH ALBUMS: A family portrait gallery is so easy in silhouette! Start by finding—or taking—photographs of each subject in profile, trying for a good light/dark contrast between subject and background. Have the shots blown up to size, then trace the outlines. Or, if you have a projector, project the slide onto a sheet of paper taped to the wall; trace.

FABRIC AND WALLPAPER: Big, splashy designs on fabrics and wallpapers are the perfect motifs for applique. Using tracing paper, trace and simplify the motif in a heavy line. Then, with lighter lines or a simple dot-dash line, mark off areas that should be embroidered to give design definition.

SIMPLE CUTOUTS: Remember cutting out "snowflakes" in school? To begin, fold a square of paper into quarters or eighths. Then cut away the center point and around the edges in any way you like. Unfold the paper, and there it is—a unique, symmetrical design.

Now that you have selected your pattern, the next step is to transfer the design onto the fabric you are using. There are several methods for transferring. Select the one that gives you the best results on your fabric.

PERFORATED PATTERN: To make a perforated pattern, trace your design on heavy quality tracing paper. Place completed tracing right side up on a well-padded surface such as a pile of newspapers or ironing board. Using straight pin, sewing needle, or unthreaded sewing machine, prick tiny holes along lines of design, about ¹⁄₁₆″ apart. When the perforating is finished, place pattern over background fabric, smooth side up, and weight it down around edges to hold it in place while transferring. The design may be transferred by means of a perforating powder called "pounce" (available at sewing notions counters), and a "pouncer." To make a pouncer, roll up a strip of flannel or felt tightly, sewing it so it remains rolled. Dip the end of the pouncer in powder, tap off excess, then dab and rub it over the perforated outline. Carefully lift up corner of perforated pattern to see if design has been transferred clearly. If not, go over outline with pounce. When the transferring is complete, carefully lift off pattern. To avoid smudging or erasure, use a fine paintbrush and watercolors to connect the dotted lines. To transfer designs to applique fabric, place pattern upside down on fabric so that drawn outline will not show on the right side of applique.

CARBON PAPER: Typewriter carbon may be used between your fabric and the tracing; however, this is apt to smudge and can soil the fabric. Dressmakers' carbon is better to use for this purpose and comes in light and dark colors. For best results, anchor the fabric to a smooth surface with masking tape; place carbon face down on fabric with tracing on top in correct position; tape in place. With a sharp, pointed instrument such as a dry ballpoint pen, carefully mark all lines of design, using enough pressure to transfer the design clearly.

BACK TRACING: A design may also be transferred to a smooth fabric by going over all the lines on the back of tracing with a soft pencil. When outline is complete, tape tracing onto your fabric, right side up, and trace over all lines again, using a hard pencil.

DIRECT TRACING: If the fabric and the tracing are not too large and unwieldy, the design can be transferred by using a light box or an ordinary glass window. With this method, the fabric must be of a light color and not very heavy. Place tracing of design (which must be marked with heavy, dark lines) right side up on light box, or tape to window in bright daylight. Tape fabric on top of tracing. With the light coming from the back, the traced design will show clearly through the fabric and can be easily traced directly onto the fabric, using a sharp pencil.

STITCH TRACING: If applique is to be a loose-weave fabric, stitch tracing will assure you an easy outline to follow. To make your stitch tracing, first draw outline of design on tracing paper. Pin tracing to fabric piece. Using contrasting color thread and sewing needle, take running stitches through paper and fabric along outline of design. When outline is completely stitched, tear away tracing paper, leaving stitched outline on fabric.

TRACING PENCIL: Trace outline of selected design on light-weight tracing paper. Using a hot-iron transfer pencil (available at sewing notions counters in both light and dark colors), go over design lines on back of tracing. Set a dry iron at wool heat (about 400°F.). To make a test sample, draw a few random lines with transfer pencil. Pin sample, pencil side down, on swatch of selected fabric; transfer with a downward stroke of your iron. If transfer lines are clear, the heat of the iron is correct. Using the same procedure, transfer pattern to fabric.

TRANSFER PATTERNS: If you do not wish to create your own designs, you can purchase one of the many designs already prepared for you as transfers. To use printed transfer patterns, always cut away the pattern name, number, and any other part that you do not wish to use. Shake the paper to remove any loose particles of transfer ink. Lay fabric on an ironing board or lightly padded surface; pin in position so it will not shift. Pin transfer pattern in place, having design side down on fabric. Following instructions that come with transfer, use dry iron to transfer ink to fabric. *Important*: Most transfer patterns include a test sample. Because of the variety of fabric blends available, it is most important to test a small piece of your fabric with the individual transfer inks. Carefully note length of time heat is applied to test sample. When you are satisfied with test sample results, use same timing and heat setting.

PATTERNS TO TRACE

Five little friends make charming appliques for children's clothes. Or, use them to create a picture, pillow, or curtain trim in the nursery.

These simple patterns are ready for you to trace and cut out. Large areas are to be appliques; details such as eyes can be embroidered.

HOW TO APPLIQUE

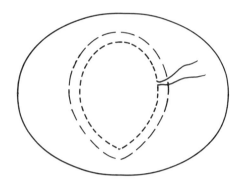

FIG. 1

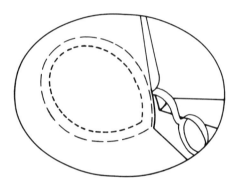

FIG. 2

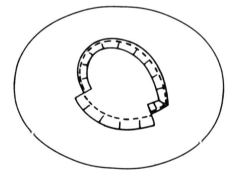

FIG. 3

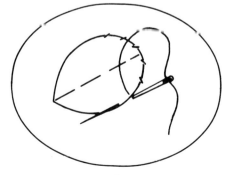

FIG. 4

Choose a fabric that is closely woven and firm enough so that a clean edge results when the applique pieces are cut. For each section of applique, cut a pattern out of thin, stiff cardboard, and mark the right side of each pattern. Press fabric smooth.

Place cardboard pattern on right side of fabric. Using sharp, hard pencils (light-colored pencil on dark fabric and dark pencil on light fabric), mark the outline on the fabric. When marking several pieces on the same fabric, leave at least ½" between pieces. Mark a second outline ¼" outside the design outline. Proceed as directed below, appliqueing by hand or by machine.

BY HAND: Using matching thread and small stitches, machine-stitch all around design outline as shown in Fig. 1. This makes edge easier to turn and neater in appearance. Cut out the applique on the outside line, as in Fig. 2. For a smooth edge, clip into seam allowance at curved edges and corners. Then turn seam allowance to back, just inside stitching as in Fig. 3, and press. Pin and baste the applique on the background, and slip-stitch in place with tiny stitches, as shown in Fig. 4.

BY MACHINE: Pin and baste appliques in place; do not turn under excess fabric. Straight-stitch around appliques on marked lines. Trim away excess fabric to ⅛" from straight stitching. Set sewing machine for close zigzag stitch as directed (¼" wide or less). Zigzag around appliques, covering straight stitching and excess fabric.

Another way to applique is with embroidery stitches.
Most stitches that seem difficult and complex are
really variations of the few basic stitches shown here.
Remember that in applique your overall design is
what's important; the stitches merely provide
the ways and means to create the design.

RUNNING STITCH

The in-and-out running stitch is the simplest and most versatile of all stitches.

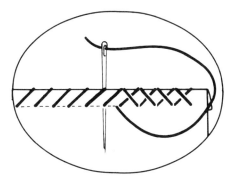

CROSS-STITCH

A decorative stitch for applying fabric firmly.

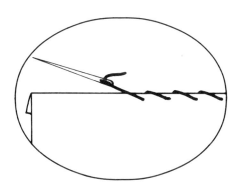

OVERHAND OR OVERLAP STITCH

An excellent slanting stitch for joining one applique fabric to another.

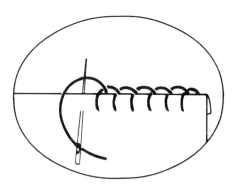

BUTTONHOLE STITCHES

Either type of buttonhole can be used for applique with stitches, reaching either over the fabric or away from it.

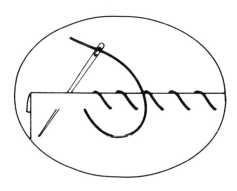

WHIPSTITCH

Another slanting stitch, which is a good strong stitch for binding edges.

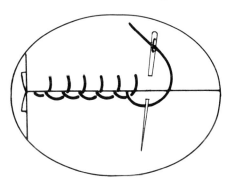

QUILTS: PUTTING IT

ALL TOGETHER

This, as the too-often-said saying goes, is it. If sound effects could be supplied with this book, we'd open this section with a blare of trumpets. Because making beautiful quilts, fully worthy of becoming heirlooms, is what this is all about. We've explored and, we hope, fully explained the creative techniques involved in quilt-making. And even included a few quilts along the way while presenting some smaller projects on which to test your mettle. But if quilting, patchwork and applique really intrigue you, you've no doubt caught the quilt-making fever that's once again sweeping the country. So here are a few final how-to's on putting a quilt together. And then comes a connoisseur's collection of the most fabulous quilts we could find, for your present and future pleasure.

PLANNING YOUR QUILT

Having studied the three colorful and historic crafts of quilting, patchwork and applique traditionally used in quilt-making, and having experimented with smaller projects to test your expertise in the different techniques, it's time to take a deep breath and decide to make a quilt. Whether you plan to do most of the work by hand or by machine, making a quilt means investing considerable time and effort in the finished product, so it's only prudent to spend a little time and thought before beginning to plan a quilt you will be proud of, and one which will give you—and/or whoever uses it—many years of enjoyable service. And while you're thinking about it, think big. In addition to being the most necessary of home furnishings, quilts traditionally were also prized heirlooms, and there's no reason why one you make shouldn't be worthy of the same status.

CONSIDER COLOR FIRST: Working with your own favorite colors is always most enjoyable, but where will the quilt be used? A bed is almost always the largest piece of furniture in a room, and whatever covers it will surely play a dominant role in the color scheme and in the total effect of the room. Keep the color wheel you learned about in school in mind and be aware of the very definite ways in which colors affect each other. You know that the primary colors, the only colors not made by mixing other colors, are red, blue and yellow. Primary colors are strong and vital, and were often used in pairs or all together in early quilt-making. Green, orange and purple are the secondary colors, each made by mixing two of the primary colors. Blue-green, blue-purple, red-orange, red-purple, yellow-green and yellow-orange are intermediary colors, each made by mixing equal parts of a primary color and a neighboring secondary.

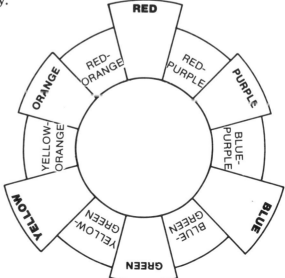

Knowing which colors are what, and where they are on the color wheel, helps in planning a color scheme—for a quilt or anything else. There are three major types of color schemes, any one of which works beautifully in a quilt.

MONOCHROMATIC COLOR SCHEME: A color scheme built around one color, with different intensities and values of that color used to achieve interest. Monochromatic color schemes are often used in contemporary rooms and are particularly effective in small areas.

RELATED COLOR SCHEME: A color scheme which emphasizes two or more colors found side by side on the color wheel, such as blue-green, green, and yellow-green. Frequently used in quilts, the related color scheme is essentially restful, without sharp contrasts.

COMPLEMENTARY COLOR SCHEME: Any color scheme which employs colors found exactly opposite each other on the color wheel, such as blue and orange, red and green, or yellow and purple. Any two complementary colors make each other stronger.

Colors are often mixed freely in quilts, without too much regard for a formal color scheme, but it's wise to consider what the predominant effect will be in relation to the rest of the room.

Remember, too, to select colors of similar intensity. The primary and secondary colors are clear and strong. They can be effective when used together, especially when relieved by lots of white. Colors with white added produce pastels, any and all of which work well together. See how congenial a rainbow of pastels can be in the Lone Star quilt on Page 109.

Placing one color next to its opposite makes both seem brighter, but mixing a color with even a miniscule amount of its opposite grays that color down and makes it dull. These are the colors to be avoided at all costs. They'll add nothing to your quilt nor to the room in which it resides.

The most important color in a quilt, as far as a room's color scheme is concerned, is the background color, which usually includes the border. When choosing additional colors for patches or appliques, always place them on the background, to see how each affects the other, and how each new color gets along with its neighbors.

DECIDING ON A DESIGN: The first element to consider, when thinking about a design for your quilt, is the size of the quilt itself. This depends, of course, on the size of the bed and the type of quilt you want to make—a complete bedcover, coverlet, or throw. See Page 103 to determine the overall dimensions that will best serve your purpose.

Whichever type quilt you decide to make, remember that the part of the quilt that covers the top of the mattress is the major design area, and the part that will display your needlework to the best advantage. Plan your quilt so that the most important elements of the design are contained within this area. For instance, unless they're part of an overall design, large appliqued flowers that droop over the edges of the bed will look just that way—droopy.

Most quilt designs are made up of blocks, as opposed to one large, non-repetitive design. If it's to be blocks, will they form an overall design, or do you want a border? How large will the blocks be, and how will they be set together? Blocks are usually from 10″ to 18″ square, but the size must be determined, in part, by how many will fit evenly into the width and length of the quilt, or within its border. Make these calculations in conjunction with deciding on the overall size of the quilt; adjusting the width or length of the quilt a few inches to accommodate the nearest number of blocks is easy to do and won't make any noticeable difference in the finished size of the quilt.

The blocks can be sewn to each other to make up the quilt top, or to contrasting lattice strips that separate and frame them. The method of joining the blocks, with or without dividing strips, must also be considered in your size calculations, as well as in planning the design. The best way to figure all this out is to plan your quilt on graph paper, which you can line up yourself if the commercially printed variety isn't available. First, lightly pencil in the size of the mattress and add side and foot drops of the desired length plus the pillow allowance, if any. This makes it easy to see how many blocks will fit best, and how large they should be. Try blocks from 12″ to 16″ square first. Lattice strips are usually from 2″ to 4″ wide, so the measurements of either blocks or strips or of both can be adjusted slightly to make your design work. The width of the border, if you're using one, is another adjustable element in your figuring. Working it all out on graph paper will help you decide if the arrangement and proportions of all these elements are pleasing. Now is the time to change them if they're not.

ESTIMATING THE YARDAGE REQUIRED: The scale drawing of the quilt top you made when planning your quilt will come in handy when it's time to estimate how much fabric you need. Most of the fabrics suitable for the top and backing come in a standard 45" width, although woolen fabrics and woolen-type blends are usually 60" or 62" wide. Sheet muslin can be purchased in 72" width, but is less suitable for hand quilting than softer fabrics.

If the top is to be quilted in an overall design, or if small pieces are to be appliqued to a background fabric, you must determine how many widths of the fabric are required to equal the width of the quilt. Multiply the length of the quilt by the number of widths required to find the total yardage. If more than one length is required, cut the second length in half lengthwise; stitch one half-width to each long side of the full width to avoid having a seam down the center of the quilt. Yardage for the backing is determined the same way.

If the quilt top is composed of pieced or appliqued blocks, the number and size of the blocks determines how much yardage they require. If the fabric is 45" wide, and the blocks, for instance, are 14½" square, including seam allowances, three blocks will fit across the width of the fabric, with 1½" left over. Determine how many rows of three blocks each will be needed to obtain the total number of blocks required. This is easy to do if you make a rough diagram on paper. In this case, if you need twenty blocks, you will need seven rows of three blocks each, and will have one block left over. Seven rows multiplied by 14½" equals 101½" of fabric, or a few inches less than three yards.

The yardage required for applique and patchwork pieces can be determined in much the same way. First, cut a full-size paper pattern for each shape in every color required. Group together all the patterns that will be in the same color; measure the size of the area each pattern requires and multiply that by the total number of pieces needed in that shape and color. If lattice strips or a border are included in the design of the quilt top, estimate that yardage separately.

As mentioned earlier, Dacron batting is generally preferred, but both cotton and polyester batting come packaged in three pre-cut sizes: 81" x 96", 81" x 108", and 90" x 108". Simply buy the next size larger than your quilt size and trim to match the quilt top.

Shown below are just three of many possible ways to plan a quilt top with the same number of blocks. In the first one at the left, the blocks are joined to each other and set in a wide border. In the second, the blocks are joined to lattice strips that separate and frame them and to a border of medium width. In the third, the border is the same width as the lattice strips.

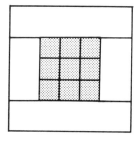 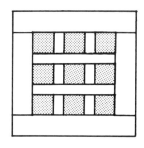 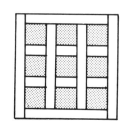

When planning how much material is required for the border and lattice strips, plan to cut all the strips on the length of the fabric to avoid piecing the long ones. But cut only the short strips to go between the blocks first, cutting just the number required to join the blocks into vertical rows. Cut each short strip as long as each block is wide; cut it the width you calculated on your scale drawing plus 1/2″, which allows for 1/4″ seam allowance along each long edge. With right sides facing, stitch the short strips to the blocks, making vertical rows. Measure the length of the completed rows before continuing. They may be slightly longer or shorter than planned if your seams varied even a fraction of an inch. Cut the long vertical strips to go between the rows to the measured length; add 1/2″ to the width for seam allowances. With right sides facing, stitch the long strips to the vertical rows of blocks. The diagrams below show how the blocks and strips are pieced together.

 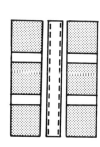

Now cut four strips the same width for the border, adding 1″ to allow for 1/4″ seam allowance along one long edge and 3/4″ along the other for finishing the quilt top later. With right sides facing, stitch the shorter top and bottom border strips to the completed center section. Then stitch the side border strips to the center section and to the ends of the top and bottom strips. That's it—you've just completed your quilt top!

If you wish to miter the border at the corners instead of butting the strips as shown at left, cut all four strips the same length; after stitching the strips to the center section of blocks, hold the ends of two strips together at each corner; pin, baste and then stitch a diagonal seam through the two ends from the inner corner to the outer corner of the border.

PUTTING THE LAYERS TOGETHER

Having assembled the top layer of a pieced or appliqued quilt, the next step is joining it to the other two layers, the batting and backing. On a quilted-only quilt (as opposed to one that's pieced or appliqued *and* quilted), this is done as the quilting pattern is stitched through all three layers, as described in the section on quilting techniques; see Page 21.

The three layers that are now ready to be put together should be approximately the same size. Do not trim the batting or backing until the quilting is completed; the layers may shift slightly as they're being quilted. Place the backing on a flat surface first, wrong side up. Place the batting on top of the backing and hold it in place with two large stitches that form a cross. Place the quilt top on the batting, right side up. Pin all three layers together temporarily with large safety pins. Starting at the center, baste the three layers together horizontally and vertically, diagonally in both directions, and around the edges, as shown in the sketches on Page 21.

Now it's the pieced or appliqued quilt's turn to be quilted. Start in the center of the piece or the section being worked on and work toward the edges. How and how much a pieced or appliqued quilt is actually quilted depends on the design and on the quilter. Appliques or quilt blocks may simply be outlined close to the seams. On a pieced top, certain patches only may be outlined. When pieced blocks alternate with plain blocks, the plain blocks only are often quilted in elaborate patterns. Or the quilt may be quilted in an allover pattern of diamonds or squares, right over the appliques or patches. Finally, the background and/or borders on pieced or appliqued quilts are frequently covered with quilting in intricate designs. It's quilter's choice—and a great way to be truly creative!

THE FINISHING TOUCH

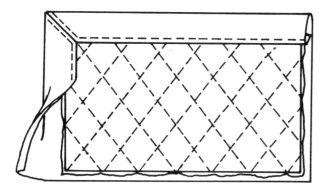

BINDING WITH THE BACKING:

The fabric used for the backing can also be used to bind the edges of the quilt and makes a very effective finish, especially if the backing is in a contrasting color. However, this method should be planned ahead so the backing can be cut large enough to allow for as wide a binding as desired; in most cases, the wider it is, the more effective it will be. (This does not apply to quilts which already have a border as part of the quilt top design.)

To finish a quilt in this manner, trim the extending backing to an even width on all sides. Turn the raw edges in 1/2″ and press in place. Bring the backing around the edges to the top of the quilt and pin and then baste in a straight, even line. Stitching along the fold, slip-stitch the edge of the backing to the quilt top, or sew in place by machine. The same method can be used in reverse to cover the edges with the fabric used for the quilt top.

BINDING A REVERSIBLE QUILT:

The simplest method of finishing the edges of a quilt is frequently used, and gives a finished look to both sides. The first step is to make sure the quilt top and the backing are equally and evenly trimmed on all four sides of the quilt. Turn the edges of both in the same amount and press. Then simply stitch the edges together, either by hand or by machine. It's a good idea to stitch two rows around all four sides of the quilt for a secure finish. Or you may prefer to add some decorative stitching that will look well on both sides. Don't think this method of finishing is only for reversible quilts; it's fast, easy and effective for almost any type of quilt.

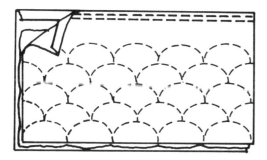

APPLYING A BIAS BINDING:

Finishing a quilt with a bias binding is an easy and effective method and allows considerable choice from the standpoint of design. You can make your own bias binding from any fabric you choose, provided it's sturdy enough to withstand the wear the edges of a quilt will be subjected to. So the color and texture of the binding, as well as whether it's printed or plain, is up to you. Bias binding can also be purchased in a fairly wide range of colors and in several different widths. It's even possible to find it in attractive calico-type prints, although the choice here is somewhat limited.

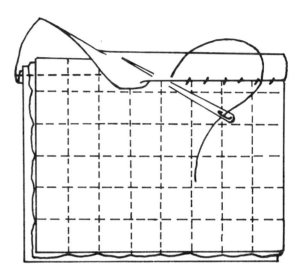

The binding can be applied from either the back or the front. To finish it with hand-stitching on the right side of the quilt, place it against the backing side with the right sides facing and the raw edges together. Baste in place and stitch 1/4" from the edges by hand or machine, using small running stitches either way. Wrap the binding around the edges onto the quilt top, turn under the remaining 1/4" raw edge, and stitch the turned edge to the quilt top, using a slip-stitch, overcasting, or small running stitches. The final stitching can also be done by machine.

BINDING A SCALLOPED EDGE:

The design of many quilts is based on circular motifs, such as the popular "Rob Peter to Pay Paul" pattern. A very attractive finish is achieved by simply outlining the outer row of half-circles with satin or zigzag stitching. The top and backing are then trimmed away together, close to the outer edge of the stitching, leaving a neatly scalloped edge.

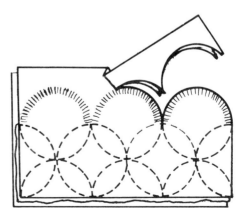

QUILTER'S CHOICE

TRADITIONAL ROSE PATTERN

Feathers, flowers and shells make successful quilting patterns in many sizes. Here are a few to trace and use or to enlarge.

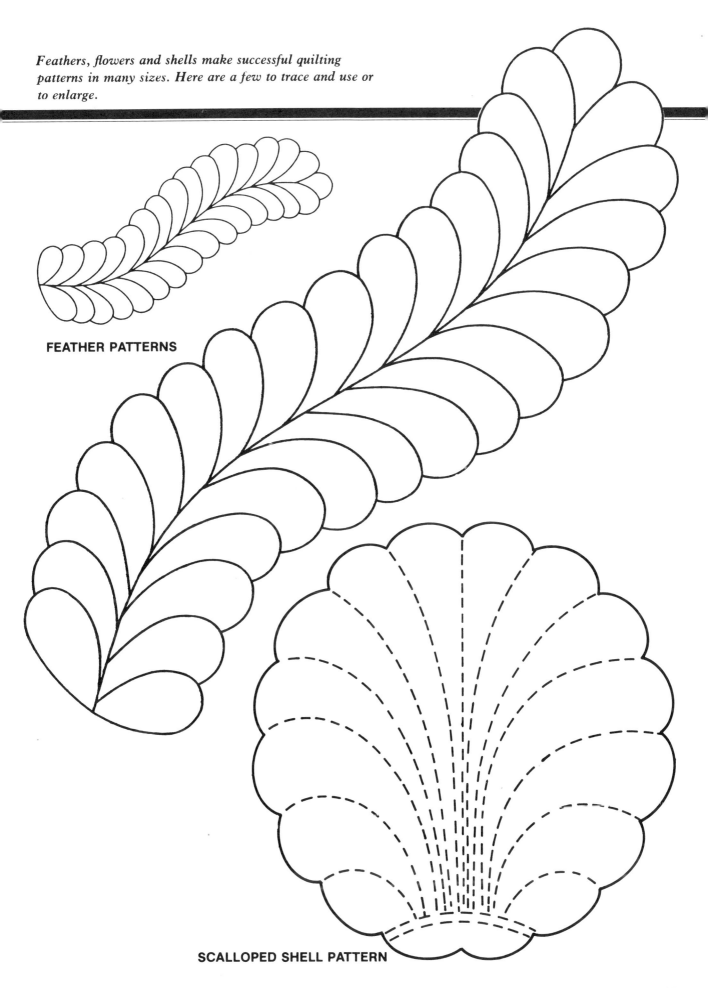

FEATHER PATTERNS

SCALLOPED SHELL PATTERN

GLOSSARY

ALBUM QUILT: A quilt composed of individual blocks made and signed by different people and then joined. Sometimes the quilt has a theme; more frequently, the designs and colors are left up to the individual contributors and so are unrelated. Usually presented as a token of esteem to a distinguished person.

AMISH QUILTING: A distinctive quilting style indigenous to the Amish people of Pennsylvania. Typically of pieced patchwork in a simple geometric pattern, and always in subtle, off-beat color combinations.

AUTOGRAPH QUILT: A quilt made up of individual blocks, each featuring one or more signatures written in India ink. Sometimes the signatures are embroidered over the ink.

BACKING: The material used for the bottom layer of a quilt. Usually made of lengths of plain or printed fabric stitched together to match the size of the quilt top.

BATTING: A fluffy polyester or cotton filler in sheet form used as padding between the top and backing of a quilt. Also called wadding or stuffing, it is usually pre-cut to quilt size and sold in cellophane bags, sometimes under the manufacturer's own trademarked name.

BLOCK: The design unit or pattern of a quilt, usually a square, rectangle or hexagon, repeated many times to form the quilt top. A block may be any size, containing any number of pieces; it may also be the entire quilt top if the design is large and non-repetitive.

BORDER: The outer margin that surrounds the major part of a quilt and serves as a frame. It may be made of plain, pieced or appliqued material and is often quilted in elaborate patterns.

COVERLET: A quilt large enough to cover the top of a bed without covering the pillows, and with less overhang than a full-size bedspread. Used primarily for extra warmth at night.

CRAZY QUILT: A quilt composed of irregularly-shaped scraps of fabric fitted together in random fashion like a puzzle; attached by stitching one to another or to a foundation block. The patches are usually of luxurious fabrics such as satin and velvet, and the joining seams are usually embellished with embroidery. Crazy quilting is actually a form of patchwork.

FOUNDATION BLOCK: A piece of muslin or other soft fabric that serves as the base or foundation for joining pieces or patches. Used in pressed quilts and crazy quilts.

FRIENDSHIP QUILT: Similar to the album quilt and the autograph quilt in purpose, the friendship quilt was usually presented to mark a special occasion or celebrate a marriage. Each block was made by a relative, neighbor or friend, who all met to set them together. Also presented to families moving away from a community, especially when "going West."

LATTICE STRIPS: Strips of solid-color fabric from two to four inches wide used to outline and join pieced blocks in a quilt. They form a grid which contrasts with the blocks; to prevent the grid from dominating the pattern, squares of another contrasting color are sometimes set into the intersections.

MARKING: The process of drawing a quilting design on the top or backing of a quilt before quilting it, or of tracing or transferring an embroidery design to fabric before stitching it. Also tracing around the outline of a template to produce a design.

MITER: The method of turning a 90° angle in a straight strip of fabric or binding at corner, or of joining two strips, with a 45° diagonal seam from the inner angle of the strip to the outer corner. The excess fabric under the seam is trimmed away and the seam allowance pressed flat. This is a desirable way to finish the four outside corners of a quilt.

MOLA: The quilt blocks and panels worked in reverse applique by the San Blas Indians and other natives of Central and South America.

PATCHWORK: The pieced-together fabric produced by stitching small pieces of material together, often in a geometric design of squares, rectangles, triangles, diamonds, hexagons or other shapes. The joinings can also be in a random pattern, as in crazy quilting. In a patchwork quilt, the small pieces of fabric are stitched together into blocks, which are then joined.

PIECE: Used as a verb, to stitch together pieces of fabric, usually to form a design block.

PRESSED QUILT: A quilt made by joining pieces or patches to a foundation block with running stitches. After the first piece, each subsequent piece is placed face down on the preceding piece; with right sides together, a seam is stitched through both patches and the foundation block. The new piece is turned to the right side and "pressed" down, ready for the next piece to be joined in the same manner.

PUTTING IN: A colloquial term meaning the attachment of a quilt to a quilting frame by securing the top and bottom edges to two muslin-covered poles. The portions of the quilt above and below the area being quilted are rolled on the poles.

QUILT: A bedcover, usually made of three layers called the top, padding and backing which are stitched together in a decorative design. Also a bedcover made of patchwork or applique which may or may not also be quilted.

QUILTING FRAME: A wooden stretcher made of four strips of wood which holds the quilt taut while it is being quilted by hand.

REVERSE APPLIQUE: An applique technique in which pieces of fabric are cut away instead of being added to form a design. Several layers of fabric, each a different color, are basted together. A design is cut *out* of the top layer, revealing the next layer of fabric. A smaller design is cut out of the second layer, revealing the third layer; and so on. The cut edges are turned under and hemmed.

SCRAP QUILT: A quilt made up of leftover scraps of fabric, regardless of color or pattern, and joined in random fashion. They utilize any scraps available and have an unplanned effect which is pleasing and entirely different than quilts with a very regular design.

SETTING TOGETHER: Sewing quilted, appliqued or patched blocks together to form the quilt top. This is done either by sewing the blocks to each other or to plain blocks or lattice strips that separate them and are part of the design.

TEMPLATE: An actual-size pattern of plastic, metal or cardboard used as a guide for cutting accurate, identically sized fabric patches.

TIED QUILTING: A quick, easy method of attaching the three layers of a quilt together, also called tufting. The layers are joined by individual, double stitches, the loose ends of which are then tied together in a knot or a bow.

TRAPUNTO: A term sometimes used for corded quilting, in which two layers of fabric are stitched together by parallel rows of running stitch or backstitch that form channels. A cord is drawn through the channels and between the top and bottom layers, forming a design which stands out in high relief.

39" x 75"	54" x 75"	60" x 80"	78" x 75"	76" x 80"	78" x 80"	72" x 84"

Size is the very first thing you must consider when you decide to make a quilt—or any bedcover. But bed and mattress sizes have become very confusing as larger and larger beds have become popular. So the first step is to accurately measure the mattress on the bed in question. Here is a list of so-called "standard" sizes, but even these vary depending upon individual mattress manufacturers, and a difference of one inch or more in either direction is not unusual. Except for the crib size, the comparative sizes are shown graphically above.

CRIB SIZE .... 27" x 48"		**DUAL SIZE** .... 78" x 75"	
TWIN SIZE .... 39" x 75"		**KING SIZE** .... 76" x 80"	
FULL SIZE .... 54" x 75"		**DUAL KING** .... 78" x 80"	
QUEEN SIZE .... 60" x 80"		**CALIFORNIA KING** .. 72" x 84"	

After determining the correct measurements of the mattress, you must decide just what type of quilt you want. A complete bedspread covers the pillows and reaches all the way to the floor on three sides, or at least far enough down to cover the top of a dust ruffle. So add twice the amount of overhang to the width of the mattress, plus seam allowances if necessary; to the length, add the amount of overhang at the foot and about 20" to cover the pillows. Then add 4" or 5" all around to make up for what will be taken up in quilting if the "quilt" is actually quilted.

A coverlet, used primarily for extra warmth at night, doesn't have to cover the pillows, but should have enough overhang on three sides to allow for what is taken up by anyone sleeping under it. So add the desired overhang, plus seam allowances if necessary, and quilting allowance all around if coverlet is to be quilted.

The usual size for throws, used for napping and such, is about 48" x 72". The same size is comfortable for automobile and stadium blankets. Always add seam allowance if seams are involved and quilting allowance if the cover is actually quilted.

APPLIQUE

is as personal as painting; in fact, think of it as painting with pieces of fabric. You'll see that some of the designs are as simple and direct as a child's artwork, and have the same forthright charm. Others are as subtle and sophisticated as the witty double project opposite—a fool-the-eye "painting," with its bird-watching feline repeated on a pillow to toss nearby. To stitch your own artistic version, see page 114.

QUILTS,

some old, some new, are always treasured. On the next pages, we show authentic antiques as well as modern translations of the traditional patterns. Whatever your penchant in quilts, we think you'll find at least one that suits it.

EAT, LEARN and be

merry—or at least enjoy mealtimes. Preschool youngsters will do all three at once if you make this clever place mat with coordinated napkin. The ultra-easy appliques are an introduction to spelling, and the embroidered place setting will teach them how to set a table. See Page 115.

To love someone is to give them room enough ... to grow

GENTLE REMINDER

This engaging wall hanging has a double purpose. In addition to being highly decorative, it says something we all should remember. The stylized tree-top is patched and padded before being appliqued; the quilted trunk adds to the three-dimensional effect. See Page 116.

NOVEL APPLIQUES

are sure attention-getters—whether they're whimsical or just plain pretty. The eye-catching unicorn overleaf, sitting in a field of printed flowers, mimics time-honored tapestry, but the 34" x 45" quilt is made of machine-appliqued fabric, and can be used as a baby cover or an amusing wall hanging. Directions, Page 117.

The stylized posies in the bouquet at the right are cut from felt and held in place with embroidery—no other stitching is needed for these novel appliques. This unusual method of applying cut-outs to fabric gives the wood-bordered wall hanging great charm and delicacy. Directions, Page 118.

OUTLINE STITCH

embroidery goes around and between the felt appliques that go in circles on this eye-spinning pillow. The appliques themselves are outlined with chain stitch for still more texture. See Page 120 for directions.

LONE STAR QUILT

is a blaze of vibrant colors exploding against a stark white background. The star is made up of 800 diamond-shaped patches, stitched together in radiating rings of color and surrounded by precise, geometric quilting. Choose from two methods of joining the patches, both clearly explained in the directions that start on Page 126.

BARN-RAISING QUILT

is one of the fascinating and intricate "log cabin" designs. All log cabin patchwork is composed of narrow strips, half light and half dark, pieced together in various patterns. Directions for 44" square crib quilt, Page 124.

HAPPY-HOME QUILT *was made by a builder's wife for her husband around 1860. Many of the fabrics have faded, but the charm is intact. Each little house is a pieced block, set into the quilt with white background strips. See Page 123.*

VIVID *red, white, and blue are combined in a patchwork quilt that's a sampler, too! Nine giant blocks, each one a variation on a thirty-six patch theme, make a king-size quilt; blocks can easily be scaled down to make a smaller quilt. Pillow is half the size of the quilt block. Directions and piecing diagram are on Page 122.*

WALL HANGING *of stark simplicity has a strong contemporary impact, but mixes well with early American or Federal furnishings, thanks to its patriotic flavor. Squares, triangles and rectangles make the stylized blue and white star, the red and white striped background. See Page 127.*

CAT-APPLIQUED PAIR

ON PAGE 105

SIZE: Wall hanging, about 36" x 43"; pillow, 17" square.

EQUIPMENT: Shallow porcelain pan. Spring clothespins. Teaspoon for dye. Iron. Paper for pattern. Pencil. Ruler. Scissors. Sewing machine with zigzag attachment. Straight pins. Sewing needle. Tracing paper. Dressmaker's carbon paper.

MATERIALS: For wall hanging: Unbleached muslin, 17" square for sky; black suede cloth, velour or velveteen, 17" square for cat; striped ribbon 2" wide, 7½ yards for window frame; printed cotton or cotton-blend fabric, 45" wide, one yard for background; compatible cotton or cotton-blend printed fabric, 45" wide, ⅝ yard for border; dark solid-color fabric, 36" wide, ⅜ yard for table; medium green cotton fabric, 36" wide, ⅜ yard for leaves; striped fabric for flower pot, 6" x 10"; scrap of beige felt for bird; heavy cotton or cotton-blend fabric, 45" wide, one yard for backing. Matching sewing thread, plus gray thread for embroidery on cat. Sky blue and dark green fabric dyes. Fusible web interfacing. For pillow: Unbleached muslin, 18" square for sky; black suede cloth, velour or velveteen, 17" square for cat; striped ribbon, 2" wide, 7½ yards for window frame; heavy cotton or cotton-blend fabric, 17" square for backing. One 16" square knife-edged pillow form. Matching sewing thread, plus gray thread for embroidery on cat. Sky blue fabric dye. Fusible web interfacing.

DIRECTIONS: To make wall hanging: Pre-wash muslin and green cotton fabric. The muslin will be dyed a mottled blue; the green cotton will be dyed a mottled darker green.

To dye fabric, dissolve one teaspoon of dye in ¼" of water; stir. Bring water to boil and simmer. Wet fabric with fresh water; bunch fabric together and hold with clothespins at random intervals. Place parts of fabric in dye; do not immerse completely. Simmer five minutes; remove fabric from dye and rinse in cold water, then dry. Iron while damp to set color.

Enlarge pattern by copying on paper ruled in 2" squares. Heavy lines are cutting lines; finer lines indicate stitching; short broken lines indicate where appliqued pieces are overlapped. Using pencil, trace each pattern piece separately onto tracing paper; cut out.

For window, cut four strips of striped ribbon for window frame, and two strips for crossbars, following pattern. Center ribbon for crossbars in place on right side of blue tie-dyed muslin square; topstitch in place along long edges. Pin strips for window frame along top and bottom edges of muslin on right side of fabric; topstitch along inner edges only. Pin one window frame strip along each side edge of muslin, overlapping top and bottom strips. Fold short edges of side strips at 45° angles to miter corners; cut away excess fabric. Topstitch along miters and inner edges.

Cut cat from black fabric and fusible web interfacing.

PATTERN FOR WALL HANGING   EACH SQUARE = 2"

Using dressmaker's tracing paper, transfer stitching lines on pattern to cat applique. Place cat applique on window with fusible web between the two fabrics; baste around edge of cat applique. Turn fabric to wrong side and, following package directions, apply hot iron to fuse fabrics together. Using gray thread, stitch with narrow zigzag stitch around cat and along fine lines of pattern. Remove basting; pull thread ends to wrong side of fabric; knot and clip. Using short, straight stitches, embroider whiskers with gray thread. Cut bird from beige felt, and zigzag-stitch in place with matching thread. Cut 36" x 43" background from printed fabric. Pin completed window in upper left of background, about 5" in from adjacent sides. Zigzag-stitch around outside of window frame, covering edges of ribbon and muslin.

Cut table from solid-color fabric. Turn curved edge under ¼" and press. Pin table to lower right corner of background, matching raw edges. Zigzag-stitch table to background along curved edge only.

Cut plant leaves from tie-dyed green fabric; cut flower pot from striped fabric. Cut fusible web interfacing same size as each piece. Place leaves and pot on background with fusible web between the two layers. Fuse pieces in place with hot iron. With matching thread and narrow zigzag satin stitch, stitch around edges of leaves and flower pot. Transfer stems to background, using carbon paper and pencil. Satin-stitch stems with green thread.

Cut 36" x 43" piece from heavy cotton fabric for backing. Pin appliqued piece to backing with wrong sides facing. For border, cut two 5" x 45" strips, and two 5" x 36" strips from compatible printed fabric. Turn under all long edges of each strip ¼" and press; then fold strips in half lengthwise, with wrong sides facing, and press. Pin shorter strips along side edges of appliqued piece first, encasing raw edges; baste in place, making sure folded edges of borders are even on front and back. Topstitch on front along inner edges, being sure to catch edges of back as well as the front. Repeat for top and bottom borders, folding ends under at each side.

For pillow: Pre-wash muslin, and dye mottled blue in same manner as for wall hanging. Enlarge pattern for window only by copying on paper ruled in 2" squares. Following pattern, cut striped ribbon for crossbars, and four 17" lengths for window frame. Assemble window with cat in same manner as for wall hanging, but stitching ribbon for window frames to blue-dyed muslin ½" in from raw edges and omitting bird. With right sides facing, stitch completed appliqued front to heavy cotton backing, ½" from raw edges along three sides. Turn right side out. Insert pillow form; slip-stitch opening closed.

EAT & LEARN PLACE MAT
ON PAGE 106

EQUIPMENT: Paper for pattern. Ruler. Hard lead pencil. Scissors. Tracing paper. Dressmaker's tracing paper. Straight pins. Sewing needle. Sewing machine with decorative stitch.

MATERIALS: Washable cotton or cotton-blend fabrics, solid and printed, each 13" x 19". Scraps of the printed fabric for letters for each place mat. Matching piece of printed fabric, 13" square, for each napkin. Matching sewing thread.

DIRECTIONS: Enlarge pattern by copying on paper ruled in 1" squares. Trace pattern, and transfer to the right side of solid fabric by placing carbon paper between traced pattern and fabric, and going over design with hard lead pencil.

PLACE MAT

Pin solid cotton fabric to printed fabric with right sides together, matching raw edges. Machine stitch together ½" from raw edges, leaving a 6" opening on one side. Turn right side out; slip-stitch opening closed. Press all edges.

Using paper pattern, cut out the letters "E", "A", "T", from printed scraps. With matching thread, baste letters on solid-color fabric in positions indicated on pattern. Set machine for zigzag satin stitch; stitch around edges of letters, and around outlines of silverware and plate.

Set sewing machine for a scallop or other decorative stitch, and embroider around mat, close to edges. Embroider another line of same decorative stitch 1" inside first line.

For napkin, make ½" hem on all edges of 13" square. Using thread to match solid-color fabric, embroider edges of napkin with same decorative stitch.

TREE-APPLIQUED HANGING

ON PAGE 106

SIZE: 41½" x 29½"

EQUIPMENT: Pencil. Ruler. Scissors. Thin, stiff cardboard. Paper for patterns. Dressmaker's tracing paper. Sewing and embroidery needles. Knitting needle. Clear nail polish.

MATERIALS: Small pieces of printed fabrics in four different colors for tree; yellow, tri-colored, red, and green were used on hanging in photograph. One 27½" x 22¾" piece contrasting print for background (blue in photograph); one 42½" x 30½" piece for border (red in photograph); and one 22¾" x 6¾" solid-color fabric for embroidered area (gold in photograph). For lining, white muslin, 42½" x 30½". Six-strand embroidery floss in green, red, and brown. Fiberfill for stuffing. Twill tape, 1" wide, 30" long. ¼" rod for hanging.

DIRECTIONS: Enlarge patterns on paper ruled in 1" squares; complete half pattern of tree trunk applique indicated by broken line. Using pattern, transfer outline of tree trunk to light green printed fabric, add ¼" seam allowance all around and mark cutting line. Using dressmaker's carbon and hard lead pencil, transfer dotted quilting lines on trunk to green fabric. Machine-stitch along marked outline of tree, using matching thread and small stitches; this makes edge of applique easier to turn and neater in appearance. Cut out applique on outside line; clip into seam allowance at curved edges and corners. Turn ¼" allowance to wrong side, just inside stitching line and press; do not turn under ¼" allowance along top and bottom of trunk. Pin and baste tree trunk in place on 27½" x 22¾" background, centering trunk along bottom, and matching raw edges; slip-stitch in place with tiny stitches. Machine-quilt along dotted lines, using green thread.

To make diamond-shaped pattern for top of tree, mark a 4½" x 2" rectangle on cardboard; mark center point on each side. Connect center points with four diagonal lines to make diamond shape; cut on marked lines for pattern. Coat edges of pattern with clear nail polish to keep from fraying. Mark pattern on wrong side of fabric; add ¼" seam allowance all around and mark cutting line. Cut patches for top of tree as follows: 5 from red printed fabric; 10 from tri-colored fabric; and 15 from yellow printed fabric. Stitch red patches together in a fan shape as shown in photograph, with long points of each diamond meeting in center. Stitch eight tri-colored patches together in pairs. Following photograph, fit pairs of tri-colored patches in place, adjacent to red patches; stitch a single patch at beginning and end of red fan-shaped piece. Stitch eight yellow patches together in pairs. Fit pairs of yellow patches into wide angles created by tri-colored pairs of patches; fit single yellow patches into remaining angles, and at each side, and stitch together to complete tree top. Press, and turn under raw edges in same manner as for tree trunk. Pin in place on background, overlapping top edge of trunk ½". Baste to background along pointed edge; unpin bottom edge. Stuff tree top with fiberfill, stuffing into points with knitting needle; do not pack filling too tightly. Baste bottom edge closed. Slip-stitch tree top to background, using tiny stitches; remove basting.

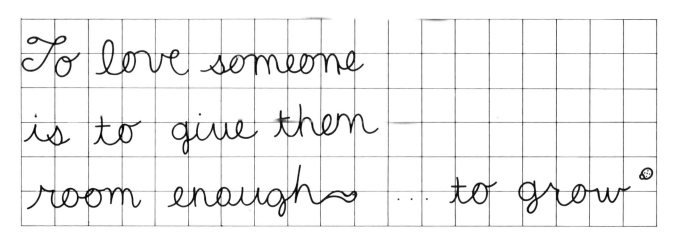

EACH SQUARE = 1"   **PATTERNS FOR TREE-APPLIQUED WALL HANGING**

Using dressmaker's carbon and hard lead pencil, transfer message to solid-color fabric; place message 1¾" from left edge, centered between top and bottom edges. Using three strands of embroidery floss in needle, embroider message in chain stitch. Embroider three dots in French knots, the worm in satin stitch, and ladybug in satin stitch and French knots. Use green and red floss for message as shown in photograph; use brown for worm's eye and dots on ladybug.

With right sides together, stitch top edge of embroidered piece to lower edge of appliqued background ¼" from raw edges; piece will measure 33¾" x 22¾".

Turn under edges of appliqued and embroidered piece ¼" all around and press. Place in center of red printed fabric and slip-stitch in place. Pin completed front to muslin backing with right sides together. Stitch together ½" from raw edges, leaving 5" opening in center of bottom edge. Trim seams, turn to right side through opening, and slip-stitch opening closed. Press edges.

To make channel for hanging rod, stitch long edge of twill tape just below top edge of wall hanging; stitch other long edge of twill tape in place. Insert hanging rod in channel created by the two rows of stitching.

UNICORN BABY QUILT
ON PAGE 107

SIZE: 35" x 45"

EQUIPMENT: Pencil. Ruler. Scissors. Paper for pattern. Thin, stiff cardboard. Sewing and embroidery needles. Dressmaker's tracing paper in light color. Tracing wheel or dry ball-point pen. Straight pins. Zigzag sewing machine. All-purpose glue.

MATERIALS: Closely-woven cotton or cotton-blend fabrics, 45" wide: 1 yard of flower print for quilt top; ⅓ yard striped fabric for fence; ⅝ yard solid-color gold fabric for unicorn; scraps of printed and solid-color fabrics for collar and horn; ¼ yard of dark flower print for border. For quilt lining, 1 yard of quilted fabric backed with batting, 45" wide. Matching and contrasting sewing thread. Six-strand embroidery floss in red and black.

DIRECTIONS: Enlarge pattern on paper ruled in 2" squares. Broken lines on pattern indicate where pieces are overlapped; dotted lines indicate embroidery. Trace each separate part of design, glue tracings to cardboard, and cut out. Place pattern on right side of fabric and

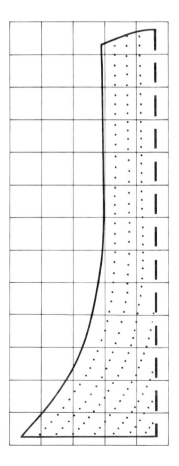

PATTERN FOR UNICORN QUILT   EACH SQUARE = 2"

117

mark around outline; mark cutting line ¼" beyond outline all around pattern and cut applique out. Cut six pieces from contrasting fabrics for unicorn's horn; with right sides facing, stitch pieces together ¼" from raw edges to make complete horn; trim seam allowances to ⅛" and press open.

Cut printed fabric for quilt top 35" x 45". Using dressmaker's tracing paper and tracing wheel or dry ball-point pen, transfer complete design to be appliqued to quilt top, centering it on the width so there is a 1½" margin on each side of design. Following numerical order indicated on pattern, pin and baste each applique in place on printed background; do not turn ¼" margin under. Using straight stitch on sewing machine, stitch around applique on marked outline. Then trim margin of excess fabric to ⅛" from stitching. Set machine for close, narrow zigzag stitch; and stitch around applique, covering straight stitching and ⅛" margin of fabric; use gold thread around fence and unicorn, red around collar. Stitch lines defining unicorn's legs and mane in red.

Embroider unicorn's face by hand, using full six strands of floss in needle. Embroider inner eye in satin stitch and outer eye in outline stitch, using black floss. Using red floss, embroider nose and mouth in outline stitch. See stitch illustrations at back of book. When embroidery is completed, press quilt top.

Cut lining to match quilt top. Pin the two layers together with wrong sides facing. Baste around all four sides, ¼" from edges, making sure both pieces are smooth and flat and edges are flush; trim edges evenly if necessary.

Edges of quilt are bound in contrasting print. Cut four 3"-wide strips from border fabric, two 45" long and two 35½" long. Turn ¼" to wrong side along both long edges of 45" strips and press. Pin a 45" strip to each side edge on wrong side of quilt, with wrong side of strip facing right side of lining and folded edge of strip 1" from edge of quilt. Topstitch close to folded edge of strip. Wrap strip around edge of quilt and slip-stitch folded edge to right side of quilt. Turn ¼" to wrong side along all edges of 35½" strips and press. Attach to top and bottom edges of quilt in same manner; slip-stitch folded ends together.

BOUQUET-APPLIQUED WALL HANGING
ON PAGE 108

SIZE: 26¼" x 15½"

EQUIPMENT: Pencil. Ruler. Scissors. Paper for patterns. Tracing paper. Thin, stiff cardboard. Dressmaker's tracing paper. Tracing wheel or dry ballpoint pen. Tailor's chalk. Sewing and embroidery needles. Glue. Rags. Staple gun.

MATERIALS: Linen or linen-type fabric in white or natural color, 17" x 24½". Small amounts of felt in a variety of colors for appliques; colors used in hanging shown: green, chartreuse, orange, mustard, yellow, gold, light blue, dark blue, light pink, medium pink, dark pink. Six-strand embroidery floss, 1 skein each of light yellow, gold, golden brown, rust, light pink, medium pink, dark pink, light blue, dark blue, green. Light beige sewing thread. Basting thread. Two pieces of clear pine wood, ¼" x 1½" x 15½". Dark green wood stain. Staples.

DIRECTIONS: Enlarge pattern for complete bouquet on paper ruled in 1" squares. Solid outlines indicate positions of appliques; broken lines indicate embroidery.

Using dressmaker's tracing paper and tracing wheel or dry ball-point pen, transfer all markings of pattern to fabric background, placing bouquet in center or slightly above center of area.

Trace actual-size patterns for flower and circle appliques, completing half patterns indicated by heavy broken lines. Lighter (and shorter) broken lines indicate embroidery. Trace triangular leaf shape, stem and half

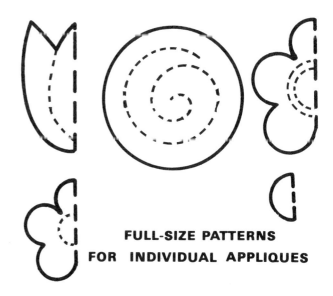

FULL-SIZE PATTERNS FOR INDIVIDUAL APPLIQUES

APPLIQUE PATTERN FOR COMPLETE BOUQUET   EACH SQUARE = 1"

of bow from enlarged pattern. Glue tracings to cardboard and cut out to use as applique patterns.

Place cardboard patterns on felt in indicated colors, mark outlines and cut out. Of large, five-petaled flowers, cut five dark blue, four gold, two light pink, and four dark pink. Of small five-petaled flowers, cut six yellow and ten light blue. Cut two light blue tulips and four mustard-colored tulips. Cut three large orange circles and two large medium pink circles. Cut 59 small chartreuse circles. Cut 16 green triangular "leaves" and three green stems. Cut two medium pink half-bows.

Using tailor's chalk, draw embroidery lines on flower appliques. Or trace and transfer to appliques by using dressmaker's tracing paper.

Referring to photograph, pin and baste the flower appliques in place on fabric background; note that the solid outlines of flowers on pattern indicate only shape and position, and are slightly smaller than the actual appliques. Using three strands of floss in needle and matching colors (except for rust on orange and golden brown on mustard), embroider appliques and attach them to background at the same time. Embroider center of each small chartreuse circle with a single lazy daisy stitch. Embroider flower appliques on marked lines with chain stitch; continue embroidery on tulips onto background as marked. Loosely outline large pink and gold five-petaled flowers with chain stitch in matching color. Embroider two rows of green outline stitch around semi-circular lower edge of bouquet and between stems. Pin and baste remaining appliques in place. Using one strand of green floss in needle, slip-stitch edges of green appliques in place. Attach and embroider both halves of pink bow by chain-stitching around appliques, ⅛" in from both edges.

To finish side edges of wall hanging, turn ¼" to wrong side and press; turn under another ½" and slip-stitch folded edge to wrong side, using matching thread. Steam-press hanging on wrong side.

Prepare pieces of wood for top and bottom of hanging by rubbing with dark green stain; wipe off excess with clean rags and allow wood to dry thoroughly. Place one piece across top of hanging, overlapping fabric by ½"; staple top of hanging to back surface of wood. Attach other piece of wood to bottom of hanging in same manner.

APPLIQUED PILLOW
ON PAGE 108

SIZE: 16" square.

EQUIPMENT: Pencil. Ruler. Scissors. Paper for pattern. Tracing paper. Dressmaker's tracing paper. Thin, stiff cardboard. Tracing wheel or dry ball-point pen. Sewing and embroidery needles. Compass.

MATERIALS: Linen or linen-type fabric in natural color, 36" wide, ¾ yard. Small amounts of felt in olive green, orange and fuchsia. Six-strand embroidery floss in golden brown, light orange and purple. Purchased cording, ¼" diameter, 2 yards. Sewing thread to match fabric. Knife-edged pillow form, 16" square.

DIRECTIONS: Enlarge pattern by copying on paper ruled in 1" squares. Heavy lines indicate appliques; lighter lines indicate embroidery; broken lines indicate quarter pattern for outer section of design. To aid in drawing pattern, use compass to make circles in following sizes: 1⅛" diameter circle for center appliques; 6⅛" diameter for inner embroidered circle; 10¼" diameter for outer embroidered circle; 13½" diameter for complete design.

All appliques are either circles or half-oblongs. Trace the two shapes from the enlarged pattern; glue tracings to cardboard and cut out to use as applique patterns.

Cut two 17"-square pieces from fabric for front and back of pillow cover. Using dressmaker's tracing paper and tracing wheel or dry ball-point pen, transfer complete pattern to right side of one piece of fabric, centering it in the square. Turn the pattern three times, matching the broken lines each time, to complete outer section of design.

To cut appliques, place individual pattern on felt of indicated color, mark outline with pencil, and cut on marked line. Cut 12 circles for center of design, six orange and six fuchsia; cut 38 half-oblongs from olive green felt. Using photograph as color guide, pin and baste appliques in place on square of fabric marked with pattern, working from the center of design outward. Applique each felt cut-out to fabric by embroidering around edge with chain stitch. Use light orange floss to embroider orange appliques; use purple floss on fuchsia appliques. As each section of appliqued design is completed, embroider marked lines in same area with outline stitch. See stitch illustrations at back of book. Embroider circle

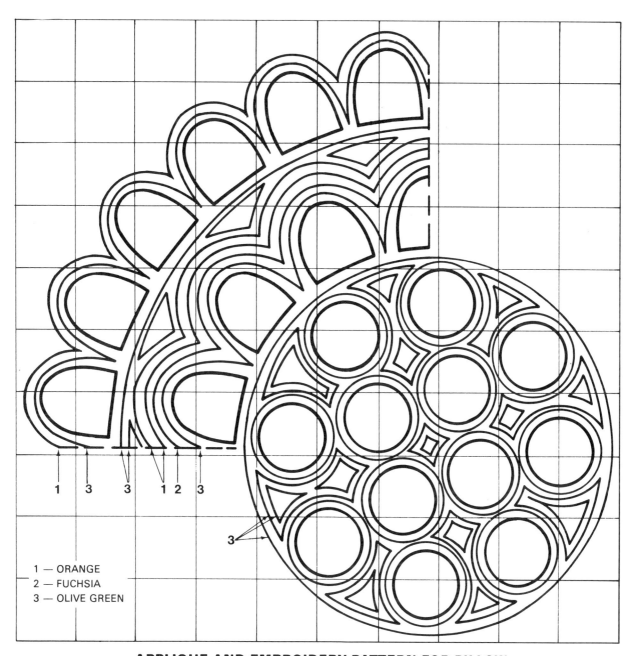

1 — ORANGE
2 — FUCHSIA
3 — OLIVE GREEN

APPLIQUE AND EMBROIDERY PATTERN FOR PILLOW   EACH SQUARE = 1"

around each center applique in matching color. See color key on pattern for remaining embroidery.

To make cording to go around edge of cover, cut 1½"-wide bias strips from remaining fabric; stitch together to make one strip 65" long. Fold strip in half lengthwise, wrong sides together, and press. Cut purchased cording 65" long and place in fold. Using adjustable cording or zipper foot, stitch close to cord without crowding against it. Trim fabric ½" from stitching for seam allowance. With raw edges of cording and fabric even, pin and baste cording around right side of appliqued cover front, rounding corners slightly. Ends of cording should over-

lap ½". To join ends, pull one end of cord out from covering and cut off ½". Turn ¼" of covering to inside, concealing raw edge. Starting with this end, stitch cording to cover front, following stitching line of cording. Where ends of cording meet at starting place, slip second end into turned-in edge of covering and continue stitching. Slip-stitch turned edge in place.

With right sides facing, baste front and back of pillow cover together, ½" from edges, enclosing cording. Stitch around three sides. Remove basting and turn cover right side out. Insert pillow form, fold seam allowances to inside and slip-stitch remaining side closed.

PATCHWORK SAMPLER QUILT

ON PAGE 112

SIZE: 110″ square.

EQUIPMENT: Pencil. Colored pencils. Scissors. Graph paper. Thin, stiff cardboard. Tailor's chalk. Sewing and quilting needles.

MATERIALS: Unbleached muslin, 60″ wide, about 9 yards, including lining. Closely-woven cotton or cotton-blend fabric in royal blue and burgundy. Scraps of fabric in blue and red prints, both light and dark backgrounds. Cotton or Dacron batting. Sewing thread to match fabrics.

DIRECTIONS: Read general directions for making quilts at the beginning of this section. This quilt is made of nine pieced blocks, set with joining strips and border. Each block is constructed differently, as indicated by piecing diagrams. The tenth diagram is for pillow design. Choose any or all of the designs shown, using your own combinations of fabric.

To make patterns for chosen designs, first copy designs on graph paper. For each design, mark a large square, made up of 36 small, equal squares, on graph paper. Then mark specific design on grid of small squares, using half a small square for triangles, two adjacent squares for rectangles, half of a rectangle for a long triangle, and one small square divided into four for tiny squares.

Next, plan the color arrangement for each block. Using colored pencils, shade each part of design to indicate color it is to be. In piecing diagrams shown, the dark shading represents a solid color, either burgundy or

blue or a combination of the two within an area; light shading represents a printed fabric—one, two or three different prints in a block, as desired; areas without shading represent white unbleached muslin. Compare diagrams with photograph.

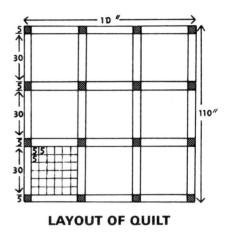

LAYOUT OF QUILT

Diagram above shows layout of entire quilt. Each pieced block of quilt shown is 30″ square; each small square of grid is 5″ square; joining strips and borders are all 5″ wide. Block for pillow is 15″ square, divided into thirty-six 2½″ squares. Note dimensions of each patch shape on graph-paper designs. Make a cardboard pattern for each one in size indicated.

Note that for a smaller quilt the same graph-paper designs can be used; simply make the large squares smaller, but still in a size that's evenly divisible by six. For instance, if large blocks are 24″ square, small blocks will be 4″ square, strips and borders will be 4″ wide, and the complete quilt will be 88″ square.

PIECING DIAGRAMS FOR SAMPLER QUILT BLOCKS

Cut patches from fabrics planned by placing cardboard pattern on wrong side and marking around outline; add ¼" seam allowance all around and cut out.

Join patches for each block in the following sequence: Join triangles and tiny squares first to make 5" squares; join 5" squares in groups of four to make nine 10" squares; joint 10" squares into three rows of three squares each; join rows to make block 30" square, plus outside seam allowance. Make nine blocks for quilt.

From muslin, cut 24 strips 5" × 30" plus ¼" seam allowance all around. From blue fabric, cut 16 pieces 5" square plus seam allowance. Join pieced blocks into three rows of three blocks each, with a strip between each two blocks. Join blue squares and remaining strips into four long strips of three strips and four squares each, alternating squares and strips. Join the four long strips and the three rows of blocks, again alternating the two, to make the quilt top, which should measure 110" square plus outside seam allowance.

To make lining, cut two 56" × 111" pieces of muslin and stitch them together along two long sides, making a ½" seam. Press seam allowances open. Cut batting to same 111" square size as lining.

To prepare for quilting, mark diagonal lines about 3½" apart in both directions on white joining strips, using ruler and tailor's chalk; use corners of 5" squares as guides.

Place lining, wrong side up, on flat surface. Place batting on top of lining, smoothing out any bumps or wrinkles. Baste batting to lining by taking two long stitches in a cross. Place quilt top on top of batting, right side up, with all edges even. Pin all layers together, then baste them together horizontally and vertically through the center, diagonally in two directions, and around the edges on all four sides. Starting in the center and working outward, quilt on marked lines and around each patch, ¼" in from each seam. If quilting by machine, use white thread in bobbin and thread to match patch in needle.

From remaining muslin, cut enough 1½"-wide bias strips to make one strip long enough to go around quilt when joined together; stitch strips together on the lengthwise grain and press allowances open. Fold strip in half lengthwise, wrong sides together, and press. With right sides together and raw edges even, stitch strip around quilt top ¼" from raw edges. Fold strip to back of quilt, turn raw edge under ¼", and slip-stitch to lining along turned edge, making ½"-wide binding on both the right and lining sides of quilt.

HAPPY-HOME QUILT
ON PAGE 111

EQUIPMENT: Pencil. Ruler. Scissors. Thin, stiff cardboard. Tailor's chalk. Paper for patterns. Compass. Sewing and quilting needles. Quilting frame (optional).

MATERIALS: Closely-woven cotton or cotton-blend fabric: small prints and solid colors in soft reds, blues, grays, and beiges, totaling about 2⅔ yards; red-and-white print for border, 1⅛ yards. 2⅛ yards white fabric, 45" wide. 4½ yards 45"-wide fabric for lining. (Blue and white checked gingham was used for lining original quilt.) Sewing thread to match fabrics. Cotton or Dacron batting. White bias binding tape, 8⅔ yards.

DIRECTIONS: Read general directions for making quilts at the beginning of this section. This quilt is constructed of 36 pieced blocks, set with white joining strips and a pieced border.

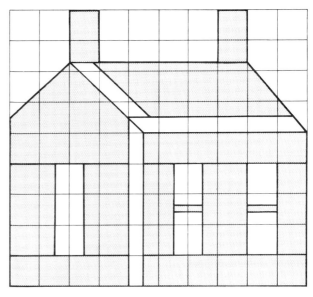

PATTERN FOR HOUSE BLOCK EACH SQUARE = 1"

Enlarge pattern for house block by copying on paper ruled in 1" squares. Make a cardboard pattern for each size patch; make one-piece windows and apply sash bars later by applique. Mark patterns on wrong sides of fabrics; add ¼" seam allowance all around each one and cut 14 patches shown shaded on pattern from one printed fabric; cut nine shown unshaded from white fabric. Assemble pieces for house block measuring 9"

123

× 10", plus outside seam allowance. Make 35 more house blocks in same manner, using one printed fabric for each house.

For joining strips, cut 30 pieces from white fabric 2¼" × 9", adding ¼" seam allowance all around. Sew house blocks into six horizontal rows of six blocks each, with a joining strip between every two blocks. Cut five strips from white fabric 2¼" × 71¼", adding ¼" seam allowance all around. Join pieced rows for main body of quilt top, with white strips between rows; note that three rows face in one direction and three rows face in the opposite direction. Piece should measure 65¼" × 71¼", plus outside seam allowance.

For white border, cut four strips 1¾" wide, two 65¾" long and two 74¼" long (measurements include ¼" seam allowance). Sew shorter strips to sides of quilt top, then longer strips to top and bottom. For pieced border, mark 1½" square on cardboard and cut square in half diagonally for triangle pattern. Cut 136 triangles from red-print fabric and 132 from white fabric, adding ¼" seam allowance. Cut triangle pattern in half and cut eight small triangles from white fabric. Join triangles into long strips by sewing short sides of red-print triangles to short sides of white triangles; make two strips, each with 32 red triangles and 31 white triangles; add a small white triangle to beginning and end of each strip. Sew a pieced strip to each side of quilt top, with the red-triangles side inward. Join remaining triangles into two strips, each with 36 red triangles and 35 white triangles; add a small white triangle to both ends of each strip. Sew strips to top and bottom of quilt top.

For outer border, cut four 2¾" wide strips from red-print fabric, two 70½" long and two 81" long; measurements include ¼" seam allowance. Sew shorter strips to sides, then longer strips to top and bottom. Quilt top should measure about 75" × 81".

For lining, cut two pieces from lining fabric 38" × 81". Sew together on long sides with ½" seams. Cut batting same size as lining and quilt top.

With ruler and tailor's chalk, mark diagonal quilting lines 1" apart in both directions over white background of quilt top, excluding white border; continue lines in one direction only onto red print border. On white border, mark a zigzag pattern, making points about 1" apart on each edge. On front of houses, mark a circle 1¼" in diameter centered between door and roof peak.

Pin and baste quilt top, batting, and lining together, following general directions. Starting in center and working around and outward, quilt on all marked lines. On houses, quilt around each colored patch, omitting window sashes, ⅛" in from seam lines. On roofs, quilt an extra horizontal line across center of piece. On pieced border, quilt around red patches, ⅛" in from seam lines.

Insert edges of quilt into fold of bias tape and stitch in place.

"BARN-RAISING" QUILT
ON PAGE 110

SIZE: 44½" square.

EQUIPMENT: Sharply-pointed pencils with light and dark leads. Scissors. Ruler. Paper for pattern. Dressmaker's tracing paper. Tracing wheel. Sewing and quilting needles.

MATERIALS: Closely-woven cotton or cotton-blend fabrics for quilt top in a variety of small prints, evenly divided between dark and light colors, totaling about 2 yards; 1¼ yards of solid dark green fabric. For lining, 2⅝ yards of printed or plain 50"-wide fabric. (Original quilt was lined in dark red print.) Cotton or Dacron batting. Sewing thread in colors to match fabrics and gray.

Note: Design will be effective if random colors are used throughout, as long as there is sharp contrast between the light and dark shades. A planned color scheme will create a more formal design. This quilt combines a planned color scheme with random colors.

DIRECTIONS: Read general directions for making quilts at the beginning of this section. Quilt consists of 36 pieced squares arranged in a geometric design, plus a border. For each square, cut sixteen ⅝"-wide strips, eight in light colors, eight in dark colors, and a 1" square. Piecing Diagram I indicates length and color of each strip; add ¼" seam allowance around each strip when cutting. The colors of the inner strips, A, B, C, D, and E, are specified on the diagram; the colors of the outer strips, F, G, H and I, may vary from square to square. All strips are cut from prints except those labeled "D" for solid dark green fabric.

With right sides together, sew strips into a 6½" square, including outside seam allowance; start piecing from the center and work around and outward. Make 35 more squares in same manner. For four of these squares, use

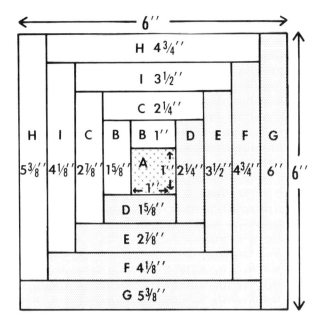

PIECING DIAGRAM 1

A = RED
B = YELLOW-GREEN
C = RED-WHITE STRIPE
D – DARK GREEN
E = NAVY
F, G = RANDOM DARK COLORS
H, I = RANDOM LIGHT COLORS

the same fabric for all G pieces; these will be corner squares. For four other squares, use the same fabrics for all except H pieces; use one fabric for H pieces on two squares and another fabric for H pieces on the other two; these will be the four center squares.

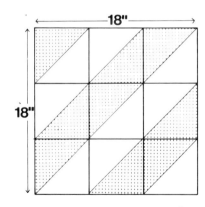

PIECING DIAGRAM 2

Sew nine squares into a block 18½" square, with right sides together and following Piecing Diagram 2; place one corner square at upper left and one center square at lower right. Make three more blocks in same manner. Sew the four blocks together to make a 36½" square piece, joining center squares as shown in photograph.

For border, cut four strips 4½" wide, two 36½" long and two 44½" long. Sew shorter strips to opposite sides of pieced square, right sides together and with ¼" seam allowances. Sew longer strips to other sides of square in same manner, sewing sides of longer strips to ends of shorter strips. Cut batting same size as quilt top. For lining, cut two pieces 46½" × 45½"; sew longer sides together with ½" seams to make piece 45½" square.

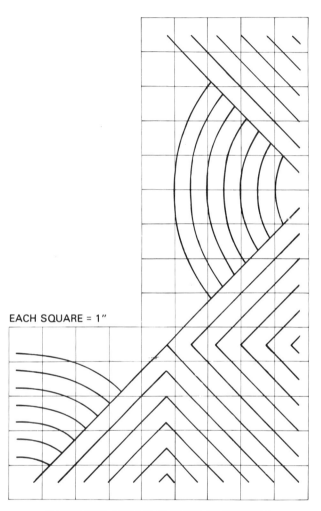

EACH SQUARE = 1"

PATTERN FOR BORDER QUILTING

Enlarge pattern for border quilting by copying on paper ruled in 1" squares. Transfer pattern to each corner of quilt-top border, ¼" from outside edge, using dressmaker's carbon and tracing wheel. Repeat design all around quilt, alternating triangles and curves.

Following general directions, center batting and quilt top over lining; pin and baste together. Quilt around all seams of pieced top and marked lines of border, using gray thread. Finish quilt by turning margin of lining to front; turn in raw edges ¼" and slip-stitch to top. Press all edges.

LONE STAR QUILT

ON PAGE 109

SIZE: 79" square

EQUIPMENT: Pencil. Ruler. Scissors. Thin, stiff cardboard. Paper for pattern. Tailor's chalk. Sewing and quilting needles. Quilting frame (optional).

MATERIALS: Closely-woven cotton or cotton-blend fabrics, 45" wide: red, ⅛ yard; bright pink and pale pink, ¼ yard each; lavender, gold and dark green, ⅓ yard each; yellow and orange, ½ yard each; medium blue, ⅝ yard; pale blue, ¾ yard. For lining, 4½ yards of 45"-wide fabric. Sewing thread to match fabrics. Cotton or Dacron batting. White double-fold bias binding tape, ½" wide, 9 yards.

DIRECTIONS: Read general directions for making quilts at the beginning of this section. Quilt is made of an eight-pointed star pieced with 800 diamond-shaped patches, set in a solid-color background.

To make pattern for diamond-shaped patches, mark a rectangle 1⅝" × 4" on paper. On each side of rectangle, mark midpoint. Draw four diagonal lines connecting points, to form a diamond shape. Cut out diamond for pattern. Each side of diamond should measure 2⅛". Cut several diamond patterns from cardboard; discard when edges begin to fray.

(Note: Before cutting fabric patches, test accuracy of pattern by drawing around it eight times, to create an eight-pointed star; there should be no gaps or overlapping of diamond-shaped segments.)

Marking patterns on wrong side of fabric and adding ¼" seam allowance all around, cut diamond-shaped patches as follows: 16 red, 32 bright pink, 48 pale pink, 64 lavender, 80 gold, 80 dark green, 96 yellow, 112 orange, 128 medium blue, 144 pale blue.

Star is made up of eight pieced diamond-shaped sections meeting at center point; each section is made up of 10 rows of 10 diamond patches each. See piecing diagram for half of one section (5 rows). Make eight sections as follows: For one section, stitch together 10 rows, following piecing diagram and color key for first five rows; for rows 6 to 10, follow photograph. Start first row with a red patch (A), second row with bright pink (B), etc. Use one of the two methods for joining diamonds described in the following paragraph. When joining diamonds to form a row, stitch patches together along sides cut on straight of goods. Stitch from the wide-angled corner towards the pointed ends. Trim seams at points as you piece. Matching corners carefully, join the 10 rows together to make a diamond-shaped section. When joining rows together, you will be stitching along the bias edges; keep thread just taut enough to prevent seams from stretching. Press pieced sections with seams to one side; open seams tend to weaken construction.

There are two methods for joining the diamonds. First method: Hold patches together, right sides facing; seam together with small running stitches on pencil lines. If the problem of sharp points and true meeting of seams proves difficult with this method, prepare each patch as follows: Second method: Cut firm paper patterns the exact size and shape of cardboard pattern. Fit paper pattern within pencil outline on wrong side of patch; hold patch with paper pattern uppermost. Fold seam allowance over each side, and tack to the paper with one stitch on each side, allowing the thread to cross the corners. Finish by taking an extra stitch into the first side; cut the thread, leaving about ¼". To make removal of tacking easier, do not knot thread or make any backstitches. Hold prepared patches right sides together, matching the edges to be seamed exactly. Whip together with fine, even stitches (about 16 to the inch), avoiding the paper as much as possible. The paper patterns may remain in place until the star shape is completed. To remove the papers, snip tacking thread once on each patch and withdraw thread; lift papers out.

Join four sections for each half of star, with red (A) points meeting in center; join halves for star. Each point of star should measure 21¼" (plus outside seam allowance) along side edges.

For background blocks, cut cardboard pattern 25½" square. Marking pattern on wrong side of fabric and adding ¼" seam allowance all around, cut four blocks from white fabric. Cut cardboard pattern in half diagonally for triangle pattern and cut four triangles from white fabric in same manner. Sew squares and triangles alternately between star points, overlapping outer angles of triangles with squares, as shown. Quilt top should measure 79" square, including outside seam allowance.

Cut two 40" × 79" pieces from lining fabric. Sew together on long sides with ½" seam. Cut batting same size.

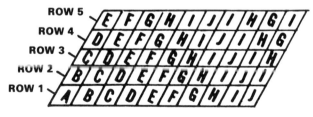

PIECING DIAGRAM

A = RED	F = YELLOW
B = BRIGHT PINK	G = ORANGE
C = PALE PINK	H = MEDIUM BLUE
D = LAVENDER	I = PALE BLUE
E = GOLD	J = DARK GREEN

Using ruler and tailor's chalk, mark design on quilt top as follows, referring to photograph. In each white corner block, draw two corner-to-corner lines through center, dividing block into four trianglar sections. In each section, draw five more triangles as shown, each one 1½" from next largest triangle; it may help in drawing lines to cut a cardboard template 1½" wide.

In each white triangle block, draw line from center angle through middle of block, to divide it into two equal triangular sections. Mark same triangle pattern in each section as for square blocks.

Following general directions, pin and baste quilt top, batting, and lining together. Starting in center and working around and outward, quilt around each diamond patch, ⅛" in from seams. Then quilt on marked lines of background blocks.

Cut white double-fold bias binding tape to fit around all four sides of quilt, covering ¼" seam allowance. Slip-stitch to lining and front of quilt.

PATRIOTIC WALL HANGING
ON PAGE 113

EQUIPMENT: Pencil. Ruler. Tape measure. Scissors. Thin cardboard. Light-colored pencil. Sewing needle. Straight pins. Sewing machine. Clear nail polish.

MATERIALS: Cotton or cotton-blend fabrics, 45" wide: white, 4¼ yards; blue, ¾ yard; red, 1 yard. Matching sewing thread. Wooden dowel, 1" diameter, 52" long.

DIRECTIONS: To make patterns, cut two 5" squares from thin cardboard. Cut one cardboard square in half diagonally to make two triangle patterns. Coat edges of cardboard patterns with clear nail polish to keep from fraying. If pattern edges become worn from marking around them, replace with new pattern.

When placing patterns on fabric, place one edge of each square on straight grain of fabric; place one short edge of each triangle on straight grain of fabric, so the diagonal edge will be on the bias. Allow ¼" seam allowance around all edges; therefore, leave at least ½" between patterns. Yardage is based on careful cutting of the patches; backing and edging strips are pieced. Do not include selvedges when cutting patches; trim them away first. (Selvedges are more tightly woven than the rest of the fabric and can cause puckering.) Eight squares will fit across the width of the fabric. Turn triangle patterns to conserve fabric if more than one row of triangles is being cut.

Press white fabric and place wrong side up on a flat surface. Using regular lead pencil, trace around and cut out twelve squares, 36 triangles, four 5½" × 10½" rectangles and four 5½" × 20½" rectangles. Press red fabric

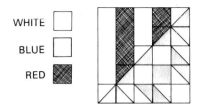

WHITE ☐
BLUE ☐
RED ▨

QUARTER-PATTERN OF PIECING DIAGRAM

and place wrong side up on flat surface. Trace and cut four squares, eight triangles, and four 5½" × 15½" rectangles. Using light-color pencil, trace and cut four squares and 44 triangles from blue fabric.

Follow quarter-pattern of piecing diagram for placement of patches. With right sides together, stitch squares, triangles and rectangles together into strips, stitching ¼" from raw edges. Stitch strips together in same manner, matching seams. Make one quarter of banner as shown in diagram, then reverse pattern and repeat for the second quarter. Reverse first half and repeat for second half. After each quarter is completed, stitch the four quarters together to form eight-pointed star in the center of the piece.

To make edgings, cut four strips from red fabric, each 1½" wide and 51½" long, piecing the fabric to obtain the 51½" length. Fold each narrow end ¾" to the wrong side and press. With wrong sides together, fold each strip in half lengthwise and press. Matching raw edges, center one folded strip along one edge on right side of patchwork, with ends of strip ¼" in from each corner. Stitch together ¼" from raw edges.

To make straps for hanging, cut six 7" × 11½" strips along lengthwise grain of white fabric. With right sides together, fold each strip in half lengthwise; stitch ¼" from raw edges along length of strip. Turn right side out; press flat with seam in center of one side. Fold each strip in half horizontally, with seam on inside. Place doubled ends of straps along top edge of patchwork, corresponding with the white patches at top of banner; see photograph for placement. With raw edges even, pin the straps to right side of patchwork over edging strip; stitch across top edge through all thicknesses, ¼" from raw edges.

To make backing, cut two 25¼" × 50½" pieces from remaining white fabric; stitch together along short sides to make a 50½" square. With right sides facing and raw edges even, place backing on top of patchwork, making sure straps and edging strips are facing inward. Stitch together ½" from raw edges, enclosing straps and edging strips; leave an 8" opening at center of bottom edge. Turn right side out through opening; fold raw edges ¼" to inside and slip-stitch opening closed.

Run dowel through the straps and rest ends of dowel on nails in desired position on wall.

ALL ABOUT

NEEDLEPOINT

Everyone is getting into the needlepoint "act"—men, women, and children. So, why not you?

There are only two basic stitches used, a slanting stitch and a straight stitch. The slanting stitch (half a cross-stitch) is called the tent or continental stitch; and the straight stitch is the gobelin stitch. These two stitches form the basis for all other needlepoint stitches. As embellishments are added to vary the stitch, the stitch is given a new name.

Our needlepoint section contains not only a variety of projects to choose from, but projects suitable for beginners as well as advanced needlepointers. In addition to actual items, we give illustrations of many novelty stitches, plus some tips on designing your own "masterpiece." You'll also find a great deal of practical information on needlepoint equipment and on blocking and finishing your needlepoint projects.

If you are a beginner, remember—the first canvas is a learning piece; it should be an uncomplicated design with about half the needlepoint area as solid background.

If you are an accomplished needlepointer, experiment with the novelty stitches given for the more complex projects. Use stitches to simulate textures or to give three-dimensional effects (see Aran Pillows, "Stained Glass" Tulips, and Contour Bargello). If you prefer to keep it simple, work in a single stitch, using vivid colors to create design interest. Change color, change stitch, change size—just let your imagination go!

If you have never done needlepoint before, now is the time to learn! And, if you've already learned the basics, look for new ideas and inspiration as well as some extra technical know-how.

Overleaf *Pastoral Landscape with Fishing Lady, sometimes called "Boston Common," was worked in tent stitch—an example of the embroidery which flourished in Boston during the 18th century. It is one of eight embroideries with a similar subject from the vicinity—dated 1743 to 1748.* (Courtesy, Museum of Fine Arts, Boston.)

THE HISTORY OF NEEDLEPOINT

As with all other types of embroidery, it is difficult to give exact dates and places where the technique of needlepoint originated. Briefly, modern needlepoint is embroidery on canvas; the most common stitch is half of a cross-stitch, also called "tent stitch."

Needlepoint as we know it began in the 16th century. An important influence was the invention of the steel needle in Elizabethan England, which replaced fishbones and thorns; thus delicate designs in fine stitches were easier to make. Needlepoint cushions, table carpets, bags, book covers, and decoration for clothing began to be made in quantity, as well as wall hangings. By the late 17th century, the gentry, at least, were filling their homes with furniture upholstered in needlepoint, often in the flame stitch type of designs which are called Hungarian, Florentine, and Bargello, depending on origin of pattern.

Needlepoint flourished in Colonial America, where it was used for pictures, as an upholstery fabric, and for fashion accessories. Most of the New England designs came from, or were strongly influenced by, England; however, importers and teachers also developed and sold their own designs.

Early needlepoint was done on a loosely woven material, such as coarse linen. Later, single-thread canvases were made especially for the purpose. After modern double-mesh canvas was invented by a French artisan in the 1860's, needlepoint enjoyed a great surge of popular enthusiasm. The double-thread canvas was often worked in a combination of fine petit point stitch for the shading of details such as faces, while gros point was used for the large, less detailed areas of garments, backgrounds, etc. To make this combination, the double-thread canvas was "split," that is, the meshes opened with a needle or pin to form a single-thread canvas for working in petit point.

During this Victorian era, Berlin work came into popularity. It is often characterized by brilliant worsteds and combinations of geometric and floral designs—a favorite theme was a cabbage rose on a black background. The majority of the designs were developed as hand-painted patterns on squared paper, especially made for copying in needlepoint or cross-stitch on canvas. Many designs came from Berlin, thus naming it.

In the beginning of our century, interest in needlepoint waned, then began to revive during the late twenties. Today, needlepoint is a favorite form of expression for the creative needlewoman. Although ready-made designs in several forms can be easily purchased, a growing number of needlepoint enthusiasts prefer to design original pieces, using their imagination and skill combined with a fascinating variety of canvas stitches.

NEEDLEPOINT EQUIPMENT

Once you decide to make a needlepoint piece, it is important to collect the proper equipment. Not many items are needed, so choose the best you can afford. Good tools produce good work. Learn to use your accessories properly and you will find your work to be neater.

Blunt needles are used for needlepoint (see Page 132). Keep a good selection of needles on hand and protect them by storing in a needle case. It is also advisable to run your needles through an emery strawberry occasionally to clean them.

You will need proper scissors. Embroidery scissors should be small, with narrow, pointed blades, and must be sharp. Protect the blade points by keeping them in a sheath.

A thimble is advisable even though little pressure is needed to make a needlepoint stitch. Generally, metal thimbles are better than plastic or bone. Be sure that the closed end and sides are deeply indented to prevent the needle end from slipping off when in use. Thimbles come in different sizes; try on a few for correct fit.

An embroidery frame is optional when making a large and heavy piece, such as a rug, or if using complicated stitches that require the use of the hand under the canvas. The round frame or hoop used for other types of embroidery is not desirable for needlepoint, as it stretches the canvas out of shape. The rectangular frame preferred for canvas work consists of four pieces: two roller pieces at top and bottom and either two screw-type ends for tightening, or flat ends with holes for adjusting. The canvas piece is tacked onto the strips of fabric on the roller pieces and laced onto the ends to hold it taut. Specific instructions for mounting the canvas will come with each frame. Rectangular frames may be mounted on a stand or held in the hand.

STARTING TO WORK YOUR NEEDLEPOINT PIECE

When starting a canvas piece, allow at least a 2″ margin of plain canvas all around the background area. Embroidering more needlepoint than will show on the surface of the finished piece is a waste of yarn and time. Before beginning, bind all raw edges of canvas, using masking tape or a double-fold bias binding—or turn the raw edges over and whipstitch to keep from raveling.

Art needlework shops, needlework departments, and mail-order houses carry single-thread (mono) and double thread (Penelope) canvas. In mono canvas the meshes are uniform in size because vertical and horizontal threads are evenly spaced in both directions; this canvas has no up and down. You can start work from any edge or in any direction. Penelope canvas has alternating large and small meshes. The selvage edges of the canvas are the sides of your piece. It is vital that the work not be turned sideways.

To follow a design from a chart, start at top right corner when working in continental or diagonal stitch and work background to beginning of design area. Then work the design area, following chart and filling in the background as you go. (Each square on the chart represents one needlepoint stitch. The chart may be given on any size graph paper; the size of the graph is not related to the size of the canvas. The number of meshes-to-the-inch of canvas being used and the number of stitches determine size of the finished needlepoint piece.) Cut yarn strands into 18″ lengths (do not break yarn, as this will stretch it). To thread yarn, double it over the end of the needle and slip it off, holding it tightly as close as possible to the fold. Push the flattened, folded end through the needle eye and pull yarn through. To start, leave 1″ of yarn at back of canvas and cover this as the work proceeds. Work needlepoint in method desired, being careful not to pull yarn too tightly. Hold thumb on yarn near stitch until you have pulled yarn through the canvas, then lift thumb and pull yarn gently into place. Keep yarn from twisting to avoid thin places in work, by letting it drop and untwist. When close to the end of a strand, fasten by weaving through a few stitches on back of work. Immediately clip ends close, to avoid tangles. When a mistake is made, pluck out yarn with blunt end of needle, or run needle under stitch and snip yarn with embroidery scissors close to needle. Do not reuse pulled-out yarn. If not using a frame, roll canvas as you work, from the bottom up or the top down.

PETIT POINT • NEEDLEPOINT
GROS POINT • QUICK POINT

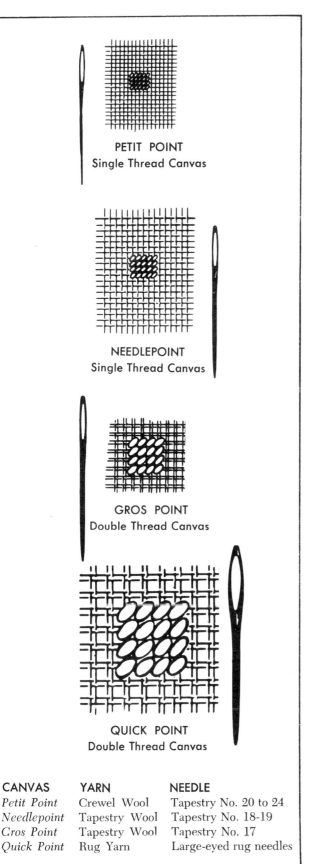

PETIT POINT
Single Thread Canvas

NEEDLEPOINT
Single Thread Canvas

GROS POINT
Double Thread Canvas

QUICK POINT
Double Thread Canvas

CANVAS	YARN	NEEDLE
Petit Point	Crewel Wool	Tapestry No. 20 to 24
Needlepoint	Tapestry Wool	Tapestry No. 18-19
Cros Point	Tapestry Wool	Tapestry No. 17
Quick Point	Rug Yarn	Large-eyed rug needles

Needlepoint is the general term for an embroidery stitch used to cover canvas, as well as for the embroidered piece. When this stitch is worked on canvas 20 meshes to the inch or smaller, it is called petit point. When worked on 14 to 18 to the inch mesh, it is called simply needlepoint. On 8 to 12 to the inch mesh, it is called gros point. Larger meshes, 5 and 7 to the inch, have been used in the past for making rugs and are sometimes referred to as large gros point. However, we prefer the name quick point.

YARNS AND CANVAS: In general, you can use a single ply of Persian yarn or split tapestry wool on canvas 18 to 22 meshes to the inch. Use a two-ply strand of Persian yarn on 12 to 16 mesh canvas. Use a full three-ply strand of Persian yarn or one strand of tapestry wool on 10 mesh canvas. For rug canvas, use rug yarn or two strands of tapestry wool. Canvas and weights of wool vary, so it is important always to experiment with the wool in relation to the canvas, to be sure the canvas will be covered but not crowded.

Persian yarn, tapestry wool, and rug yarn may be combined in one needlepoint piece if special colors are unobtainable in the correct yarn. Care must be taken, however, that sufficient strands of the finer yarn are used to balance the weight. Fine yarns may be doubled or tripled to cover the canvas, but a heavy rug yarn cannot be used on a fine canvas. Other types of yarn may be used only if they have a tight, firm twist. Knitting worsted, for example, is not suitable for most needlepoint, because the twist is not firm enough and it wears thin from constant pulling through the canvas. However, if a special color is needed when making a picture, which does not require durability, knitting worsted may be used by working with short strands.

Canvases range in width from 18 to 54 inches, or from 14 to 80 inches for rug canvas. When buying canvas, look for the best quality available. It is important that the mesh be regular, with no weak or tied threads. Choose the canvas with a glossy finish.

NEEDLES: A blunt tapestry needle is always used. Needles range in size from fairly fine to the large rug needles. Sketches at left show actual sizes in relation to the various types of canvas. The needle to use with each yarn should have an eye large enough to accommodate the yarn, but not larger than needed. Chart relates threads and needles to type of work. In embroidery and sewing needles, the largest number indicates the finest needle.

You may have a favorite needlepoint design that you would like to use again in another size. Any design can be enlarged or reduced by using a canvas with a larger or smaller mesh count than that of the original design. To illustrate, a rose motif worked on petit point canvas is shown at upper right, with three actual-size details of variations shown below it.

To figure the overall size of your design on the new background, count the number of stitches lengthwise and crosswise on the original. Then count off an equal number of meshes on the new background.

ESTIMATING THE AMOUNT OF YARN: Select the type of yarn best suited to the mesh of your canvas. Work a 1″ square and note the amount of yarn used. Figure the number of square inches to be covered by each color in your design, then multiply by the amount used to work the 1″ square. This gives you the approximate yardage for each color. To figure the number of skeins needed, divide the yardage by the number of yards in a skein.

SPLITTING DOUBLE-THREAD CANVAS: Parts of a design on gros point canvas may require more detail than can be obtained with the gros point stitch as it is worked over double threads—for instance, facial or floral details. To accomplish this, the double threads of the canvas may be split and petit point worked in these particular areas. To split the double threads, mark the design area first, then run the blunt end of your needle between the vertical and horizontal threads of the canvas to separate them. Keep the split threads just within the marked area. The petit point stitch is worked over each single split thread, thus making twice as many stitches per inch as in the gros point parts; see stitch detail below. A single ply of Persian yarn, or six strands of six-strand embroidery floss, or silk floss may be used on the petit point parts, while tapestry yarn or a full three-ply strand of Persian yarn may be used for the remainder.

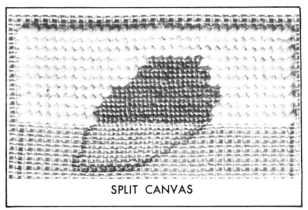

SPLIT CANVAS

ADAPTING A DESIGN TO A DIFFERENT SIZE

Petit point worked in crewel wool on a 22-to-the-inch single-thread canvas.

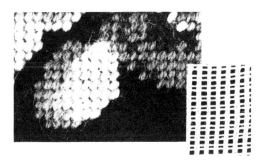

Gros point worked in tapestry yarn on 10-to-the-inch double-thread canvas.

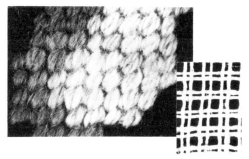

Quick-point with wool rug yarn on a 5-to-the-inch double-thread rug canvas.

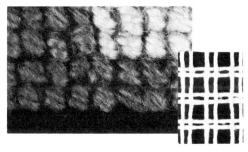

Cross-stitching with rug yarn on 3½-to-the-inch double-thread rug canvas.

THREE METHODS FOR WORKING BASIC NEEDLEPOINT STITCH

HALF CROSS-STITCH

Needle is vertical when making stitch.

HALF CROSS-STITCH Start at upper left corner of canvas. Bring needle to front of canvas at point that will be the bottom of first stitch. The needle is in a vertical position when making stitch (see detail). Always work from left to right; turn work around for return row. Catch yarn ends through finished work on back.

CONTINENTAL STITCH

DETAIL 1   DETAIL 2

Detail 1 shows starting new row below finished portion. Detail 2 shows starting a new row above finished portion.

CONTINENTAL STITCH Start design at upper right corner. To begin, hold an inch of yarn in back and work over this end. All other strands may be started and finished by running them through wrong side of finished work. Details 1 and 2 show placement and direction of needle; turn work around for return row. Always work from right to left. Finish design, then fill in background.

DIAGONAL STITCH

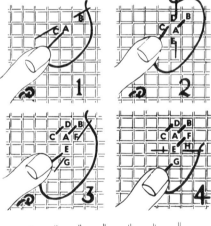

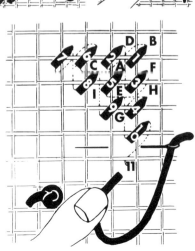

DIAGONAL STITCH Begin by tying a knot at end of yarn and putting needle through canvas to back, diagonally down from upper right-hand corner of work. Never turn work; hold it in the same position. Step 1: The knot is on top. Bring needle up at A, down through B and out through C. Step 2: Needle in D, out through E. Step 3: Needle in F, out through G. Step 4: Start next row in at H and out through I.

You are now ready to work from the Big Diagram. Each stitch is drawn on Big Diagram with blunt and pointed ends. Put needle in at pointed end, out at blunt end.

Stitch No. 5 is your next stitch. It extends from space I to A. Complete the stitches to 10 on diagram in numerical order to finish the diagonal row. Stitch No. 11 starts the next row diagonally upward.

After starting row going up, needle is horizontal. Needle slants diagonally to begin new row down, as in Step 1. Going down, needle is always vertical, as in Step 2: and again, when the last stitch is made, the needle slants diagonally to begin next row up, Step 3.

Work as far as knot; cut off. All other strands of yarn may be started and ended by running them through the finished work on the back. Work background to design; then work design. Fill in remaining background.

WHICH METHOD SHOULD BE USED?

The stitch used in working needlepoint has a great deal to do with the wearing quality of the embroidery. The three most familiar methods are the half cross-stitch, the continental stitch, and the diagonal stitch, all described on opposite page. Each has certain advantages:

The half cross-stitch does not cover canvas as well as the continental or diagonal stitch and must be done carefully for good coverage on front; there is practically no yarn on back (see right). It works up quickly, saves yarn, and is practical for pictures or areas that receive little wear.

HALF CROSS-STITCH

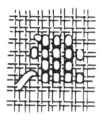

BACK

The continental stitch uses more wool than the half cross-stitch; however, it covers the canvas both front and back (see right). As a result, the finished piece is more attractive, with better wearing quality. The slight padding on the back makes it durable and practical for upholstery and pillows.

CONTINENTAL STITCH

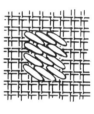

BACK

The diagonal stitch, contrary to popular belief, does not use more wool than the continental stitch, but the same amount. It covers the front of the canvas well, and, being actually woven into the canvas, forms a durable web to reinforce the back (see right). This method is best for needlepoint that will receive a lot of wear, particularly rugs, chair seats, or any other items to be upholstered.

DIAGONAL STITCH

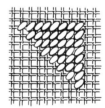

FRONT

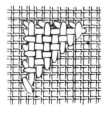

BACK

A variety of novelty stitches can be combined on canvas to produce an interesting range of textures (see Tulip Sampler on Page 146).

Often the novelty stitches are combined with a plain needlepoint background, thus making the design area more prominent.

CROSS-STITCH COUCHING Lay a heavy yarn along canvas for length desired; run ends to back of canvas. Bring a finer yarn out in mesh at bottom left of laid yarn. Make a cross-stitch over the laid yarn, taking stitches in meshes at each side and up over three meshes. Skip number of meshes desired; couch with another cross.

THREE-STITCH CROSS Starting at the bottom, make a diagonal stitch in third mesh over and up. Bring needle out two meshes to the left at top. Make second half of cross to the lower right and bring needle out on left at center of the cross. Make a horizontal stitch across to right and bring needle out in same mesh as top left of cross for beginning of the next stitch. Continue to top.

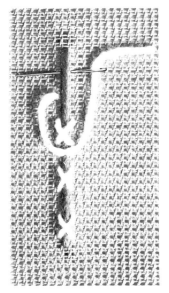

CROSS-STITCH
COUCHING

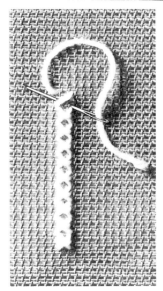

THREE-STITCH
CROSS

CASHMERE STITCH VARIATION Starting at bottom, take a diagonal stitch over one mesh of the canvas; bring needle out at lower left of the first stitch. Make a longer diagonal stitch over two meshes and up one. Continue with the longer diagonal stitch to the top; complete the row with a diagonal stitch over one mesh of the canvas.

LAID STITCH WITH BACKSTITCH Bring the needle out at bottom for the first row. Insert needle in fourth mesh above and bring out between strands of the first mesh to the left. Insert needle between strands of first mesh to left at bottom and bring out in the next mesh. Insert needle in second mesh at top and out between the strands of next mesh. Continue in this manner; make each row with the bottom of stitches in same meshes as top of last row. Make backstitches between rows, over one mesh.

CASHMERE STITCH
VARIATION

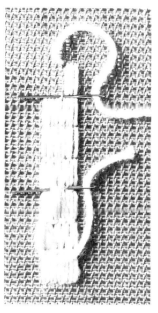

LAID STITCH
WITH BACKSTITCH

CANVAS STITCHES

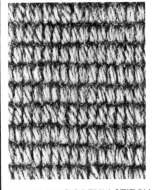
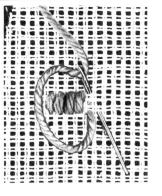

UPRIGHT GOBELIN STITCH

UPRIGHT GOBELIN STITCH Bring the needle out at bottom of row at left and work to the right. Take an upright stitch over two meshes of canvas; bring needle out at bottom of row one mesh to the right. Continue across in this manner. Top of the stitches of succeeding rows are in the same mesh as bottom of the stitches of last row.

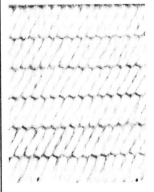
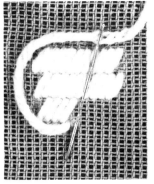

WIDE GOBELIN STITCH

WIDE GOBELIN STITCH This stitch is slightly slanted as it is worked over three horizontal and two vertical meshes of the canvas. Work across from left to right in the same manner as for Gobelin Stitch; turn the canvas upside down to work next row in the same manner.

ENCROACHING GOBELIN STITCH

ENCROACHING GOBELIN This stitch is worked over five horizontal and one vertical mesh of the canvas and is slightly slanted. Work the first row as for Wide Gobelin Stitch. For the second row, bring needle out only four meshes below and work as before over five horizontal meshes, thus making the encroaching stitch.

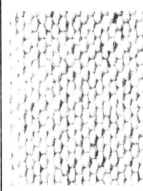

BRICK STITCH

BRICK STITCH A variation of the Gobelin Stitch. Upright stitches are all the same length. Work first stitch over two meshes of canvas; bring needle out to right one mesh down. Make next stitch over two meshes; bring needle out one mesh up to right. Continue across. On next row, work from right to left; top of stitches are in same mesh as bottom of stitches of the first row.

HUNGARIAN STITCH Starting at the left, work upright stitches—the first stitch over two meshes, the second stitch over four meshes, and the third stitch over two meshes, making a diamond shape. Skip one vertical mesh and repeat; continue across to the right. On second row, work a longer center stitch in open mesh between diamonds of first row, using second color if desired.

HUNGARIAN STITCH

STEM STITCH Work diagonal stitches from the top to bottom, over two meshes of canvas each way; make each stitch one mesh below last. Work second row in diagonal stitches in opposite direction, with lower end of stitches in same meshes as first row. To square off beginning or end of row, work the stitch over one mesh.

STEM STITCH

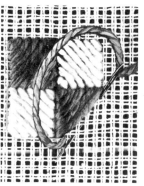

CHECKERBOARD STITCH Starting in the upper left corner, work diagonal stitches from left to right over first one mesh, then two meshes, three meshes, four meshes, five meshes, four, three, two and one mesh, forming a square. Make three more squares in the same manner, alternating direction of stitches and making ends of stitches of adjoining squares in same meshes of canvas.

CHECKERBOARD STITCH

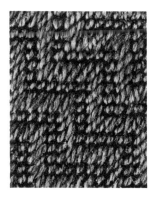

JACQUARD STITCH Starting at the upper left, work diagonal stitches over two horizontal and two vertical meshes of canvas. Make six stitches down, then six stitches to right; continue down and across for desired length. For next row to right, work diagonal stitches over one mesh of canvas, making same number of stitches down and across. Repeat these two rows alternately.

JACQUARD STITCH

CANVAS STITCHES

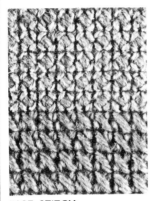 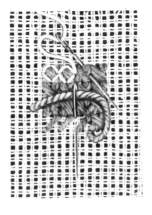

RICE STITCH

RICE STITCH Working from left to right, make the bottom half of crosses diagonally over two meshes to the right. Return to left, making top half of crosses diagonally to left. Using a finer yarn, take a small diagonal stitch over each arm of crosses, having the stitches meet in the meshes between the arms of crosses.

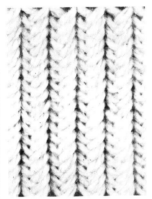 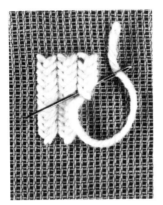

FERN STITCH

FERN STITCH Work rows from top to bottom. Bring the needle out at top left. Take a diagonal stitch two meshes down and two meshes to the right and bring needle out one mesh to left. Make second half of stitch up over two meshes of canvas each way and bring out at left side in the mesh below last stitch. Continue in this manner to bottom. Make next row in same way, with ends of stitches in the same meshes as the stitches of last row.

STAR STITCH

STAR STITCH Each star consists of eight stitches all meeting in the center; make each star in the same way. Work over two meshes of canvas for each stitch of star, bringing the needle down through center mesh each time, and working around to complete the star. Backstitch may be worked around the completed stars in another color.

MOSAIC STITCH

MOSAIC STITCH Consists of long and short stitches taken alternately in diagonal rows. Insert the needle one mesh to the right, going up one mesh for a short stitch and two meshes for a long stitch. In each succeeding row, a short stitch is worked into the end of a long stitch and a long stitch into the end of a short stitch.

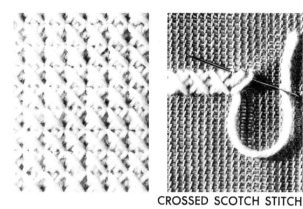

CROSSED SCOTCH STITCH   Starting at the left, make a diagonal stitch up over two meshes of canvas; bring needle out in mesh to left below first stitch. Make a longer diagonal stitch up over three meshes, then bring out below one mesh to right of the last stitch; make another short diagonal stitch up. Cross these stitches with a diagonal in opposite direction, going into open meshes at corners. For plain Scotch Stitch, do not cross stitches; make a short diagonal stitch in two open corners, same direction as previous stitches.

CROSSED SCOTCH STITCH

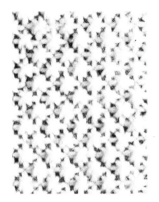

DOUBLE CROSS Starting at left, make a horizontal stitch over four meshes of canvas and a vertical stitch across the center over four meshes; bring the needle out at upper left one mesh from the center. Cross over diagonally to lower right. Make other half of diagonal cross in the opposite direction in open meshes at each side of center. On the next row, make top and sides of upright crosses in the same meshes as the last row.

DOUBLE CROSS-STITCH

LEAF STITCH Starting at the bottom center of leaf, make a diagonal stitch three meshes to right and four meshes up. Bring the needle out one mesh up at center. Make next stitch one mesh above to right; make another stitch the same. Make next stitch one mesh up and one mesh to left of last stitch; make another stitch in the same way. For top center stitch, bring needle out two meshes up at the center and make an upright stitch over three meshes. Complete the other side of leaf the same. Make sides of adjoining leaves in the same meshes.

LEAF STITCH

KNOTTED STITCH Starting at the left, bring needle out at bottom of row; make a diagonal stitch one mesh to the right and five meshes up. Bring needle out two meshes down on left. Cross over vertical stitch one mesh to the right and one mesh down; bring out two meshes below. Continue across row to the right. On succeeding rows, bring top of stitch one mesh up from bottom of last row between stitches, as for Encroaching Gobelin Stitch.

KNOTTED STITCH

CANVAS STITCHES

Fig. 1   Fig. 2

OBLONG CROSS-STITCH WITH BACKSTITCH Make the long cross-stitches over four horizontal meshes and one vertical mesh of the canvas. Starting at left bottom, make first half of each cross to right end of the row (Fig. 1). Work back to left, making second half of cross (Fig. 2). Over the center of each cross-stitch, make a backstitch, going in and out of meshes at each side of cross (Fig. 3). Make tops and bottoms of each row of crosses in same meshes. Work row of backstitch between rows of crosses.

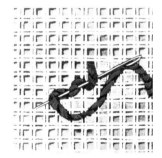

Fig. 3

OBLONG CROSS-STITCH WITH BACKSTITCH

Fig. 1   Fig. 2

Fig. 3   Fig. 4

TWISTED KNOT STITCH

TWISTED KNOT STITCH Bring yarn to the front at upper right. Wind yarn toward you loosely, twice around needle (Fig. 1). Turn the needle counter-clockwise, twisting yarn; insert needle one mesh to right above and bring out one mesh to the left of beginning (Fig.2). Continue making knots in this manner across to the left. Turn canvas around for next row. Wind yarn around needle and take a horizontal stitch to left (Fig. 3), working below last row as shown. Make succeeding knots, taking a diagonal stitch upward into bottom of last knot (Fig. 4).

WEB STITCH Take diagonal stitches across the canvas, laying rows of yarn to form a square of desired size (Fig. 1). To couch laid yarn down, start in the upper right corner and make stitches as for diagonal method of needlepoint (see page 8). Work to the opposite corner (Fig. 2). Two colors are effective for this stitch, but it may be done in one color. Alternate Web Stitch squares with Velvet-Stitch Loop squares for a high-low texture.

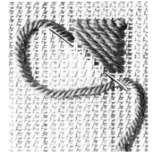 

Fig. 1   Fig. 2

WEB STITCH

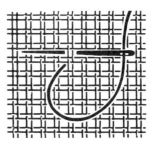

Fig. 1   Fig. 2

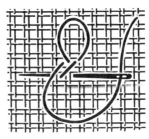 

Fig. 3   Fig. 4

VELVET-STITCH LOOPS Starting at upper right, make first half of cross over one mesh of canvas (Fig. 1). Take a stitch one mesh to right above half cross and bring needle out in same mesh (Fig. 2); form a loop ¼" long while completing the cross (Fig. 3); bring needle out one mesh to the left to begin next cross. Continue across, forming cross-stitch loops. For the next row, turn the canvas and work as shown in Figs. 4, 5, and 6, holding the loops below the work with your left thumb.

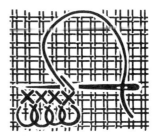 

Fig. 5   Fig. 6

VELVET-STITCH LOOPS

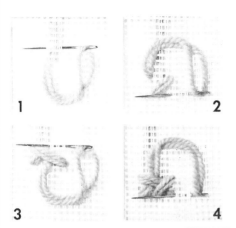

GREEK STITCH Start in fourth mesh below top left corner of area to be embroidered. Insert needle at top, into fourth mesh from corner; bring out in corner (Fig. 1).

At bottom of row, insert needle in seventh mesh from left side; bring to front in fourth mesh from left (Fig. 2).

At top of row, insert needle three meshes to right of completed stitch; bring out in same mesh as last stitch completed (Fig. 3).

At bottom of row, insert needle three meshes to right of completed stitch; bring out in same mesh as last stitch completed (Fig. 4). Continue across. See Figs. 3 and 4.

To start next row, begin three meshes below worked row (upper part of stitches will be in same meshes as bottom of stitches of last row).

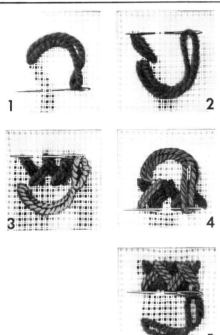

TWO-TONE HERRINGBONE With purple yarn, start in upper left corner of area to be embroidered. Insert needle six meshes down from corner and five meshes to right; bring out in third mesh from left side (Fig. 1).

At top of row, insert needle six meshes to right of last stitch at top; bring out two meshes to left (Fig. 2). *At bottom of row, insert needle four meshes to right of last stitch at bottom; bring out two meshes to left. At top of row, insert needle four meshes to right of last stitch; bring out two meshes to left. Repeat from * across.

With fuchsia yarn, start six meshes down from left corner. At top of row, insert needle in fifth mesh from corner; bring out two meshes to left (Fig. 3). Work across, following Figs. 3 and 4.

To begin next row, with purple yarn, start five meshes below last row (top of stitches will be in same mesh as bottom of stitches of last row, Fig. 5).

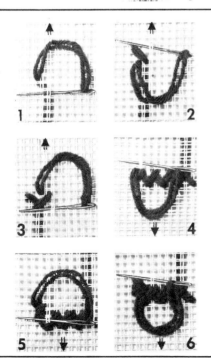

HERRINGBONE-GONE-WRONG Start at top left corner of area to be embroidered. Insert needle three meshes below and three meshes to right; bring out in next mesh to left (Fig. 1). At top of row, insert needle in fourth mesh from corner; bring out in next mesh to left (Fig. 2). *At bottom of row, insert needle two meshes to right of completed stitch; bring out in next mesh to left (Fig. 3). At top of row, insert needle two meshes to right of completed stitch and bring out in next mesh to left. Repeat from *.

To start next row, turn canvas so that completed row is at bottom. Insert needle one mesh to right in row above; bring out in next mesh to left (Fig. 4). Insert needle in empty mesh inside point of first stitch; bring out in next mesh to left (Fig. 5). Insert needle in mesh directly above next point; bring out in next mesh to left (Fig. 6). Continue across. Turn canvas for each row.

NEEDLEPOINT,

a relaxing way to while away the hours, is the art of covering canvas with a variety of stitches. Stitches can be traditional or innovative, but combined with the rich colors of yarn, a finished needlepoint piece is surely something to be treasured. On the next few pages you'll see just how varied needlepoint can be—from the traditional sampler at right to the brilliant four-way bargello mirror frame, to the elegant floral repeat design for upholstery.

SAMPLER DONE IN NEEDLEPOINT

repeats the alphabet theme of traditional samplers—which served the double purpose of teaching young needleworkers how to embroider and how to read. Here, the idea is old, but the colors are new—making this 17" x 19" sampler an amusing accent piece for a contemporary room. Directions, Page 166.

"STAINED GLASS" TULIPS are worked in richly textured
needlepoint that can be framed as a picture or used to top a pillow. Black "leading,"
worked in continental stitch, is filled in with seven different novelty stitches, making
the 12" x 12" piece a needlepoint sampler. Directions, Page 167.

PILLOWS FROM A GARDE

Trellis- and lattice-patterned pillows, opposite, have an airy garden look that
well with today's light-handed decorating. The flowers are done in embroid
stitches, just as they would be on fabric. Directions are on page

DESIGNED BY GENIA WIDDER

BARGELLO PATTERNS _work beautifully with either traditional or contemporary designs. The colorful repeat patterns are worked in upright stitches over two or more meshes of needlepoint canvas, with all stitches starting and ending in the same meshes as the stitches above and below._

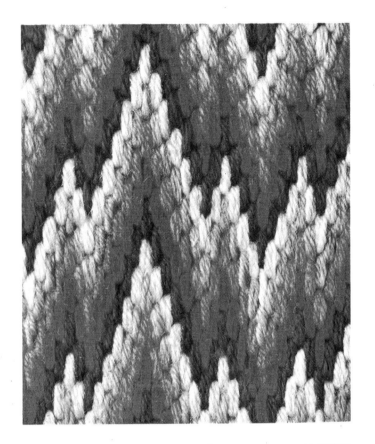

Flame stitch is worked over four meshes. Going upward, each stitch starts one mesh over, four meshes up from preceding stitch.

Stitches forming concentric squares go over four meshes. Each stitch starts one mesh up or down. Stitches in centers vary in length.

Subtle shading from dark to light in monochromatic or related colors is characteristic of bargello. These typical patterns, worked on 10-mesh-to-the-inch canvas with tapestry yarn double in the needle, can be used for pillows, upholstery or fashion accessories. The design is usually established by the first row; succeeding rows follow the same pattern.

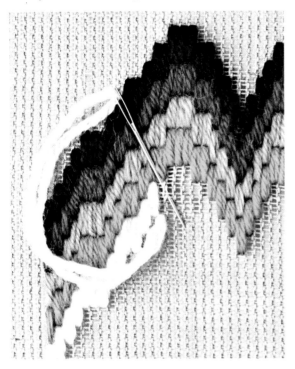

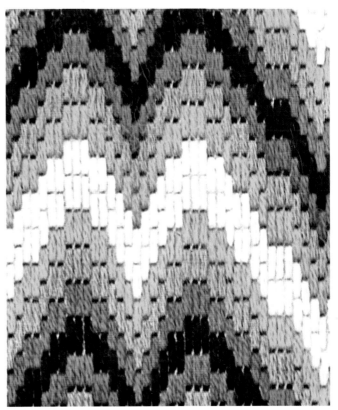

Stitches of zigzag pattern go over four meshes. Each stitch or group of two or three starts at center of previous stitch.

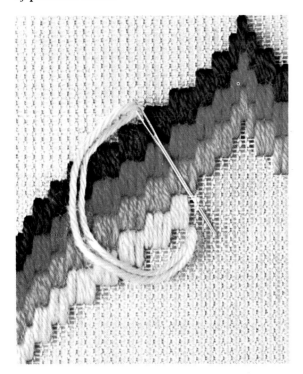

Stitches of chevron pattern go over four meshes. Each stitch or group of stitches is one mesh over, two meshes up or down.

CONTOUR BARGELLO

*gives a rounded, three-dimensional look to
needlepoint planned for pillows and
upholstery. Undulating bands of bargello
curve around lavender anemones and frame a
pair of brilliant poppies. Additional contrast
and dimension are achieved by working the
centers in continental stitch with two plies of
three-ply yarn, the bargello with three.*
Directions, Page 170.

DESIGNED BY SUZY GIRARD

FABULOUS FRAME *for a mirror or a picture is done in bargello with a dramatic, radiating effect. The subtly shaded pattern is repeated on all four sides, meeting at the corners for a mitered look. Directions, Page 172.*

VICTORIAN PICTURE

of an exotic parrot perched on a crescent of brilliant blossoms is typical of the era's passion for naturalistic design. Worked on 10-mesh-to-the-inch canvas, the 18½" square would also make a charming pillow. Directions, Page 173.

UPHOLSTERY *done in needlepoint has great decorating status. Here, tulips worked in stripes make easy repeat patterns. Start with a small project, such as a footstool, then "graduate" to larger pieces. For upholstery hints, see page 158. Directions for Tulip Upholstery are on Page 173.*

ARAN ISLE DESIGNS

echo the distinctive knitted stitches originated by the artisans of the famed Irish islands. Reproduced in needlepoint, using heavy rug yarn, they retain their sturdy character and richly textured look. Used in fascinating variety, they make veritable needlepoint samplers of the two pillows seen here. Directions begin on Page 175.

DESIGNED BY JACK BODI

VEGETABLE QUARTET *of home-grown beauties in brilliant natural colors will thrive however you plant them— as check-bordered pillows, as pictures, or as wall hangings. Finish pillows with cording and backing of contrasting fabric; frame pictures in the same accent colors. See Page 179 for directions and charts.*

HOW NEEDLEPOINT DESIGNS ARE SOLD

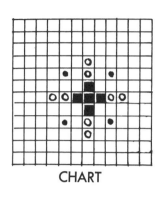

CHART

EMBROIDERED CENTERS: These are pieces with the center design already worked. They're available in a wide range of subjects and sizes. Backgrounds may be worked in one of the tent stitches (half-cross, continental, diagonal), or in one of the novelty stitches.

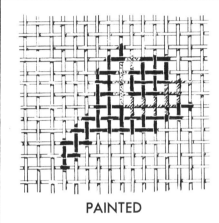

PAINTED

CHARTED DESIGNS: Many designs for pictures and other needlepoint pieces are available in chart form. Following a chart, a design may be worked on any-size canvas mesh desired to produce a large or small piece. Each square on the chart represents a corresponding stitch to be taken in the canvas.

WORKED FROM CHART

PAINTED PIECES: The design is painted directly on the canvas in colors approximating the colors to be used in working the needlepoint. You can paint your own designs on needlepoint canvas, with acrylic paints and a fine nylon brush. Be sure to thin the paint with water so it does not clog the canvas mesh. Permanent felt-tip marking pens may be used, but the ink should be tested to make certain it will not run in water.

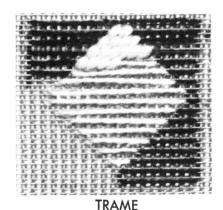

TRAME

TRAME PIECES: The design has yarn laid in long stitches across the canvas in the exact pattern. The colors used in tramé patterns are approximately the colors to be used in working the piece in needlepoint. The needlepoint is worked over the long laid stitches, following the correct color arrangement. This helps to pad the piece for a richer look and makes it very easy to follow the colors.

DESIGNING NEEDLEPOINT

Today, more and more women are interested in finding a medium of self-expression. Needlepoint is one way to fill this need. Once the basic stitches are mastered, the competent needlewoman is ready to take the further step of creating her own designs. Therefore, we offer some how-to suggestions on creating individual needlepoint designs. It is really quite a simple matter to design a piece of needlepoint to fit your personal requirements and taste. The satisfaction of "making your own" is well worth the effort and time.

WHERE TO FIND A DESIGN

Those who are talented in drawing will have no trouble creating an entirely original needlepoint design. Others may wish to obtain the aid of an artist friend, or the art teacher in a local school. However, even those who have no creative talent and wish to "do it themselves" may still obtain distinctive results by using the following suggestions.

1. Take your inspiration from something purely personal—a favorite picture in your home, your pet, a pictorial representation of your hobby, a sampler of daily activities, your coat of arms.

2. Work out a design inspired by your decor—repeat a motif taken from your wallpaper or drapery fabric. Change the size or proportion to suit your needs and to fit the item you plan to make. You can enlarge a small design for a bold, contemporary effect or reduce a large one to repeat for an allover pattern. Use the colors of your decorating scheme.

3. Research designs—look up and copy old designs from books on needlepoint in your library, or study actual pieces in museums. Use them as shown, or vary designs to suit your own taste. Usually illustrations have been reduced from the size of the original; perhaps your library or museum has a photostating service, so that you can get the design you wish to use blown up to full size. If not, enlarge by squares. Trace the design carefully and do the enlarging at home. (Note: When making a copy, remember not to use someone else's design for an item to be sold unless the design is in public domain.)

4. Adapt designs from other needlework. Cross-stitch designs, for example, can be adapted easily to needlepoint by using them as a chart for counting.

CHOOSING YOUR MATERIALS

For delicate, traditional designs, small stitches are most suitable; simple, bold, contemporary designs should be worked in large stitches.

Petit point employs the smallest stitches, and is suited to small designs, detailed traditional designs and delicate effects, such as are used on evening bags and French boudoir chairs. Choose a fine canvas and fine yarn such as crewel wool.

Needlepoint is suited to upholstery, pictures, etc. Use a medium single or double thread canvas, and a two-ply strand of Persian yarn, or one strand of tapestry yarn.

Gros point is suited to upholstery, as well as to pictures, pillows and rugs. Use medium large double thread canvas, one or two strands of tapestry yarn.

Quick point is especially suited to bold designs and for making rugs. Use a large mesh canvas and rug wool, or two or more strands of tapestry yarn. In using this for upholstery, care should be taken that when mounted on a chair or stool seat, it is not too bulky for inserting into the frame.

PUTTING A DESIGN ON CANVAS

There are three ways of getting your design on the canvas. One is to make the design into a chart or graph, each square of which represents one stitch, with symbols to indicate the colors; you follow this chart in working the canvas. Another way is to work from a design with outlines filled in with color. You draw the design outlines on your canvas and fill in the colors with embroidery. The easiest method for the needleworker to follow is to have the design painted on canvas, with various areas colored to correspond exactly to the wools to be used.

1. How to Make a Chart or Graph
Draw the design on a piece of graph paper with the count the same as your canvas (i.e., 10-squares-to-the-inch paper represents 10-mesh-to-the-inch canvas); each square represents a stitch. On most graph papers you can
continued

fill in color areas with water colors. If paper buckles, use colored pencils.

Another method is to rule lines representing canvas threads over the design, scaled to exact size of finished piece. If necessary, enlarge or reduce design before ruling lines.

2. How to Mark Outline on Canvas

Place design, heavily outlined, under canvas; trace lines that show through; complete outline with Permanent (waterproof) felt tip marking pen, or India ink and a very fine brush. In using this method (particularly good for coarse canvas), paint curved lines as curves; do not attempt to indicate where individual stitches fall. Planning placement of stitches while working is interesting.

With small meshed canvas, you can transfer your design directly to the canvas. Thumbtack canvas to a flat surface; establish a vertical and horizontal center as placement guides. Cover canvas with carbon paper; center pattern over carbon, and trace around outline of design with a blunt point such as tip of a knitting needle. After transferring is completed, paper towels should be placed over

outline and pressed with a hot iron to remove any excess carbon that might discolor yarn. Go over outlines with a waterproof India ink.

HOW TO PAINT IN THE DESIGN

1. For a sample design with few colors, color areas can be filled in with wax crayons. Fix color by pressing canvas under paper towels with warm iron.

2. Designs can be painted on canvas with acrylic paints and a fine nylon brush, but paint should be thinned with water so it goes on easily and does not clog the canvas mesh.

3. For complex designs, painting design on canvas with oil paints is not difficult. It can be used on all canvases, but the paint must be thinned. Turpentine or Japan drier can be used as a thinner. If turpentine alone is used, allow forty-eight hours to dry. Japan drier will darken the color slightly, but will dry in twenty-four hours or less. Try thinning the oil color with a little of both to get a drying time between the two mentioned. Test on canvas scraps to find the one you prefer. Use a fine brush for detail and a slightly wider brush for filling in larger areas.

French period chair, ideally upholstered with petit point.

Medium-weight chair with a seat covered in gros point.

AIDS TO UPHOLSTERING

Designs become bolder and simpler with large stitches and finer and more detailed with small stitches. The character of the design is thus in keeping with the stitch count of the needlepoint which in turn should harmonize with the character of the furniture.

Petit point is ideal for very delicate furniture such as French chairs. Needlepoint and gros point are well suited to average weight chairs such as Chippendale and Queen Anne. Quick point goes well with bulky, unembellished contemporary furniture and Provincial styles.

Technically, almost any chair can be upholstered with petit point and gros point. However, the bulkiness of quick point limits its uses slightly. It is not recommended for upholstering chair seats or stool tops which fit down into a frame unless the stool or chair has been specially built to allow for the extra bulk. If a piece of needlepoint too bulky for such a chair is forced into its frame, the frame may split when the chair is used.

*Contemporary chair, with
a removable seat, boxing,
is suitable for quick point.*

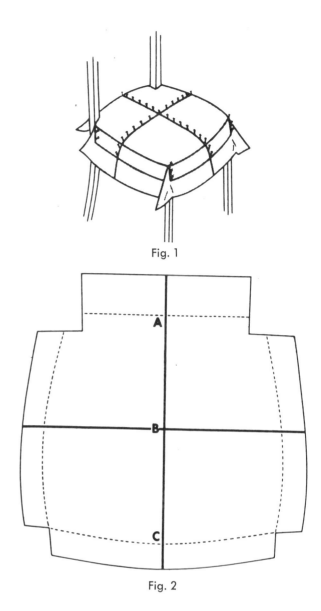

Fig. 1

Fig. 2

In order to work needlepoint only in the area of the canvas that will show after the piece has been upholstered, it is necessary to make a pattern. It is important in time and money saved and the appearance of the finished upholstery to work only the necessary area of canvas. Remember to allow at least 2″ margin of canvas around pattern for blocking.

To make a muslin pattern, use a piece of muslin a little larger than the area of a seat, for instance of a chair, to be upholstered. Mark a vertical and horizontal line at center. Draw corresponding center lines on chair seat. Place muslin on chair, matching lines. Beginning at center, pin muslin to seat along lines, Fig. 1, spacing pins 3″ apart. Slash muslin to fit around back posts and tuck it down. Pin corners to make miters if necessary.

Mark all around lower edge of chair seat; mark around back posts, reaching down into tucked-in area; mark on both sides of mitered corners; make a line to indicate top area of seat to be used in placing design for needlepoint. Remove muslin from chair and pin down on a board with threads straight. You will find that despite great care, the shape of the muslin is slightly irregular. Make a perfectly symmetrical paper pattern from muslin version, making sure measurements check with chair seat. Mark horizontal and vertical lines and outline of top area. Cut out paper pattern, Fig. 2.

Mark center horizontal and vertical lines on canvas. Place paper pattern on canvas; horizontal line on paper should be placed ½″ behind horizontal line on canvas for proper placing of chair design. Leave a 1½″ margin all around for blocking, Fig. 3. Mark pattern outline on canvas. Save paper pattern to use later as a guide in blocking needlepoint piece.

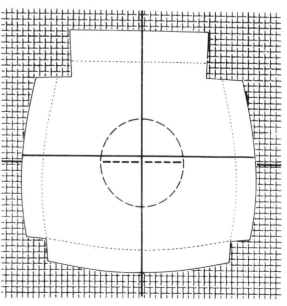

Fig. 3

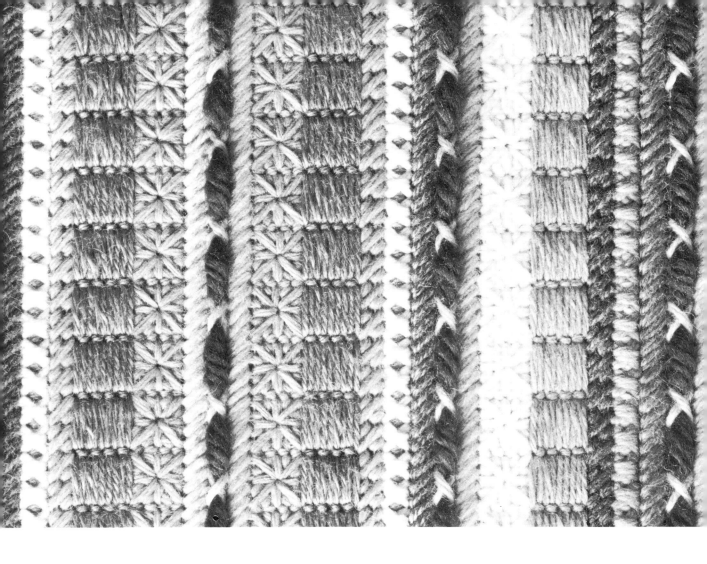

SIX-STITCHES — *cross-stitch couching, three-stitch cross, cashmere stitch variation, laid stitch with backstitch, star, and mosaic—are repeated in several colors for an exciting design that is ideal for a pillow or upholstery. Use this combination—or make up your own. Remember, couched stitches are not practical for upholstery that will receive hard use.*

FLORENTINE WORK

Florentine, Bargello, or Hungarian work is of ancient origin and was generally used for covering cushions. Later it came into use for upholstery fabric and such personal items as handbags. It is also known as Flame Embroidery, because of the distinctive zigzag patterns which characterize this work. Traditionally, several shades of one color are used to give a soft and gradual ombre effect, but for a more striking effect, several different colors may be combined in one design. The work consists of perpendicular stitches which can be made all the same length, or in a combination of long and short perpendicular stitches, covering from two to six meshes of the canvas. The canvas used is usually single thread, 10 meshes to the inch. Depending on the color combinations and stitch arrangements, various effects are obtained which give names to the patterns, such as diamond, skyscraper and sawtooth.

Bargello stitch is easily worked from a graph pattern. Work the first row in peaks, following chart below; starting at the center, work to right and then left to finish row and establish the pattern. For succeeding rows, follow first row, in long or short stitches as indicated on chart, until all the surface is covered. Fill in the corners of the design to completely cover the area.

A Bargello design may be carried out for chair upholstery to cover both seat and back as shown. It is advisable to plan the color scheme and work a small section of one seat to determine how much yarn will be required. Suppose you are working the chair seat and back shown here. Outline areas on your canvas to correspond with seat and back of chair. Work one-quarter of the back and determine how much yarn you used. Then purchase enough to cover that area, multiplied by the number of times necessary to cover all of back and seat, before continuing with the work.

Chair covered with Bargello work

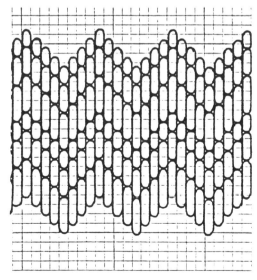

CHART FOR BARGELLO DESIGN

HOW TO MAKE A NEEDLEPOINT CHART FROM ANY DESIGN YOU CHOOSE

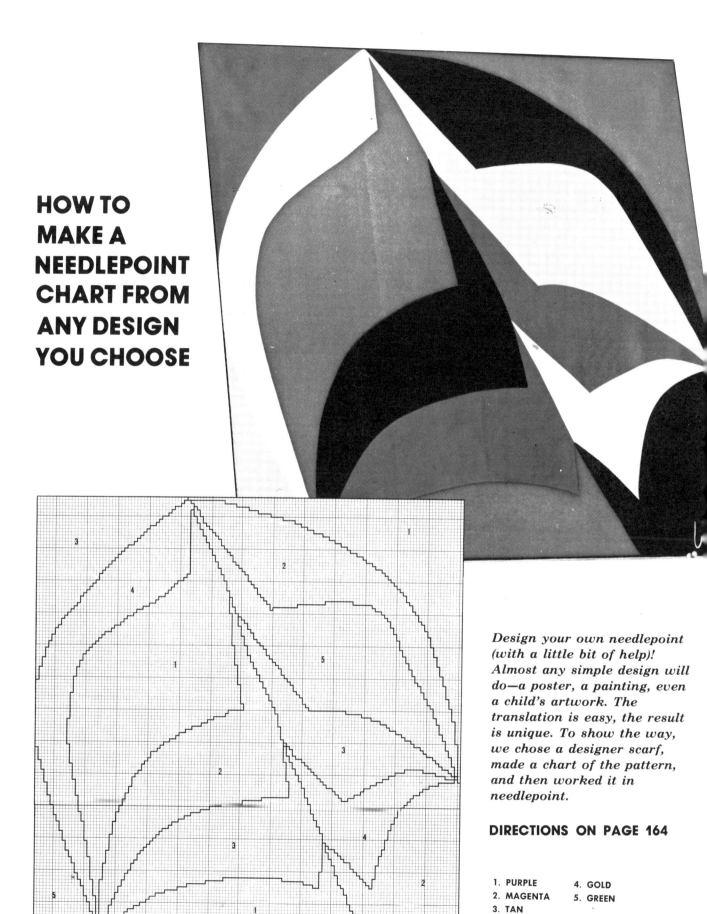

Design your own needlepoint (with a little bit of help)! Almost any simple design will do—a poster, a painting, even a child's artwork. The translation is easy, the result is unique. To show the way, we chose a designer scarf, made a chart of the pattern, and then worked it in needlepoint.

DIRECTIONS ON PAGE 164

1. PURPLE
2. MAGENTA
3. TAN
4. GOLD
5. GREEN

CHART FOR SCARF DESIGN

HOW TO TRANSFER A DESIGN WITHOUT MAKING A CHART

Motif for Magnolia Pillow was adapted from wallpaper, using a unique and simple method. Illustration shows our design being traced from the wallpaper onto nylon web, which is then basted to canvas; needlepoint is worked right over the pattern!

METHOD DEVELOPED BY LENORE FOMON

Many of our readers have asked about ways of transferring designs to canvas for a special needlepoint project. The most commonly used methods are often either not accurate enough to obtain the necessary detail, or are impossibly frustrating for anyone without an art background. We have come across a method developed by Lenore Fomon that we think is exciting in it's simplicity, and entirely within the capabilities of even those who say they cannot draw a straight line. With this method a floral motif, scene, or geometric design you have admired can be put on your canvas accurately and easily.

The materials required are minimal. You will need a piece of tracing nylon (Trace-A-Pattern™), a web-like material which can be purchased by the yard at pattern counters. It

HOW TO TRANSFER A DESIGN WITHOUT A CHART

is quite strong and has no tendency to stretch. Although it is not entirely transparent, it is clear enough to see a design placed under it. You will also need a set of colored, waterproof lead pencils. It is essential that they be waterproof; if not, the colors may bleed into the design during the blocking process. Test the pencils on a scrap piece of nylon and wash with soap and water. In addition, you will need masking tape and a clear spray adhesive, needlepoint canvas and sewing thread.

Lay the design down on a flat, hard surface and cover it with tracing nylon the same size as design. Tape the edges securely together to keep them from slipping. Keeping the colored pencils sharpened to a fine point, trace the outlines of design onto the nylon with the appropriate color pencil. Do not fill in areas with color yet.

Carefully separate the nylon from the design. Save the design for color reference a few steps later. If it is necessary to retouch any outlines, lay the nylon over a sheet of white paper for better visibility.

Spray the canvas with adhesive and place the marked nylon web over it, pressing and smoothing it lightly until it adheres; let dry.

Baste the nylon web to canvas around all edges outside of design area. Using the flat surfaces of the points of the colored pencils, fill in each area outline and background with the color in which it is to be worked, referring to the original design whenever necessary. Light even pressure of the pencil on the nylon web over the surface of the canvas will color the crossing threads and leave the meshes transparent, thereby sharpening the working surface.

Now you are ready to work your needlepoint directly over the nylon-covered meshes. The web material is so thin that it is not difficult to pass the needle through the mesh of canvas and web.

Use the needlepoint method desired, working through the canvas meshes as usual, and making stitches over the nylon web. Follow the colors drawn on the web. Where detailed color changes occur across a mesh of canvas, be guided by the shape and contour of the design to determine which color to use. Do not remove the nylon web; work entire design and background over the web. When the needlepoint is completed, the nylon web will not be visible. Finish your needlepoint piece as desired, for a pillow or picture, etc.

HOW TO MAKE A NEEDLEPOINT CHART

You don't have to be an artist to design your own needlepoint. The easiest way to begin is to pick a design you especially like from another medium—a scarf, an illustration, wallpaper, etc.—then translate it into needlepoint. When you have found the right design, decide on the size of your intended needlepoint piece. You may need to change the size of the original design. If so, the next step is to have a photostat made, enlarging or reducing the design to your specifications.

Making a Chart: Buy translucent graph paper (available at art supply stores). The number of squares per inch on the graph paper must equal the number of meshes per inch of the canvas, since each square represents one stitch on the canvas. Center a sheet of graph paper on top of the design or photostat; secure with tape. Using a soft pencil, trace the outlines of the design onto the paper, square by square (see illustration). If

desired, darken the outlines with a fine waterproof felt-tipped pen. Choose the colors for your needlepoint; don't hesitate to depart from the original colors. If you like, you can block in the colors on the graph paper; use crayons or pens. You now have a chart.

MAKING A CHART

JOINING CANVAS, BLOCKING, AND MOUNTING

The technical know-how for making up needlepoint is what gives the finished product a professional look. Each step should be given the utmost attention, from the choice of design to the finishing trim. For best results, read our general instructions carefully (see pages 131 to 143) before starting work on your needlepoint piece.

JOINING CANVAS

It is not always convenient to work an entire piece of needlepoint on one piece of canvas, as, for example, when making a large rug. If working in sections, be sure to use canvas of the same mesh and weight for all pieces. Plan to work five rows of needlepoint over the joined sections; if using a chart, mark chart with parallel lines enclosing the five rows. Start needlepoint for each section 2″ from edge to be joined. When each piece has been worked, block separately. To join, carefully cut away all but four rows of unworked mesh on one of the two edges to be joined. Lap cut edge over corresponding edge so that the four rows of meshes on top coincide with the four rows of meshes below. Be sure both sides of both pieces line up correctly, matching warp (vertical) and woof (horizontal) threads. Pin pieces together, with large needles or pins, through center of lapped edges. Following pattern, work five rows of needlepoint over double thickness of canvas.

For bags or similar items made of more than one piece, another technique for joining is used. Finishing each piece as a separate section, trim unworked canvas margin to ½″ or 1″; turn margin to back and whip to embroidery. Join pieces at the edges with a connecting row of needlepoint; or sew together by hand with a slipstitch and cover the joining with a twisted cord. When joining, match design stitch by stitch.

If a canvas thread is weak or has been accidentally cut, it is advisable to patch the area. Cut a piece of matching canvas ½″ larger than the weak spot. Baste the patch to the wrong side of the canvas with matching wool, aligning the mesh of the two pieces. Continue working in pattern, stitching through both layers of canvas. Trim away the ends of any canvas threads that may show through.

CLEANING AND BLOCKING

Try to keep your needlepoint clean; store it in a plastic bag between work sessions. If your piece should need a little freshening, however, simply brush over the surface with a clean cloth dipped in cleaning fluid. Colors will brighten and return to their original look.

No matter how badly a piece is out of shape, it may be blocked squarely. Cover a soft-wood surface with brown paper. Mark size of canvas on paper, keeping corners square. Place needlepoint right side down over marked guide. (If piece has been worked with raised stitches, block right side up, to preserve texture.) Stretch canvas to guidelines and fasten with thumbtacks ½″ apart, near edge of canvas. If necessary, needlepoint area may be straightened by pulling in place and adding tacks near the needlepoint. Wet thoroughly with solution of 1 tablespoon salt to quart of cold water; let dry. If badly warped, repeat.

Wetting needlepoint for blocking softens glue sizing of the canvas. When piece dries, canvas resets, and holds its shape unless it is unmounted, as in rugs, or subject to handling, as with handbags. For such pieces, it is advisable to stiffen the back of the work with glue while it is wet and fastened face down. Dry glue can be obtained at a hardware store. Mix one-half cup of dry glue with one-half cup of boiling water, then thin with three cups of cold water; mixture should be brushed onto the back only.

TO MOUNT PICTURES

After canvas has been blocked, stretch it over heavy cardboard or plywood cut same size as worked portion of canvas. Use heavy cardboard for small pictures (12″ or less); for larger pictures and panels, use ¼″ plywood. If cardboard is used, hold canvas in place with pins pushed through canvas into edge of cardboard. If canvas is mounted on plywood, use carpet tacks. Push pins or tacks only part way into edge; check needlepoint to make sure rows of stitches are straight. Carefully hammer in pins or tacks the rest of the way. Using a large-eyed needle and heavy thread, lace loose edges of canvas over back of cardboard or plywood to hold taut; lace across width then length of picture.

ALPHABET SAMPLER

ON PAGE 145

SIZE: 17" x 19", unframed.

EQUIPMENT: Ruler. Pencil. Scissors. Tapestry needle. For blocking: Soft wooden surface. Brown wrapping paper. Square.

MATERIALS: Needlepoint canvas, 10-mesh-to-the-inch, 22" x 24". Tapestry yarn, 8.8 yard skeins: 35 skeins gray-blue; 4 skeins bright green; 4 skeins orange; 2 skeins watermelon; 2 skeins fuchsia; 1 skein light yellow; 1 skein gold. Masking tape. For mounting: heavy mounting board, 19" x 17". Straight pins.

DIRECTIONS: Read directions for working needlepoint starting on page 131. Using pencil, outline a 17" x 19" rectangle in center of canvas, leaving a 2½" margin all around. Start in upper right corner. Following chart and color key, work design in Continental stitch; see page 134. Each square of chart represents one mesh of canvas.

Block and mount finished piece following directions on page 165. Frame as desired.

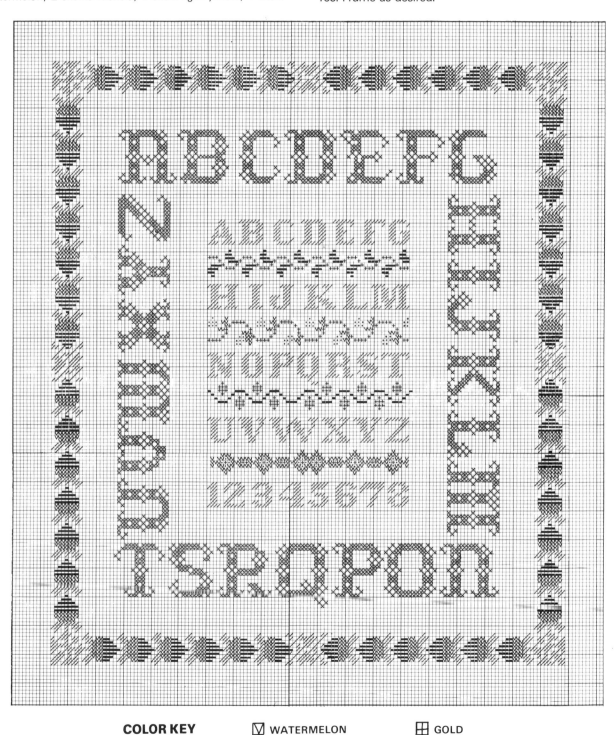

COLOR KEY

- ☒ FUCHSIA
- ☑ WATERMELON
- ☒ ORANGE
- ☑ GREEN
- ⊞ GOLD
- ☐ BLUE
- ⊡ YELLOW

"STAINED-GLASS" SAMPLER

ON PAGE 146

SIZE: 12" x 12"

EQUIPMENT: Tapestry needle. Scissors. Pencil. For blocking: Rustproof thumbtacks. Soft wooden surface. Ruler. Square. Brown wrapping paper.

MATERIALS: Needlepoint canvas, 10-mesh-to-the-inch, 17" x 17". Tapestry yarn, 8-yard skeins: 1 skein red; 2 skeins purple; 3 skeins shocking pink; 1 skein coral; 3 skeins white; 6 skeins black; 2 skeins medium yellow-green; 1 skein light yellow-green; 1 skein dark green; 5 skeins gold. For mounting: Heavy mounting board, 12" x 12" rabbet size.

DIRECTIONS: Read directions for working needlepoint starting on page 131. Tape edges of canvas. Cut yarn into 18" lengths. Using pencil, outline a 12" x 12" square in center of canvas, leaving a 2 ½" margin all around.

Following chart, work all black dividing lines in Continental stitch; see Page 134. Referring to Stitch Key below, and photograph on page 146 for placement of colors, fill in background, flowers, leaves and stems in novelty stitches; see diagrams and descriptions starting on page 136. Note: When working leaves in cashmere stitch variation, turn canvas one quarter turn to the left.

Block and mount needlepoint as directed on page 165; frame as desired.

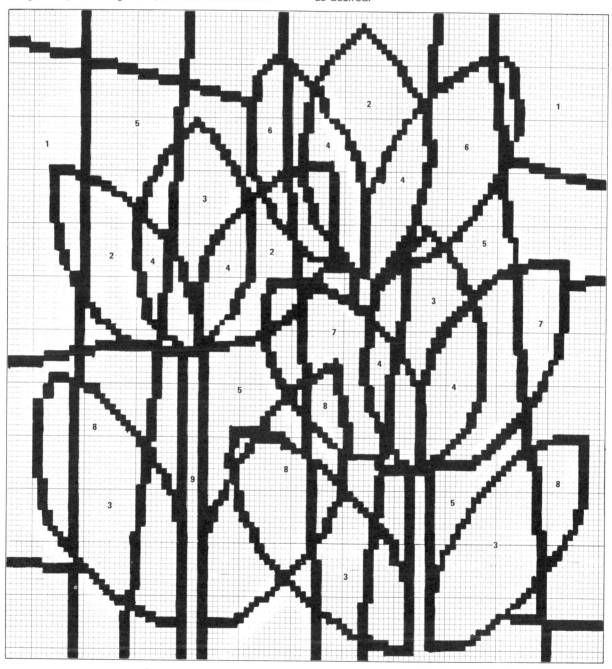

STITCH KEY

1 MOSAIC STITCH	**4** LAID STITCH WITH BACK STITCH	**7** CROSS-STITCH
2 STAR STITCH	**5** CONTINENTAL STITCH	**8** CASHMERE STITCH VARIATION
3 OBLONG CROSS-STITCH WITH BACKSTITCH	**6** KNOTTED STITCH	**9** CROSS-STITCH COUCHING

TRELLIS PILLOWS

ON PAGE 147

SIZE: 15" x 15"

EQUIPMENT: Pencil. Ruler. Scissors. Waterproof, felt-tipped pen. Tapestry needle. For blocking: Soft wooden surface. Brown wrapping paper. Rustproof thumbtacks. Square. For finishing: Sewing needle. Straight pins.

MATERIALS: Mono needlepoint canvas, 12-mesh-to-the-inch, 20" x 20" for each pillow. Three-ply Persian yarn, 100 yards white and 33 yards either cyclamen pink or green for each pillow. Small amounts of left-over yarn (such as tapestry wool, velours or Persian yarn) in bright green and three shades of either pink or yellow. White fabric for backing, 36" wide, ½ yard for each pillow. Cable cord, ¼" diameter, 1¾ yards for each pillow. Muslin, 36" wide, ½ yard for each inner pillow. White sewing thread. Polyester fiberfill for stuffing. Masking tape. Paper for patterns.

DIRECTIONS: Tape edges of canvas to prevent raveling. Using pencil, outline 15" x 15" square in center of canvas. Enlarge embroidery pattern for flowers by copying it on paper ruled in ½" squares.

To work flowers: Place canvas over enlarged flower pattern so that flowers are 2" in from right side of outline and 2"

up from bottom of outline. Using waterproof pen, copy pattern onto canvas. Following Color and Stitch Keys, work flowers and leaves in embroidery stitches; see diagrams and descriptions starting on page 230; see page 134 for Continental stitch. The embroidery stitches are worked in the same manner as they would be on fabric, taking stitches through the canvas instead of through fabric. Work stitches closely for Turkey work centers, then clip loops and trim ends to form a rounded pompon; see diagrams. Trace reversed flower pattern in opposite corner of square outline; work in same manner or vary stitches and placement of color as desired.

To work background: Mark exact center of outlined area on canvas by lightly marking diagonal lines from corner to corner in both directions. The point where they meet is indicated on chart by a small black dot; chart shows center square of pillow bordered by double diagonal lines and parts of eight adjoining squares. Using full three-ply white yarn in needle, start at center and fill in squares with small blocks of vertical stitches as indicated on chart. (Two different symbols are used to differentiate between blocks, but the stitch is the same.) Work diagonal lines with vertical stitches over two threads of canvas in cyclamen pink or green. Fill in spaces between diagonal lines with vertical stitches over four threads of canvas in white. When working around embroidered flowers and leaves, be sure needlepoint stitches meet edges of embroidery; fill in with short stitches if necessary.

TURKEY WORK

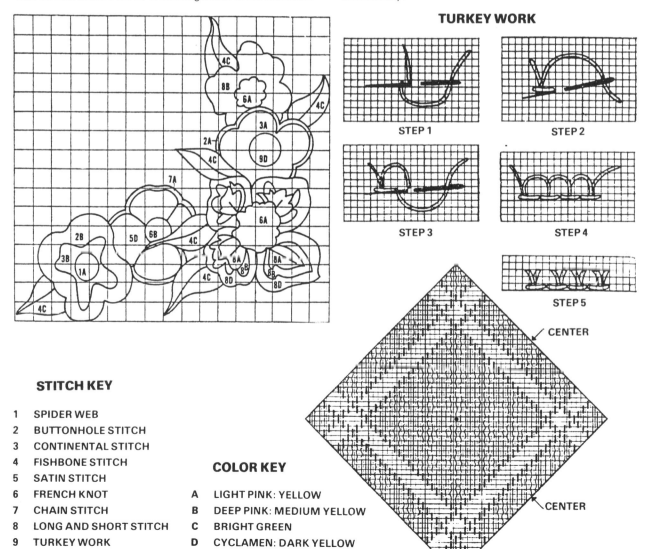

STEP 1

STEP 2

STEP 3

STEP 4

STEP 5

CENTER

CENTER

STITCH KEY

1 SPIDER WEB
2 BUTTONHOLE STITCH
3 CONTINENTAL STITCH
4 FISHBONE STITCH
5 SATIN STITCH
6 FRENCH KNOT
7 CHAIN STITCH
8 LONG AND SHORT STITCH
9 TURKEY WORK

COLOR KEY

A LIGHT PINK: YELLOW
B DEEP PINK: MEDIUM YELLOW
C BRIGHT GREEN
D CYCLAMEN: DARK YELLOW

TRELLIS PILLOWS

CONTINUED

Block needlepoint following directions on Page 165. Trim edges of canvas to ½".

To back and finish pillows: Cut fabric for backing to same size as embroidered canvas. To cover cording, cut remaining fabric into 2"-wide bias strips; stitch ends of longest strips together diagonally with ¼" seams until you have a strip 64" long; press seam allowances open. Fold strip in half lengthwise, wrong sides together; place cording inside fold and stitch fabric together close to cording. Starting at the center of one side, baste cording around right side of needlepoint, with cording covering the edges of needlepoint and seam allowances to outside. Pull one end of cord out of covering and cut off ½". Turn ¼" of covering to inside, concealing raw edge. Starting with this end, stitch cording in place, with seam against edges of needlepoint. Where ends of cording meet, slip second end into turned-in edge of covering and continue stitching.

With right sides facing and raw edges even, baste needlepoint and backing together, enclosing cording. Stitch together as close as possible to cording, leaving an 8" opening in center of one side. Trim seam allowances diagonally at corners and turn cover to right side.

To make inner pillow, cut two 16½" × 16½" pieces of muslin and stitch together ½" from edges, leaving a 6" opening at center of one side. Turn right side out and stuff with fiberfill. Turn raw edges in and slip-stitch opening closed. Insert inner pillow in needlepoint cover. Turn edges of opening in and slip-stitch embroidered pillow cover closed.

LATTICEWORK PILLOWS

ON PAGE 147

SIZE: 14½" × 15½"

EQUIPMENT: Pencil. Ruler. Scissors. Tapestry needle. Sewing needle. For blocking: Soft wooden surface. Brown wrapping paper. Rustproof thumbtacks. T-square.

MATERIALS: Mono needlepoint canvas, 14-mesh-to-the-inch, 19½" × 20½". Three-ply Persian yarn, 2½ ozs. each of white and bright pink. Velveteen for pillow backing and cording, 45" wide, ½ yard. Cable cord ¼" diameter, 64". Polyester fiberfill for stuffing, one lb. Sewing thread to match. Masking tape.

DIRECTIONS: Tape canvas edges to prevent raveling. With pencil mark a 14½" × 15½" area in center of canvas; mark a vertical and horizontal line down center of canvas. Cut yarn into 18" lengths. Following motif and layout charts, begin at center; with a full three-ply strand of yarn in needle, work the pink stitches in upright and horizontal Gobelin stitch (see 1A and 1B below) over the number of meshes and in the direction indicated on graph chart. The white areas are worked in Brick stitch (Diagram 2) and Gobelin stitch. The rows marked by arrows on chart are common rows between motifs; do not repeat when working subsequent motifs. Continue working motifs until the marked area on canvas is covered. When needlepoint is complete, block following directions on Page 165. Trim canvas margins to 1". To make inner pillow: Cut two pieces of muslin 16½" × 17½". Stitch together making ½" seams and leaving a 6" opening on one side. Turn to right side; stuff fully. Turn raw edges in; slip-stitch closed. To back and finish pillow cover refer to directions for Trellis Pillows.

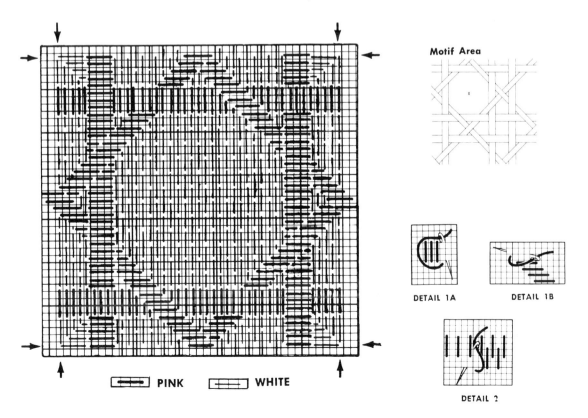

PINK   WHITE

Motif Area

DETAIL 1A   DETAIL 1B

DETAIL 2

CONTOUR NEEDLEPOINT
ON PAGE 150

EQUIPMENT: Pencil. Ruler. Scissors. Tapestry needle. For blocking: Rustproof thumbtacks. Soft wooden surface. Brown paper.

MATERIALS: See materials listed for each piece of needlepoint. Amounts of three-ply Persian yarn given take regrouping of plies into consideration.

GENERAL DIRECTIONS: Read directions for working a needlepoint piece on page 131. Mark outline of area to be worked on canvas, allowing at least 2½″ for unworked margin on all sides. Mark exact center of area to be worked; mark center of each side on marked outline. Center rows of design are marked by stars on charts; exact center of area to be worked is point at which the two starred rows intersect.

Use two plies of three-ply yarn for center motif and center background of each design. Use full three-ply yarn for bargello pattern. Following chart and Color Key for each design, first work center motif in Continental stitch, starting at exact center of design. Chart for each design includes one quarter of bargello pattern, which is also one quarter of outline for background of center motif. Mark this outline on all four sides around center motif. After completing motif, work background of center area in Continental stitch. Begin bargello pattern at left side of chart and work to the right. After completing first quarter of pattern, continue pattern for second quarter by repeating it in reverse, omitting those stitches which are worked over center mesh. Repeat in reverse for remaining half of pattern. To complete bargello on anemones piece, see individual directions.

When embroidery is completed, block needlepoint piece, following instructions on page 165.

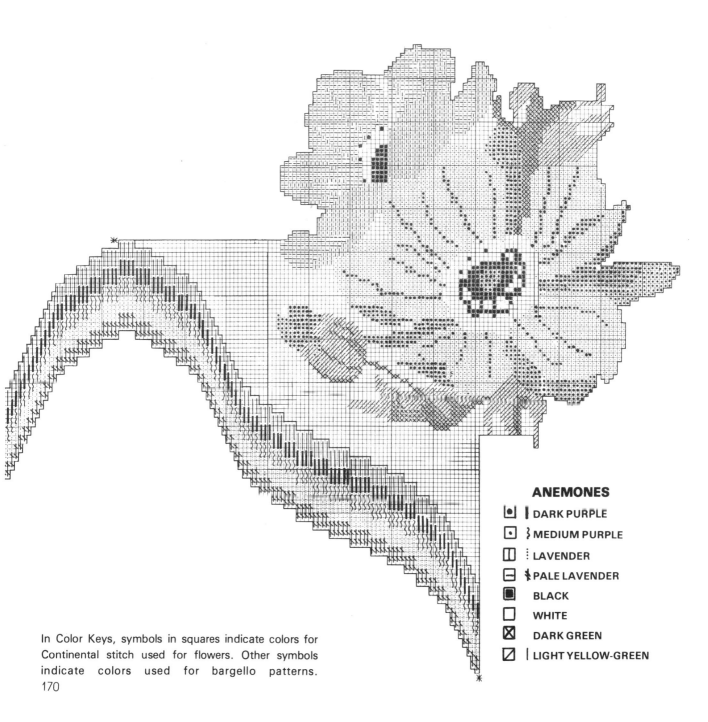

ANEMONES

▣ ❘	DARK PURPLE
⊡ ⸨	MEDIUM PURPLE
◫ ⋮	LAVENDER
⊟ ⸩	PALE LAVENDER
◼	BLACK
☐	WHITE
⊠	DARK GREEN
⊘ ❘	LIGHT YELLOW-GREEN

In Color Keys, symbols in squares indicate colors for Continental stitch used for flowers. Other symbols indicate colors used for bargello patterns.

To make needlepoint pillow: After needlepoint piece has been blocked, trim canvas margins to about 1". Cut backing fabric to same size as trimmed canvas. With right sides facing, stitch needlepoint piece and backing together about 1" from edges, leaving opening at center of one side for inserting inner pillow. Trim off corners of canvas diagonally and apply a little glue to trimmed edges. Whip canvas margins to wrong side of piece and turn cover right side out. Insert inner pillow through opening. Add stuffing to corners if needed. Turn in raw edges of opening and slip-stitch opening closed.

NEEDLEPOINT WITH ANEMONES

SIZE: 17½" x 15½"

MATERIALS: Mono needlepoint canvas, 14-mesh-to-the-inch, 22½" x 20½". Backing fabric, 20" x 18". Three-ply Persian yarn; amounts given in yards: dark purple,

45; medium purple, 54; lavender, 44; pale lavender, 160; dark green, 6; light yellow-green, 28; black, 3; white, 94 (for center background).

To continue bargello, repeat pattern in reverse, omitting pale lavender; then repeat pattern as charted, omitting yellow-green. Continue bargello pattern out to outline in pale lavender.

NEEDLEPOINT WITH POPPIES

SIZE: 15¾" x 15¼"

MATERIALS: Mono needlepoint canvas, 14-mesh-to-the-inch, 20¾" x 20¼". Backing fabric, 18½" x 18". Three-ply Persian yarn; amounts given in yards: dark orange, 15; light orange, 20; dark pink, 67; medium pink, 64; pale pink, 78; very pale pink, 24; dark green, 7; light green, 39; black, 4; white, 94 (for center background).

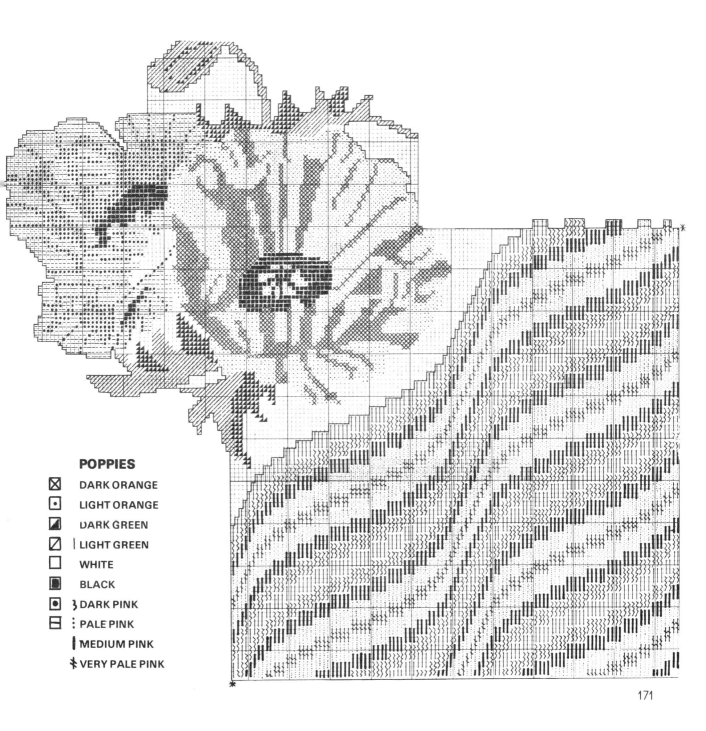

POPPIES

⊠ DARK ORANGE
⊡ LIGHT ORANGE
◪ DARK GREEN
◩ LIGHT GREEN
☐ WHITE
◼ BLACK
◉ DARK PINK
⊟ PALE PINK
❙ MEDIUM PINK
⚹ VERY PALE PINK

BARGELLO FRAME

ON PAGE 151

SIZE: Approximately 12" x 12".

EQUIPMENT: Scissors. Ruler. Pencil. Tapestry needle. Straight pins. For blocking: Soft wooden surface. Brown wrapping paper. Square. Rustproof thumbtacks. For frame: Utility knife. Staple gun.

MATERIALS: Mono needlepoint canvas, 12-mesh-to-the-inch, 19" x 19". Persian-type yarn: Pale blue, 14 yards; light blue, 28 yards; medium blue, 34 yards, plus about 29 yards for twisted cord; dark blue, 54 yards. Mirror to fit center unworked area. Piece of plywood, about 14" x 14". Masking tape.

DIRECTIONS: Read directions for working needlepoint starting on page 131. Chart is for one half of upper right-hand corner of frame and is repeated eight times by reversing it for each adjoining section. The horizontal graph lines on chart represent horizontal threads of the canvas; vertical lines represent vertical threads.

Determine center of top edge of canvas; mark a vertical pencil line between threads to bottom edge. Starred vertical row on chart corresponds to this marked line on canvas.

Tape edges of canvas to prevent raveling. Measure down marked line on canvas 3½" from top edge. Using a full three-ply strand of yarn in needle, begin at upper left corner of chart (at top of starred vertical row), and work pattern row of dark blue bargello from left to right. Work the same dark blue row in reverse, omitting the starred vertical row, to establish the pattern across top of frame. Following chart and Color Key, work subsequent rows with stitches starting and ending in same holes as adjoining rows. This will com-

plete one quarter of design. Turn canvas one-quarter turn to left and repeat the whole process, working second side of frame in exactly the same manner as first. Work remaining two sides the same way.

Divide dark blue yarn and use a two-ply strand to work two rows of Continental stitch all around outer edge of bargello. Divide strands of dark blue yarn and use a two-ply strand to work two rows of Continental stitch all around outer edge of bargello; see page 134. Then work six additional rows on each side, starting and ending flush with beginning and ending of previously worked two rows, thus leaving a completely unworked square at each corner. (This will reduce bulk and make it possible to miter corners neatly on back of plywood.)

Cut plywood to exactly the same size as perimeter of bargello. Stretch needlepoint over plywood; tape edges temporarily to back. Starting at center and working toward corners, staple two opposite sides to back of plywood close to last row of needlepoint. Remove tape on these two sides and trim unworked canvas margins to 2". Repeat on remaining two sides. Trim unworked corners diagonally, cutting away half of the square, and crease canvas sharply to miter corners.

Measure center unworked square on front of frame for size of mirror. If required size is not available, use slightly smaller size and work rows of Continental stitch around inner edge of bargello so mirror will fit. Coat unworked area with glue and press mirror into place; weight down with books or a heavy object until glue is thoroughly dry.

Using five strands of medium blue yarn, make two twisted cords, one to go around edge of mirror, the other to go around outer edge of frame; see directions on page 303. Glue cords in place around edges, butting ends at center of lower edges after applying a touch of glue to each end.

Center cardboard on back of plywood and glue in place, covering the cut ends of canvas.

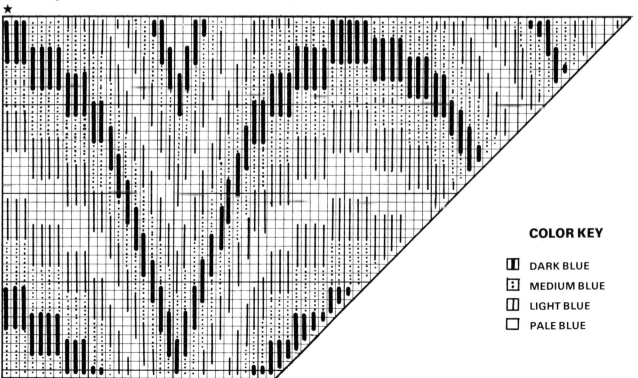

COLOR KEY

- ⊞ DARK BLUE
- ⊡ MEDIUM BLUE
- ⊞ LIGHT BLUE
- ☐ PALE BLUE

TULIP UPHOLSTERY

ON PAGE 153

EQUIPMENT: Scissors. Pencil. Ruler. Tapestry needle. For Blocking: Soft wooden surface. Brown wrapping paper. Square.

MATERIALS: Needlepoint canvas 10-mesh-to-the-inch; see directions below for figuring amount. Tapestry or Persian yarn (approximate yardage given for one repeat only; work out amount needed according to number of repeats): 14 yards beige, 6 yards greenish brown, ½ yard antique gold, 2 yards marigold, 2 yards yellow, 4 yards medium green, 2½ yards dark green, 4 yards black. Muslin. Paper for patterns.

DIRECTIONS: Read directions on page 131 for working a needlepoint piece. To figure amount of canvas required, measure chair seat or stool to be upholstered, allowing suffi-

cient amount to cover thickness of seat filling. Allow 2½" extra all around, outside widest part.

Make muslin and paper patterns for each piece to be upholstered; mark on canvas following directions for Upholstery Pieces on page 158.

Work needlepoint design within marked area, using continental or diagonal stitch; see page 134. Start at top right of canvas and follow chart below, repeating motif for first vertical row. Begin second vertical row at heavy black lines in center of chart, and then repeat whole chart as before for remainder of second row, thus staggering flowers and leaves in adjacent rows. Repeat first and second vertical rows until marked area of canvas is completely filled. Fill in background with beige yarn as you complete design.

Block piece following directions on page 165, use paper pattern.

VICTORIAN PARROT

ON PAGE 152

DESIGN AREA: 18½" square.

EQUIPMENT: Masking tape. Tapestry needle. Pencil. For Blocking: Thumbtacks. Soft wooden surface. Brown wrapping paper. Ruler. Square.

MATERIALS: Needlepoint canvas, 10-mesh-to-the-inch, 28" x 29" (design area about 18½" square). Tapestry yarns, 8 yard skeins: 2 skeins pale grey-green; 2 skeins medium grey-green; 3 skeins dark grey-green; 1 skein each apple green; medium bright green; deep green; pale yellow green; light olive green; olive green; deep olive green; pale cocoa; light cocoa; medium cocoa; dark cocoa; light red-brown; medium red-brown; dark red-brown; tan; gold; antique gold; pale mauve; light mauve; medium mauve; dark mauve; lavender; purple; deep purple; light blue; medium blue; dark blue; light coral; medium coral; red; maroon; black for background, 47 skeins. Heavy cardboard or ¼" plywood for mounting, 22¾" x 23½".

DIRECTIONS: Read directions on page 131 for working needlepoint piece. Mark outline of picture 22¾" x 22½", allowing 2½" margin all around. Following chart on page 174, work parrot design, using one strand of tapestry yarn in needle. Find center of chart and center of outlined area of canvas. Work design from center to right side. Continue working design to left, then fill in background to marked outline.

Block and mount picture, following directions on page 165. Frame as desired.

COLOR KEY

- ■ BLACK
- ◪ GREENISH BROWN
- ⊠ MEDIUM GREEN
- ▨ DARK GREEN
- ☐ BEIGE
- ▨ GOLD
- ▨ MARIGOLD
- ⊡ YELLOW

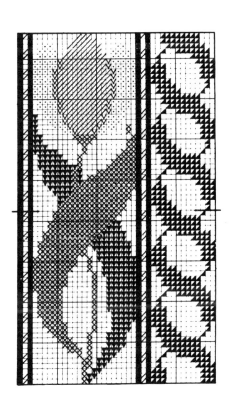

COLOR KEY

Symbol	Color	Symbol	Color	Symbol	Color	Symbol	Color
O	PALE GRAY-GREEN		DEEP OLIVE GREEN	—	GOLD		LT. BLUE
/	MED. GRAY-GREEN	I	PALE COCOA		ANTIQUE GOLD	W	MED. BLUE
	DK. GRAY-GREEN	V	LT. COCOA	·	PALE MAUVE		DK. BLUE
X	APPLE GREEN		MED. COCOA		LT. MAUVE		LT. CORAL
Z	MED. BRIGHT GREEN		DK. COCOA		MED. MAUVE	Y	MED. CORAL
	DEEP GREEN	+	LT. RED-BROWN	S	DK. MAUVE	=	RED
	PALE YELLOW-GREEN		MED. RED-BROWN		LAVENDER		MAROON
	LT. OLIVE GREEN		DK. RED-BROWN	II	PURPLE		
•	OLIVE GREEN		TAN		DEEP PURPLE		

"ARAN" PILLOWS

ON PAGE 154

SIZE: Each pillow approximately 19½" square.

EQUIPMENT: Yarn needle. Scissors. Ruler. Pencil. For blocking: Soft wooden surface. Brown wrapping paper. Rustproof thumbtacks. For finishing: Straight pins. Sewing machine. Sewing needle. Two pencils.

MATERIALS: Double-thread rug canvas, 5 mesh-to-the-inch, 23" square for each pillow. Heavy rug yarn, off-white, 1½ lbs. for each pillow (includes enough for pillow, twisted cord, tassels). For finishing: Off-white wool or wool-blend fabric, one 20¼" x 20¼" piece for each pillow. Matching thread. Muslin, two 20¼" x 20¼" pieces for each pillow. Polyester filling, 1½ lbs. for each pillow. Masking tape.

GENERAL DIRECTIONS: Read directions for working a needlepoint piece on page 131. Tape edges of canvas. Mark exact center of canvas and begin working there; work outward in concentric rows, following chart below and stitch diagrams for specific pillow. Work with one strand of yarn in needle, no longer than 18" for most stitches; exceptions are noted in specific directions. Charts show upper left quarter of each pillow. The double threads of the rug canvas are shown on charts and in stitch diagrams as single lines. Each pair of crossed double threads is considered one mesh.

Note: Before starting each new stitch pattern, check chart. Some stitch patterns continue around corners, while others stop at corners, change direction, and then go on to next corner.

When needlepoint is completed, block right side up, following directions on page 165. When dry, trim canvas margins to ¾".

To finish pillow: Center needlepoint over outer fabric, right sides together; stitch together along each side between last two rows of Continental stitch, leaving a 12" opening in center of one side. Trim corners of fabric seam allowance; turn cover to right side.

To make inner muslin pillow, place right sides of two muslin pieces together; stitch together ½" from edges, leaving a 6" opening in center of one side. Turn right side out; stuff fully and slip-stitch opening closed. Insert inner pillow in embroidered cover; slip-stitch opening closed except for 1".

To make twisted cord: Using six strands of yarn, each six yards long, make twisted cord following directions on Page 303. Stitch cord around edge of pillow, inserting ends into 1" opening; slip-stitch opening closed, catching ends of cord on inside.

To make tassels: Make four 6" lengths of twisted cord, using one 24"-long strand of yarn for each one. Cut thirty-six 12" strands of yarn for each tassel. Fold twisted cord in half; center 12" strands of yarn across cord near looped end. Draw ends of cord through loop, encircling strands of yarn, and pull tightly. Bring ends of strands together and wrap a piece of yarn around them several times, about 1" from looped end of tassel; tie in a knot. Trim ends of tassels to an even length. To attach a tassel at each corner of pillow, tuck ends of twisted cord on tassel under twisted cord around pillow and stitch securely in place.

CHARTS FOR "ARAN" PILLOWS

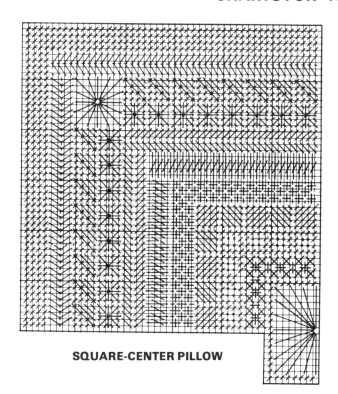

SQUARE-CENTER PILLOW

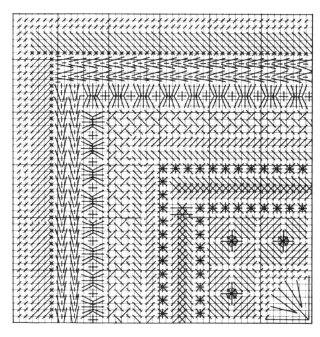

ROUND-CENTER PILLOW

ROUND-CENTER PILLOW

ON PAGE 154

ROUND SPIDER-WEB CENTER: Using 60"-long strand of yarn, bring needle up seven meshes to left of center, leaving 5" end of yarn hanging on back of work. Stitch foundation spokes as shown on chart into center area. Horizontal and vertical stitches go over seven meshes; long, slanted stitches go over five meshes; shorter slanted stitches go over four meshes. Anchor final stitch firmly. Turn work over and thread needle with the 5" end of yarn that was left hanging on back. Fasten end firmly by weaving through stitches on back.

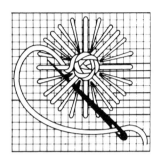

ROSETTE STITCH: Use another 60"-long strand of yarn. Making sure end of yarn is secured on back of canvas, bring needle up through canvas as close to center as possible. Carry thread across two of the longer spokes and back under one. Continue around center, working over and under only the longer horizontal, vertical and slanted foundation stitches, until you complete six rounds. Fasten off at back of canvas.

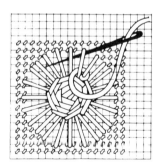

WHIPPED SPIDER-WEB STITCH: Using another 60"-long strand of yarn and starting where rosette stitch ended, cover all 24 spokes, carrying thread forward under two spokes and back over one. Continue until you have completed four or five rounds, covering spokes completely. Fasten off securely. Outline completed round spider web with Continental stitch, filling area 16 meshes square as shown on chart.

SCOTCH STITCH VARIATION: This pattern consists of a block of four Scotch stitch squares with a knotted upright cross-stitch in the center. Two blocks fit directly above completed center. To make first square, work from left to right, following diagram below; make slanted stitches over one mesh, then over two, three, four, three, two, and finally one, until one Scotch stitch square is complete. Work next

square with diagonal stitches slanting in the opposite direction. Work two more squares, reversing direction each time; see chart. Make knotted upright cross-stitch in center as directed below.

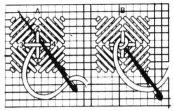

KNOTTED UPRIGHT CROSS-STITCH: Make upright cross-stitch over four meshes at center of Scotch stitch block, coming up at 1, down at 2, up at 3, and down at 4 (Diagram A above). Bringing needle up in center hole, slide it out below horizontal stitch at left of vertical stitch, then slide it under upper half of vertical stitch from right to left, as shown in diagram. Bring yarn around to lower right and insert needle into same hole where knot began (Diagram B).

REVERSED SMYRNA CROSS-STITCH: Work this stitch in one direction around all four sides of pillow, so all top stitches slant the same way. Work each upright cross-stitch over two meshes (Diagram A). Work diagonal cross-stitch over upright cross-stitch (Diagram B).

VAN DYKE STITCH: This stitch pattern must be worked downward in vertical rows. The first row begins four meshes to the left of the upper row of the preceding stitch pattern; see chart. Begin with two straight horizontal stitches across four meshes. These two stitches are used only when beginning each row. Then bring needle up at 1, down at 2, up at 3, and down at 4 as shown in diagram. This is the anchor stitch for the stitches which follow and is the only one where the needle goes under meshes at top of stitch. Bring needle up at 5 to begin next stitch. Slide needle under only crossed yarn portion of the previous cross-stitch and bring needle down at 6. All succeeding stitches are worked in this manner. End the row four meshes below preceding stitch pattern. Turn canvas a quarter turn to right when you finish a row, so the completed row is at top of canvas. Repeat at each corner.

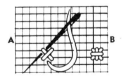

SMYRNA CROSS-STITCH: Work this stitch in one direction on all four sides of pillow, so that top stitches all go the same way. First, work diagonal cross-stitches, then work upright cross-stitches over diagonals, ending with horizontal stitches on top.

KALEM STITCH: This row begins four meshes to the left of the upper left corner of preceding stitch pattern and is worked down from top of row; see chart. The stitch pattern consists of two vertical rows of diagonal stitches, each row over two meshes — one with stitches slanting up to the left, the other with stitches slanting up to the right, both sharing the same center holes. End row four meshes below lowest mesh of preceding stitch pattern. Turn canvas a quarter turn so finished row is at top.

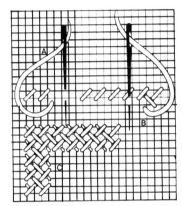

WOVEN PLAIT STITCH: Work pattern in same direction on all four sides of pillow, so that pattern continues around corners without interruption. Starting four meshes above and four meshes to left of preceding pattern, work diagonal stitch over two meshes as shown in Diagram A. In first row, stitches slant up to right; in next row, stitches slant up to left (Diagram B). Repeat until four rows of meshes are covered; see Diagram C. Fill in edges of inner and outer rows with half stitches.

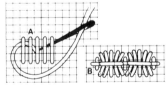

SHEAF STITCH: This row begins just above preceding stitch pattern and four meshes to the left. Working from left to right, make five upright stitches over four meshes (Diagram A). Bring needle up in center hole behind the five stitches. Slide needle under stitches to the left and out, then across all stitches to the right. Insert needle in same center hole behind stitches and draw yarn firmly to back. The first upright stitch of each group begins and ends in the same holes as the last stitch of the preceding group. Work upright cross-stitches between sheaves to complete the pattern. End row even with right-hand edge of preceding stitch pattern. Turn canvas a quarter turn to the left so finished row is at left.

KNIT STITCH: This is a three-part pattern which begins two meshes above and four meshes to left of preceding stitch pattern and ends even with right-hand edge of it.

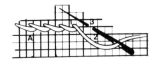 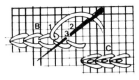

Working from left to right, come up at 1, down at 2, up again at 3 (Diagram A). Repeat until row is complete. Go back to beginning of row and come up at 1, down at 2, up again at 3 (Diagram B). Repeat to end of row. Cover meshes in center of stitch with backstitches (Diagram C). This completes one whole row of knit stitch pattern. Make another whole row above it; see chart. Turn canvas a quarter turn to left so finished rows are on your left.

FISHBONE STITCH: Starting four meshes to left and four meshes above preceding stitch pattern, bring needle up at 1, down at 2, up at 3, down at 4; see diagram. Work to right, ending row even with preceding stitch pattern. Fill in with shorter slanting stitches at beginning and end of each row. Turn canvas a quarter turn so finished row is on your left.

Complete embroidery for pillow top with two rows of Continental stitch around all four sides. Block and finish as described in general directions.

SQUARE-CENTER PILLOW
ON PAGE 154

LARGE SQUARE SPIDER WEB: Using a 60"-long strand of yarn, bring needle up seven meshes to left of center, leaving 5" end of yarn hanging in back of work. Make foundation stitches into center hole as shown on chart. All 24 stitches are worked over seven meshes. Anchor final stitch firmly. Turn canvas over; thread needle with 5" end left hanging on back when you began. Anchor firmly, weaving needle through stitches on back.

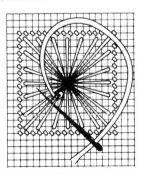

WHIPPED SPIDER WEB STITCH: Use another 60"-long strand of yarn. Making sure end is secured on back of canvas, bring needle up as close to center as possible. Carry yarn forward under two stitches and back over one. Continue around until all 24 stitches are completely covered, approximately eight rounds, giving corner spokes two or three extra wraps of yarn. Finish square with one row of Continental stitch all around.

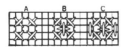

FALSE RICE STITCH: Working over two meshes, make four cross-stitches forming a square, with all top stitches slanting out to sides of the square (Diagram A). Cover center of square with an upright cross-stitch, making top stitch the upright one (Diagram B). Fill in between squares with a single straight vertical stitch over two meshes of canvas (Diagram C). Repeat pattern all around whipped spider web center; see chart.

FRENCH KNOT SQUARES: Using Continental stitch, work outlines of squares four meshes by four meshes; see A on diagram. Fill center of each square with four French knots; see B on diagram. To make French knots, bring needle up at 1 and loop thread once around needle as shown in C; go back down at 2, drawing thread firmly to back until knot is formed. Repeat pattern all around; see chart.

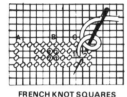

FRENCH KNOT SQUARES

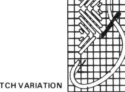

SCOTCH STITCH VARIATION

SCOTCH STITCH VARIATION: Starting four meshes above and four to left of preceding pattern and working down on left side of canvas, make slanted stitches over one mesh, then two, three, four, three, two, and finally one until Scotch stitch square is formed. The next Scotch stitch square is worked with stitches slanting in the opposite direction, with stitches ending in same holes as stitches of previous square. Work one row of Scotch stitch squares all around; see chart.

UPRIGHT CROSS-STITCH PATTERN: Hold canvas in same position when working all four sides so that pattern will be uniform, going around corners without interruption. Bring needle up at 1, down at 2, up at 3 and down at 4. Work three alternating rows of crosses as shown in diagram. Fill in blank spaces on inner and outer edges of pattern with half-stitches.

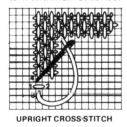

UPRIGHT CROSS-STITCH PATTERN

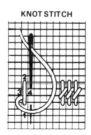

KNOT STITCH

KNOT STITCH: Row begins four meshes to left of preceding stitch pattern; see chart. Working from left to right, bring needle up at 1, down at 2, up at 3, down at 4. Repeat to end of row, finishing even with outer edge of preceding stitch pattern. Turn canvas a quarter-turn to left so finished row is at your left; repeat on all sides.

KALEM STITCH: See description and diagram under round-center pillow.

MOSAIC BLOCKS: Starting directly above completed kalem stitch and working from left to right, work mosaic stitches in blocks of four, alternating directions; see A in diagram. Repeat pattern until row of 16 blocks is even with outer edge of preceding stitch pattern. Go back to beginning of row and finish blocks with a knotted upright cross-stitch in center of each; see below.

KNOTTED UPRIGHT CROSS-STITCH: Make upright cross-stitch over four meshes; see B and C in diagram. Bring needle up in center hole behind cross-stitch; slide needle out below horizontal stitch to left of vertical stitch; slide needle under top half of vertical stitch from right to left: see D in diagram. Bring yarn around to lower right and insert needle in same hole where knot began; see E in diagram.

MOSAIC BLOCKS

COMBINATION BLOCK

COMBINATION BLOCK: Work pattern in same direction on all four sides of pillow so that slanting stitches of all blocks go the same way; see chart. Starting directly above completed mosaic blocks, work from left to right. Combination blocks are made of overlapping triangles, the lower triangle worked in Continental stitches, the upper triangle worked in diagonal stitches. Repeat pattern until row of 16 blocks is even with end of preceding stitch pattern.

SQUARE SPIDER WEB CORNERS: Using a 60"-long strand of yarn, bring needle up four meshes to left of center hole; see chart. Make 16 stitches, each one over four meshes, into center hole. Using another 60"-long strand, bring needle up as close as possible to center. Carry yarn forward under two stitches and back over one. Continue around until all 16 stitches are completely covered, approximately five rounds, giving corner stitches one or two extra wraps of yarn.

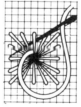

SPIDER-WEB CORNERS

FLY STITCH

FLY STITCH: This pattern must be worked down from top of row, starting four meshes to left of square spider web corner; see chart. Bring needle up at 1, down at 2, up in center at 3, down again at 4. Repeat to bottom of row, ending four meshes below lower edge of square spider web in corner. Use small slanting stitches to fill in at beginning and end of each row. Turn canvas a quarter-turn to right so that finished row is at top.

Complete embroidery for pillow top with four rows of Continental stitch around all four sides. Block and finish as described in general directions.

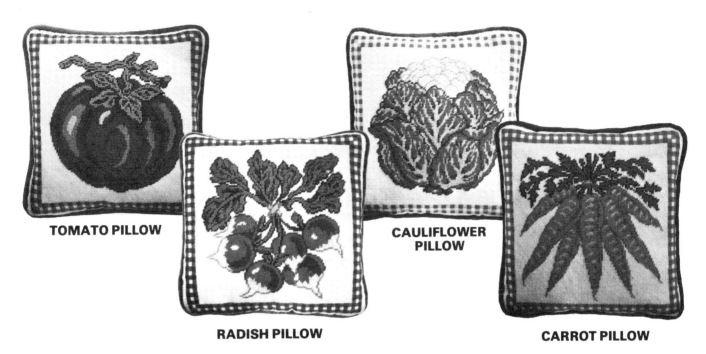

TOMATO PILLOW

RADISH PILLOW

CAULIFLOWER PILLOW

CARROT PILLOW

VEGETABLE PILLOWS

ON PAGE 155

SIZE: 14" x 14"

EQUIPMENT: Tapestry needle. Scissors. Pencil. Ruler. For blocking: Soft wooden surface. Brown wrapping paper. Rustproof thumbtacks. Square.

MATERIALS (for each): Mono needlepoint canvas, 10-mesh-to-the-inch, 18" x 18". Three-ply Persian yarn: See chart for colors and yardage. Velveteen for pillow backing and cording, ½ yard. (We used the following: Tomato pillow, orange. Radish pillow, hot pink. Cauliflower pillow, purple. Carrot pillow, green.) Cable cord, ¼" diameter, 1¾ yards. Muslin for inner pillow, ½ yard. Sewing thread to match backing. Polyester fiberfill for stuffing. Masking tape.

DIRECTIONS: Read directions for working needlepoint on page 131. Mark an area 14" x 14" on canvas, leaving equal margins on all sides. Tape canvas edges to prevent raveling. Cut yarn into 18" lengths; use full three-ply strand of yarn in needle.

Following chart and Color Key for individual pillow, work design in Continental stitch; see page 134. When Needlepoint is complete, block according to directions on Page 165; trim margins to 1".

Cut 16" x 16" piece of fabric for pillow backing. Cut remaining fabric into 1½"-wide bias strips. With right sides facing, join strips together on lengthwise grain to make strip long enough to fit perimeter of pillow with ½" overlap. Lay ¼"-thick cable cord along center length of strip on wrong side of fabric. Fold strip over cord and stitch along length of strip close to cord.

With raw edges of cording facing out, baste cording to right side of blocked and trimmed canvas, keeping cording seam along edges of needlepoint and rounding corners slightly. Overlap cording ends ½" on one side; trim off any excess. To fit ends together, cut off one end of cord ½" inside fabric casing; turn in casing ¼". Insert other end and slip-stitch fabric of both ends together. Stitch cording to needlepoint. Pin finished canvas and fabric together with right sides facing and edges even, enclosing cording. Stitch together 1" from edges; leave an 8" opening in center of one side. Trim allowances to ¼"; clip canvas at corners. Turn to right side.

To make inner pillow: Cut two 16" x 16" pieces of muslin. With right sides facing, sew edges together with ½" seams; leave a 6" opening in center of one side. Turn to right side and stuff fully with fiberfill. Turn in raw edges of opening and slip-stitch closed. Insert inner pillow into needlepoint pillow cover. Add stuffing in corners if necessary. Turn in raw edges of opening and slip-stitch closed.

TOMATO PILLOW

COLOR KEY	YARDS	COLOR KEY	YARDS
☐ WHITE	150	⊠ MAROON	15
⊙ LIGHT TANGERINE	2	⊡ MINT GREEN	13
⊘ DEEP TANGERINE	30	⋎ EMERALD GREEN	6
⊙ BRIGHT RED	80	⊞ PINE GREEN	6

CAULIFLOWER PILLOW

COLOR KEY	YARDS		COLOR KEY	YARDS
☐ WHITE	150		⊞ DARK GREEN	18
▨ LIGHT LIME	60		☒ LIGHT PLUM	6
◉ LIME	66			

RADISH PILLOW

COLOR KEY		YARDS
□	WHITE	165
⊠	PALE HOT PINK	6
◨	MEDIUM ROSE	60
◙	MAROON	24
⊡	LIME	23

COLOR KEY		YARDS
▽	MEDIUM GREEN	7
⊞	DARK GREEN	12
⊟	PALE GOLD	1
◎	PECAN	1
◭	PURPLE	3

CARROT PILLOW

COLOR KEY	YARDS		COLOR KEY	YARDS
☐ WHITE	165		◪ ORANGE	75
⊡ BRIGHT GREEN	25		⊙ DARK BITTERSWEET	25
⊻ MEDIUM GREEN	6		⊟ PALE GOLD	1
⊞ KELLY GREEN	6		◎ PECAN	1
⊠ BRIGHT YELLOW	8			

ALL ABOUT

EMBROIDERY

As one of the oldest decorative handcrafts, embroidery is being rediscovered today in both its traditional forms and in new creative styles for decorating the home, clothing, and accessories.

Embroidery is a versatile and personal needlecraft, whether you do it by hand or by machine. A beginner can learn embroidery by making an interesting sampler of the simple basic stitches; an accomplished embroiderer can paint a picture in yarns of various textures, choosing from a large range of stitches to obtain subtle and meaningful effects.

The embroidery stitches are your tools. Basic stitches (straight, satin, outline, chain, and lazy daisy) are included in this section as well as more intricate stitches. Begin by practicing the basic stitches, or, if you know them already, learn new stitches.

The secret is to learn by doing! Learn to choose the correct yarn to use with background fabric, and what weight and textures of yarns will best express the subject. Learn ways to work cross-stitch by counting the design from a chart onto a variety of fabrics. Experiment with embroidering on checked materials, using the fabric as a guide and as part of the design. Begin by decorating a simple patchwork afghan or pillow. Or tackle an intriguing type of embroidery you've never done before, such as cutwork or drawn work. Start right now by selecting your first embroidery project!

THE HISTORY OF EMBROIDERY

ANCIENT EMBROIDERY

The origins of embroidery are lost in obscurity. The few existing examples of early Egyptian, Greek, and Roman embroideries often show fine strips of pure gold or other metals wound around a foundation thread of linen. These gold-covered threads were couched to the surface of the fabric to cover certain areas in a solid gold effect, or were used to outline colored silk, wool, or linen embroidery. There are also rare examples of fabric appliques which were used for wall hangings or to decorate garments.

Silk embroidery was developed in the Orient along with silk fabrics. The earliest Oriental garments of richly hued silks were embroidered with silk, metallic thread, or jewels. Seed stitch, chain stitch, outline stitch, featherstitch, and satin stitch were used, and tiny bits of metal similar to modern sequins were often added to the design. Mirror fragments were used in some of the embroideries of India, held in place by close chain stitching. And the Punjabs in India used a darning stitch to create fine allover ornamentation. Although European styles have changed through the centuries, Oriental designs and workmanship still follow the old traditions, colors, and designs.

When silkworms were first smuggled out of the Orient, they were cultivated in Italy and southern France. Fine silk fabrics, brocade, and velvet were made up into wall hangings or garments, all richly embroidered with silk floss and metal threads.

Embroidery and applique formed a part of the early wall decorations in European homes.

Castles during the Middle Ages and up to the 17th century were built of stone, sometimes without mortar. Drafts blew through the walls unless hangings were used. One of the most famous early pictorial hangings is the Bayeux Tapestry, which is not a tapestry at all, but an embroidery in wool on linen worked in outline, rope stitches, and laid work. It tells the story of the Norman conquest of England in the 11th century.

THE ENGLISH TRADITION

During the 16th century, Catherine of Aragon, the first wife of Henry VIII, introduced Spanish "black work" in England. Turkey tufting, which is believed to have been an imitation of Turkish carpets, was also popular in the Tudor period. Elizabeth I and her cousin, Mary Queen of Scots, were both skilled needlewomen. Many embroideries of their time were done in wool or silk on a coarse linen similar to a very fine canvas with threads of an even count; this was called "canvas work." It was popular to make samplers or "exemplars" of the variety of stitches one could work on canvas. While many stitches were used, the most important one was tent stitch, the forerunner of needlepoint.

Another early form of embroidery in England was "needle worke cruell," which derived its name from the type of wool used, "a thin worsted yarn of two threads." This embroidery was worked on a linen background in various stitches. It reached its height of popularity during the early 17th century at the time of James I and is often called Jacobean work. Today the name "crewelwork" refers to

Detail from a colorful crewel-embroidered border on a petticoat made in New England between 1725 and 1750 includes trees, flowers, a waiting dog and a building set in a rolling rural landscape.

embroidery of the same type as the early work. A very good example is shown on **Page 191**.

Bed hangings of the 17th and 18th centuries, often worked in crewel, provided the sleeper with privacy and kept out cold night breezes. When heavy fabric was not available, several thicknesses of material were layered together and held with stab stitching, thus popularizing the quilting technique.

or Roumanian stitch to replace the long-and-short stitch. The New England needlewoman found that she could conserve her crewel and still obtain a charming effect by executing this stitch so that she picked up with her needle only a few threads of linen ground, allowing most of the woolen threads to lie on the surface. Among interesting examples of early crewel embroidery in this country are the narrow embroidered bands running around

Sampler embroidered by Eliza J. Benneson in 1835 combines simple cross-stitch lettering with a stylized border of flowers, foliage and a pineapple, in satin stitch, stem stitch and French knots.

COURTESY OF THE COOPER UNION MUSEUM, NEW YORK

EARLY EMBROIDERY IN AMERICA

American embroideries are descended from so many others that it is very difficult to know just where our individuality begins. For example, during the early 1700's our ancestors were making samplers similar to those being made throughout Europe at the time; crewel-embroidered bedspreads were closely related to the Jacobean designs being embroidered in England; needlepoint (then called "tent stitch") chair seats and pictures were as popular here as abroad. Most of the New England designs either came from or were strongly influenced by England.

Early American crewel embroideries showed slight changes from those in England both in design and stitches, the most notable difference being the use of a modified Oriental

the hemlines of petticoats. These designs are less formal than the English, and sometimes the borders showed landscapes with beasts and buildings, as well as floral ornaments. See the detail from a petticoat border opposite.

Many of the crewel designs were worked in native dyed wools. The early settlers who found it expensive to import yarns from England had to depend on their own inventive ability, and a number of colors used by them were discovered by accident or through experiment. Many a New England colonist raised her own indigo plants and boasted the possession of an indigo tub in the rear kitchen. Here lambs' wool was tinted various shades of blue. Attempts were made to match the Canton blues of the chinaware from the Orient, and crewel embroideries worked in these shades were called "Blue and White Work."

Instruction in embroidery was part of the education of every well brought up young girl in America. Their samplers varied according to the part of the country where they were made. The young girls of New England were apt to combine only a few simple stitches, using them for a small picture, a flower border, and an alphabet. There might also be a rather lugubrious verse along with the embroiderer's name and date of working.

Many of the samplers made by the early Pennsylvania Dutch settlers are long, narrow strips of linen in a fairly open mesh. These show drawnwork and a variety of quite complicated stitches. Samplers from various parts of the country were genealogical charts, with sturdy trees, each branch labeled with the names and dates of each ancestor.

An interesting type of embroidery sprang up from the teaching of the Moravian sect. These people migrated from Moravia in central Europe and settled in Bethlehem, Pennsylvania, in 1740. The art of embroidering memorial samplers was taught in their schools. Later, this kind of embroidery became a fad in other areas, with less morbid subjects, such as ships and pastoral scenes. These pictures were a combination of a tinted satin background and silk embroidery in a variety of stitches.

In the early 1800's, the alphabet samplers became more elaborate and often had rich floral borders requiring skillful workmanship. One made in 1835 is shown on page 187. While young girls were making their samplers, there was a great deal of embroidery being done for practical use in the home. Cross-stitch was worked on canvas to produce large carpets. Chairs and benches were upholstered with canvas worked in Bargello or flame stitch; see page 161. Turkey work was used as an upholstery fabric, for bed covers and rugs.

Popular in Europe at this time, and widely used here, was a kind of embroidery called "tambour." This is an embroidered chain stitch worked with a fine needle resembling a crochet hook. The Casell carpet opposite is a unique example.

Just as white quilts were popular in the 18th century, so were other types of "white work." This term applies to white embroidery in general, which was greatly influenced by the French; some of the best examples come from Louisiana. It is interesting to note that the tambour stitch used to embroider the Caswell carpet was equally popular in white work for embroidering dainty veils, shawls, and collars of fine net. Interest in white work continued until about the middle of the 19th century.

EMBROIDERY IN THE 20th CENTURY

During the last quarter of the 19th and first quarter of the 20th century, needlewomen did a great deal of knitting, crocheting, and tatting. They also made embroidered antimacassars, bureau runners, doilies, and other household linens, known as "fancy work." Designs were available stamped on material, as perforated patterns, or as hot iron transfers. They were used for both white work and embroidery in silk on linen, using Kensington stitch in the realistic colors of flowers and fruits.

Starting in the 1920's, there was a revival of interest in crewel embroidery and needlepoint. Most of the designs were copies of old pieces and were used to upholster both antique furniture and reproductions. At the same time, many needlewomen embroidered unique designs which were created to their specifications by artists who either painted the needlepoint designs on canvas or made perforated patterns to stamp the designs on linen.

During World War II, merchandise was scarce and kits containing both patterns and materials were produced, thus making certain that the customer had the yarns in the right colors. This service may have been responsible for a steady increase in handcrafts since the beginning of the 1950's.

Today there is an ever-increasing demand for unusual and well designed needlework patterns. Top artists not only design for other needlewomen, they themselves are literally painting with yarns, creating contemporary rugs and wall hangings which are museum pieces. Right now we are in the most exciting period of all needlework history. We have a vast heritage of handwork techniques, a limitless variety of yarns and other materials with which to work, and the needle arts are recognized by museum authorities as fine arts media of the 20th century.

The Caswell carpet, made by Zeruah Higley Guernsey Caswell, is one of the best-known large-scale embroideries. Squares worked in tambour stitch were joined to make the 12' x 13½' carpet. It is recorded that two young Patawatomi Indians who lived with Zeruah's family while attending Castleton Medical College worked on the carpet, designing the two squares marked with their initials. This impressive embroidery was completed in 1835, after two years' work.

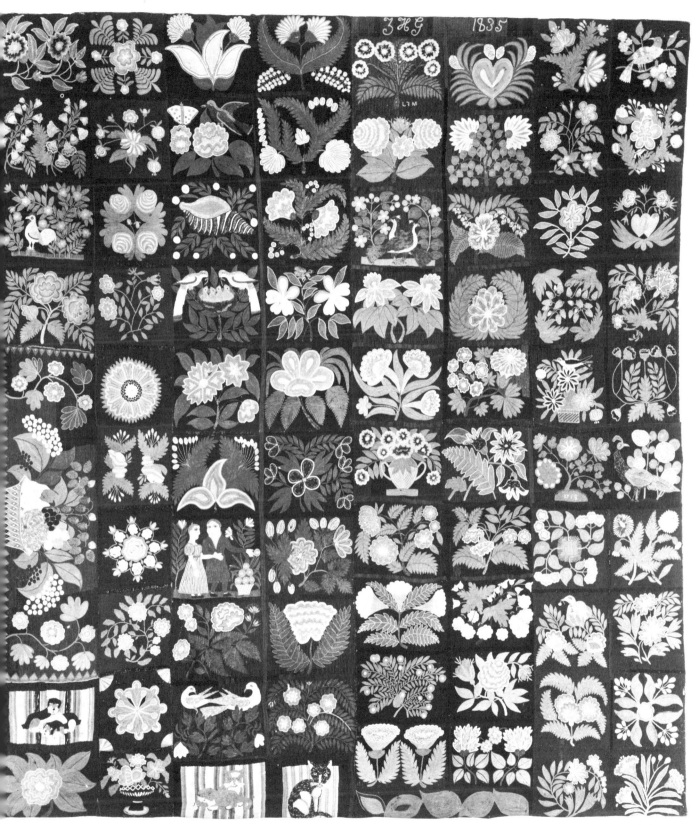

COURTESY OF THE METROPOLITAN MUSEUM OF ART, NEW YORK.   GIFT OF KATHERINE KEYES, 1938, IN MEMORY OF HER FATHER, HOMER EATON KEYES

ASSISI EMBROIDERY

Assisi work, named for the Italian village of its origin, is a very distinctive type of needlework. Traditionally, it was done on pale ivory linen and embroidered in red, blue, and black, or in a combination of two colors. The designs were worked from charts and embroidered by counting the threads of the linen. Today, the same method is used on any even-weave fabric. Simplicity of design is important to show the true character of this technique and its charm lies in the artistry, neatness and skill of the embroiderer.

The design is first outlined with a running stitch or straight stitches and then worked in reverse to fill in the outline between the first stitches. When finished, the outline resembles backstitch. The background is then filled in solidly with cross-stitch, leaving the design area unworked. The cross-stitch must be done carefully, counting an equal number of threads vertically and horizontally for each stitch, and making all stitches even. Work first half of all crosses in one direction and the second half in the opposite direction. After the Assisi work is completed, narrow borders can be added in cross-stitch and straight stitch in simple repeat patterns.

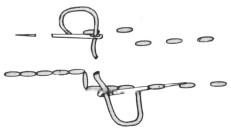

ASSISI OUTLINE STITCH

CROSS-STITCH

190

TREE OF LIFE DESIGN   COURTESY OF THE METROPOLITAN MUSEUM OF ART, NEW YORK

Crewelwork, or Jacobean embroidery, first became fashionable in the 17th century and expressed the extravagant taste of the time for richly-embroidered decorations. Early designs, which customarily featured exotic flowering trees combined with birds and animals, resulted from an exchange of ideas between Asia and Europe. Although the first crewel embroidery was worked in shades of one color, generally blue or green, later designs sometimes used varied and brighter coloring, but greens and blues still predominated.

The exotic Tree of Life was, and is, the most popular basic design. An elaborate example is the hanging shown above from the Metropolitan Museum of Art. The odd thing about these trees is that a single trunk with its many branches will carry a wide variety of flowers and fruits. Even the leaves vary in shape. Thus crewel embroidery gives you a chance to express your own individual design ideas, since the kind of forms you use is limited only by your own imagination.

Swirl the trunk gracefully up the center of the area, decreasing its diameter as you get to the top of the tree. At the base of the trunk, embroider satin stitch scallops of brown and green to represent earth and grass, and add flora and fauna.

CROSS-STITCH EMBROIDERY

Cross-stitch is easy to do and can be used effectively on clothing, for monogramming, and for decorating household furnishings. It can be worked successfully on almost any type of fabric, as illustrated opposite. Whatever the background fabric, make sure the strands of embroidery floss or yarn lie smooth and flat, and all stitches are the same length. Avoid making knots on back of work. When beginning, leave end of strand on back and work stitches over it; finish by running end of strand under the work on back of piece.

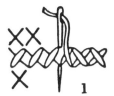

CROSS-STITCH

CROSS-STITCH OVER CANVAS

When working cross-stitch, make all crosses on entire piece in same manner. Work all underneath stitches in one direction and all top stitches in opposite direction. Make all crosses touch by inserting your needle in the same hole used for the adjacent stitch.

Cut strands of yarn or floss 18″ to 20″ long. To keep fabric from raveling as you embroider, bind edges with masking tape and remove when design is completed. An embroidery hoop will help keep the fabric taut and stitches even.

ON MONK'S CLOTH: The mesh of a coarse, even, flat-weave fabric such as monk's cloth makes it easy to follow a design, which can be worked from a chart simply by counting each square of fabric. Count two horizontal and two vertical threads for one stitch.

ON GINGHAM: A checked fabric such as gingham makes a good guide for cross-stitch. Make crosses over checks, from corner to corner, following a chart.

ON EVEN-WEAVE FABRIC: Count the threads of an even-weave fabric such as heavy linen or hardanger cloth to make every cross-stitch exactly the same size. For instance, in the photograph below, a three-thread square was counted for each stitch.

OVER PENELOPE CANVAS: Penelope cross-stitch canvas makes it possible to do cross-stitch on closely-woven and unevenly-woven fabrics because it is basted to the fabric on which the design is to be embroidered and later removed. Center the canvas over the fabric, making sure that the horizontal and vertical threads of canvas and fabric are parallel. Stitch basting lines diagonally in both directions and around edges of canvas. Work crosses from a chart, taking each diagonally over the double mesh of the canvas and through the fabric, being careful not to stitch through the mesh of the canvas.

CROSS-STITCHING ON DIFFERENT FABRICS

ON MONK'S CLOTH

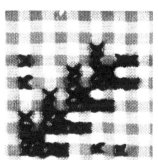

ON GINGHAM

ON EVEN-WEAVE FABRIC

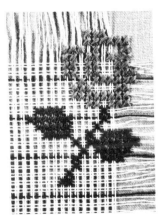

OVER PENELOPE CANVAS

CROSS-STITCH ON TRADITIONAL SAMPLERS

COURTESY OF THE SMITHSONIAN INSTITUTE

A custom-made sampler that celebrates a baby's birth or commemorates a marriage day is a traditional and prestigious gift—and more. It's also a stimulating challenge and an opportunity for the embroiderer to display her talents as both designer and creative artisan. Personalized samplers can also be planned around a particular hobby or interest of the recipient. And in spite of being so impressive, samplers are easily worked on even-weave fabric or by using Penelope canvas. Some suitable motifs are shown in chart form opposite. These can be combined with the cross-stitch alphabet charted on Page 35 or with those used in the alphabet sampler shown on page 240 and charted on pages 86–87.

Other old samplers similar to the one above can be found in many museums, and are an excellent source of design inspiration. Your public library may have books illustrating old samplers, parts of which you can copy or trace to work out your own individual design.

Here are a few motifs which could be used in cross-stitch samplers. Select the ones you like and combine with the alphabets mentioned opposite and with other motifs to create your own design. Each symbol on these charts represents a different color. Other motifs can be found in cross-stitch booklets. Or, using these as samples, create your own motifs on graph paper.

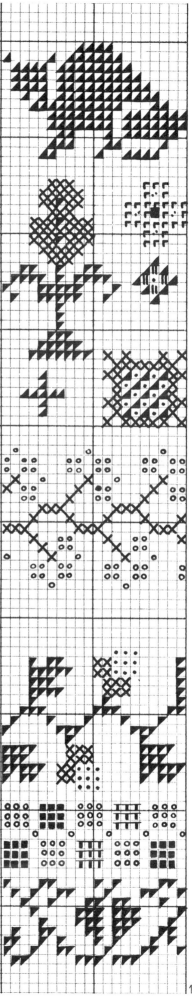

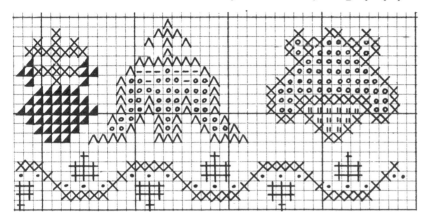

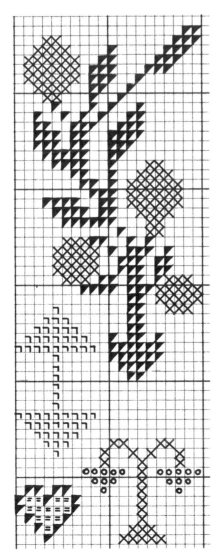

CROSS-STITCH ADDS A BRIGHT TOUCH TO APRONS

Checked gingham presents an easy, ready-to-use guide for working cross-stitch designs. And there's something particularly appealing about the fresh, forthright simplicity of cross-stitch embroidery against a background of crisp, white-checked fabric. Each cross is worked within a check of the gingham, with both diagonal stitches starting and ending precisely at opposite corners of the check.

Gingham is available with checks in various sizes, all the way from tiny 1/16″ checks to sizeable 1″ checks. Big, bold cross-stitch

designs can be worked on 1/4″ checks, but 1/8″ checks are more suitable for most designs. Some cross-stitch designs created especially for gingham call for stitching on the white checks only. But almost any design can be used, utilizing both the white and colored checks.

The attractive green-and-white checked apron above is embroidered with a row of yellow and green daffodils, accented by simple cross-stitch borders. This design would also be charming on a little girl's gingham dress, as would most of the motifs and borders on the previous page.

Gingham with eight or ten checks to the inch is most suitable for working the cross-stitch designs used on the apron shown opposite. On eight checks to the inch, use all six strands of six-strand embroidery floss. On ten checks to the inch, use only three strands of floss.

Place fabric in an embroidery hoop to make it easier to take exactly even stitches and to avoid pulling the floss. Work all bottom stitches of crosses in one direction; com-plete crosses with top stitches in opposite direction, as indicated by small sketch below.

Follow the charts to work the cross-stitch designs. When the design is all in one col-or, an X symbol is used to indicate each cross stitch. If more than one color is used, X is used for one color and a different sym-bol is used for each additional color. You may find embroidering easier if you first mark the designs on the fabric with a hard pencil.

CROSS-STITCHING ON CHECKS

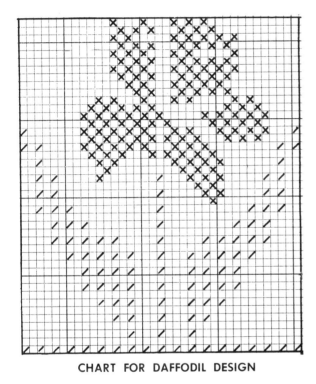

CHART FOR DAFFODIL DESIGN

⊠ YELLOW

⧄ GREEN

CHART FOR BORDER DESIGN

MATERIALS: Gingham with 8 or 10 checks to the inch, 3/4 yard, Matching sewing thread. Six-strand embroidery floss in yellow and green. White medium-width rickrack.

DIRECTIONS: Cut piece of gingham for apron 29″ wide x 22½″ long. Cut two pieces for ties, each 3½″ x 28″. Cut piece for waist-band 3½″ x 16½″. Cut pocket 5½″ x 6″.

Starting 5½″ up from one 29″-long edge, em-broider daffodil design across apron. Em-broider border design immediately below daf-fodils. Stitch white rickrack in place below border design, with upper points of rickrack just meeting lower edge of border design.

Fold piece for waistband in half lengthwise as a guide for placement of border; embroider border half-way between fold and one raw edge. Then stitch white rickrack just below embroidered border.

Embroider border across piece for pocket, 2″ down from one 5½″-long edge. Stitch rickrack in place just below border. Turn ¼″ to wrong side along all four edges of pocket and press; turn top edge under another 1″ and hem. Pin to apron 3½″ down from top edge and 6″ in from one side edge. Stitch around three sides close to fold.

Make double ¼″ hems along side edges of apron. Turn ½″ to wrong side along bottom edge; turn up another 2″ and hem. Gather top edge to measure 16.″ With right sides facing, stitch waistband to gathered top edge of apron, ¼″ from raw edges. Fold ¼″ under along each end and remaining long edge of waistband; press. Fold waistband in half lengthwise, en-closing raw edges, and slipstitch turned edge to wrong side of apron. Make double 1/8″ hems along both long edges and one end of each tie. Insert raw edges of ties into open ends of waistband and stitch close to folds.

CUTWORK EMBROIDERY

Cutwork, also known as Richelieu embroidery, is worked from designs stamped or traced on linen. The design is worked in buttonhole or overcast stitch, sometimes with bars bridging open areas. The background fabric is then cut away, leaving the embroidered design in relief.

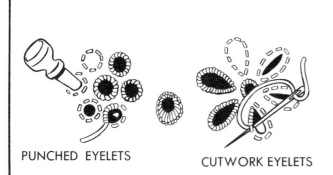

PUNCHED EYELETS   CUTWORK EYELETS

PUNCHED EYELETS can be made up to ¼″ in diameter. Mark placement of each eyelet and, before punching holes, outline eyelet with running stitches to support the buttonhole stitches. Then whip punched edges with buttonhole stitching or close overcasting. Shaded eyelets can be made by embroidering one side with longer stitches than the other. Note small sketch of separate eyelet shaded this way.

CUTWORK EYELETS are made by slashing the center and trimming fabric to fit after the outline has been reinforced with tiny running stitches. As the edge is buttonholed or whipped, the fabric is pulled back to the running-stitch outline.

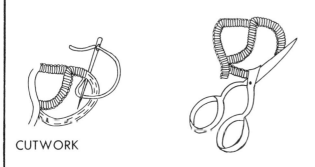

CUTWORK

CUTWORK other than eyelets is done by outlining the entire design in buttonhole stitch and then trimming the background away to leave the design in relief. If desired, make a running stitch first and work buttonhole stitch over it for a more raised effect. If large areas are to be cut away, make connecting bars between embroidered edges before trimming away background. Cross back and forth with embroidery thread several times, then cover bar with buttonhole stitching, being careful not to catch fabric.

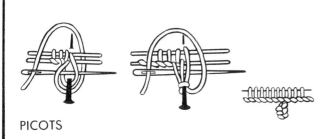

PICOTS

BUTTONHOLE PICOTS can be used to embellish connecting bars or the buttonholed edges of cutwork. Insert a straight pin in work as shown. Slip the thread carefully under the head of the pin from left to right, then take it up over the bar and out again under the pin. Pass the thread under the head of the pin again, from left to right, and insert the needle into the two loops as shown at left. Diagram in center shows a knot formed at the head of the picot, and diagram at right shows buttonhole stitch worked up the length of the picot.

The type of cutwork above, based on round and oval eyelets, is sometimes called Madeira work. The eyelets are beautifully worked in overcast stitch, with leaves and dots in satin stitch. The photograph is actual size; the design can be traced and used for a border or as a corner motif.

The photograph at right shows an actual-size detail of contemporary cutwork in a rose pattern. Here, the embroidery is done almost entirely in buttonhole stitch, with touches of satin stitch and outline stitch.

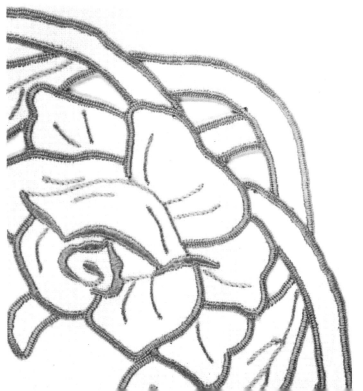

DRAWN WORK—HEMSTITCHING

Hemstitching is a basic form of drawn work in which some threads are drawn out from the background fabric and the remaining threads are pulled together into groups, using a fine needle threaded with a matching or contrasting color. It is most often used to finish hems and make borders. The grouped threads may also be worked upon in various ways to make a more elaborate border.

PLAIN HEMSTITCHING

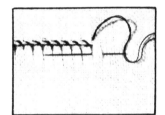

FIG. 1

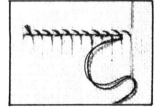

FIG. 2

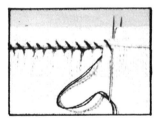

FIG. 3

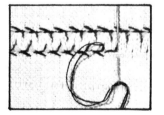

FIG. 4

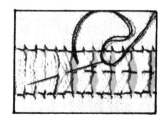

FIG. 5

Hemstitching can be worked on any type of even-weave fabric, either fine or coarse. The thread used should be smooth and very strong; choose pearl cotton or from three to six strands of six-strand embroidery floss if working on coarse fabric; use one or two strands if working on fine fabric. To draw out threads, insert a pin under one thread near side edge of fabric and pull it up; then carefully draw the thread from the fabric across the entire width. The hemstitching is done on the wrong side of the fabric, from left to right.

To do plain hemstitching, draw out two or three threads, depending on the coarseness of the fabric. Secure thread in needle at left edge of drawn section without making a knot by taking a few stitches over end of thread. Pass needle under three or four upright threads of drawn section from right to left. (Fig. 1). Pull thread taut, insert needle in second row of threads above drawn section (Fig. 2) and pull thread tight. Continue across, as in Figs. 1 and 2, always picking up same number of threads. Secure thread at end. Bottom edge of drawn section may be hemstitched also as shown in Fig. 4.

A hem may be made at same time hemstitching is done. Turn fabric over twice to make hem desired width, and baste. Draw out threads just below edge of hem. Starting at left, hemstitch as in Figs. 1 and 2, inserting needle in 2nd row of threads above and through bottom edge of hem (Fig. 3). Repeat these two steps across, catching hem edge and picking up same number of threads each time.

For a more decorative border (Fig. 4), pull out about eight threads and work across in same manner as Figs. 1 and 2, picking up six threads at a time. To hemstitch lower edge of drawn section and make zigzag design, pick up first three threads only, then continue across, picking up six threads at a time (Fig. 4).

To make twisted groups of hemstitched threads (Fig. 5), pull out 10 or more threads and work plain hemstitching evenly at top and bottom of drawn section, picking up four threads at a time. Turn work over to right side, secure thread at right-hand edge in middle of drawn section. Pick up second group of threads at left with needle pointing from left to right. Bring this group of threads over and to the right of first group by inserting needle under first group and turning it to the left, keeping second group on needle. Continue across in same manner, always picking up second group of threads first.

Italian Hemstitching: This is based on the same two steps as plain hemstitching, except in the second step, the needle points downward instead of upward, unless otherwise stated.

To make border shown in Fig. 6, baste hem. Draw out two threads just below hem, skip three threads, draw out next two threads, skip three, etc., for desired width. Make first row of hemstitching, picking up four threads at a time. With needle pointing downward for second step, insert needle in hem first, two threads up from fold, then through all thicknesses and out at drawn section. Continue across in same manner. To make succeeding rows, insert needle in space between groups of threads of preceding row (Fig. 6).

A wide decorative border, the right side of which is shown in Fig. 7, is worked as follows: Baste hem. Draw out two threads just below hem, skip three threads, draw out ten threads, skip three threads, draw out two threads. Work first two rows of hemstitching as shown in Fig. 6, picking up four threads at a time. On next row, fasten thread at base of wide drawn section and work a row of plain hemstitching as in Fig. 4, picking up eight threads at a time. On last row, fasten thread in last drawn section and work a row of hemstitching like second row, inserting needle in space between groups of threads and at base of groups.

To make border in Fig. 8, baste hem. Draw out ten threads just below hem, skip four threads, draw out two threads, skip four threads, draw out ten threads. Work first row as for Fig. 6, picking up nine threads at a time. Turn work around. Work second row along other edge of same drawn section, picking up three threads at a time and inserting needle in second row of threads above. Turn work around. Work third row in narrow drawn section, picking up three threads at a time and inserting needle in second row above. Turn work. Make fourth row in same drawn section along other edge in same manner. Turn work. Make fifth row in next wide drawn section, picking up three threads at a time and inserting needle in second row of threads above. Turn work. Make last row along other edge of wide drawn section, picking up nine threads at a time and inserting needle in second row of threads above. Be sure that nine-thread groups are in line with groups in first drawn section.

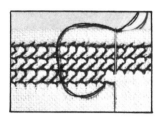

FIG. 6

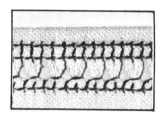

FIG. 7

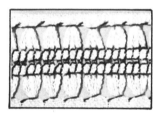

FIG. 8

Many other decorative borders may be made by combining examples above and drawing out different numbers of threads.

DRAWN WORK—NEEDLEWEAVING

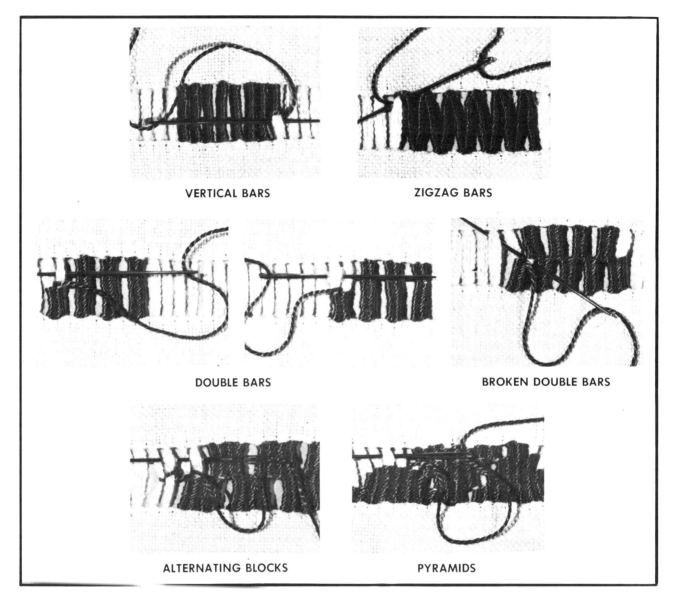

VERTICAL BARS

ZIGZAG BARS

DOUBLE BARS

BROKEN DOUBLE BARS

ALTERNATING BLOCKS

PYRAMIDS

Needleweaving, a form of drawn work, has been a favorite method of making colorful borders on linens for centuries. The technique of drawing threads from a fabric and then replacing them by weaving a design over the remaining threads can produce striking contrasts in color and texture, especially when the thread used is heavier than the threads removed. Practice the six basic patterns shown on this page before starting to work the simple repeat borders opposite.

Choose coarse linen or a loosely woven fabric from which threads can be drawn easily. Use pearl cotton or all six strands of six-strand embroidery floss and a blunt needle.

Draw out enough horizontal threads to make a narrow border, usually ½″ to ¾″ wide. Both edges of the drawn section should be hemstitched first; see Page 200. Use thread that matches the fabric for hemstitching and take an equal number of vertical threads in each stitch usually three, four or five, depending on the weight of fabric being used. Then do the needleweaving on the right side of the fabric, over and under each group of threads divided by hemstitching; never split these groups. Keep weaving threads close together so they cover the vertical threads of the drawn section.

To begin, fasten end of thread by placing it along first group of threads and working over it. To finish, run needle back into weaving for about four rows; cut thread close to work.

VERTICAL BARS: Fasten thread at lower right and work closely around first group of hemstitched threads from bottom to top. Finish off and cut thread as described above. Make each bar separately in same way.

ZIGZAG BARS: Fasten thread at lower right and work one vertical bar, but do not cut thread. Work two stitches around first bar and second group of threads at the same time, then work down second group of threads. Work around bar just completed and next group of threads at same time, and continue making zigzag bars in same manner.

DOUBLE BARS: Fasten thread at lower right, weave under first group of threads and over second group. Then weave back under second group and over first group. Continue weaving closely, under and over first and second groups from bottom to top, then finish off and cut thread. Make each double bar separately.

BROKEN DOUBLE BARS: Fasten thread at lower right and weave double bar as described half-way up drawn section; then weave under first group of threads, over second and under third. For remaining half of bar, weave over third group of threads and under second, then back over second and under third. Continue weaving third and fourth groups of threads halfway up and continuing to top on fourth and fifth groups. Work across in same manner. Finish first bar by working to top.

ALTERNATING BLOCKS: Fasten thread at lower right, weave under first group of threads, over second group, under third, over fourth. Then weave back under fourth, over third, under second, and over first. Continue weaving in this manner halfway up drawn section. Then weave under first group, over second, under third, over fourth, under fifth, over sixth. Weave back under sixth, over fifth, under fourth and over third. Continue weaving to top on third, fourth, fifth and sixth groups of threads. Fasten off thread. Start next block at bottom on fifth, sixth, seventh and eighth groups of threads and weave halfway up. Then weave on seventh, eighth, ninth and tenth groups of threads to top. Continue weaving across in this manner. Finish first two groups of threads as a double bar.

PYRAMIDS: Fasten thread at lower right, weave under and over first eight groups of threads and back under and over to first group. Weave back and forth for one-quarter depth of drawn section. Then weave over and under one group less on each side (six groups) for second quarter of depth. Weave under and over one less group on each side (four groups) for third quarter of depth. Weave over and under two center groups for last quarter, to top of drawn section. Fasten off thread. Start next pyramid upside down at bottom of drawn section. Weave under and over two groups of threads for first quarter; over and under four groups for second quarter; under and over six groups for third quarter; over and under eight groups for last quarter. Fasten off thread. Continue weaving across in same manner.

Many interesting designs can be made from these basic patterns.

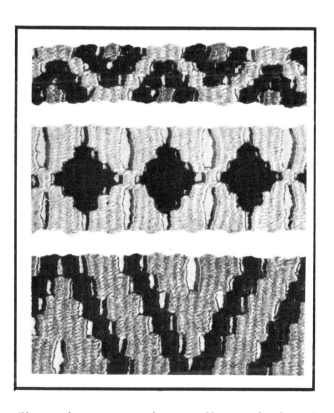

Shown from top to bottom: Narrow border of triangles worked in three colors; medium border of vertical diamonds in two colors; wide border of reverse V's in two colors. Photographs have been enlarged for greater clarity and detail.

FAGOTING

Joining pieces of fabric together with decorative stitching that gives an open, lacy effect is called fagoting. This technique can be used instead of conventional seams to join two pieces or sections of an article, or to add a hem. Or—a much more ambitious project—strips of fabric can be fagoted to each other to produce open-work yardage from which a blouse, for instance, could be made. Almost any fabric can be used, but silk, satin, linen, or linen-like weaves are most suitable. The decorative stitching can be done with embroidery silk, pearl cotton or six-strand embroidery floss.

The first step is to hem the two edges to be joined with fine slip-stitches that aren't noticeable on the right side. Then baste the two pieces of fabric to a piece of stiff paper, leaving the desired amount of space between the two edges. The space may vary, depending upon the weight of the fabric and the amount of openness desired, but it should be kept the same on any one article. The tension of the embroidery should also be kept the same throughout. When the fagoting is completed, clip the basting and remove the work from the paper.

At the right, four varied fagoting stitches; Trellis Stitch, Twisted Bars, Grouped Buttonhole Stitch, and Knotted Insertion Stitch. The first two, explained in detail below, are the most popular fagoting stitches.

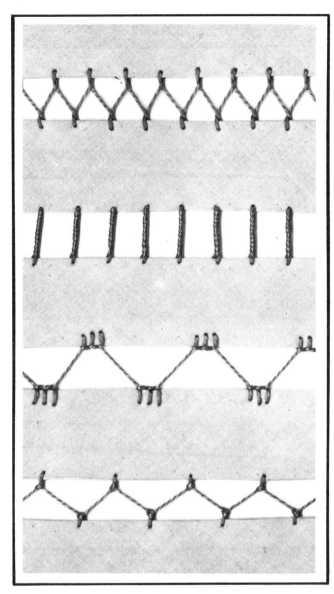

Fagoting stitches shown actual size, with space the width of bias tape between the hemmed edges.

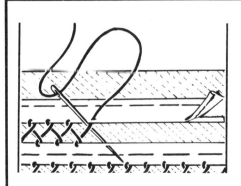 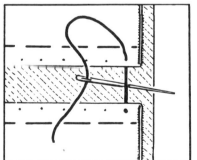 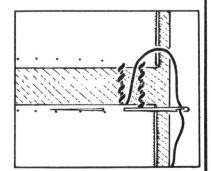

Trellis Stitch: Insert needle from underside of lower piece, carry diagonally across opening, insert in upper piece from underneath, pass under thread from left to right and back down through lower piece. Twisted Bar: Make straight stitch from lower to upper piece, overcast top to bottom; next bar to left.

HARDANGER WORK

Hardanger work based on a typical block design that features both open and ornamented squares.

Hardanger embroidery is easily recognized because it is always worked in squares. It was originally done in ancient times in Asia and Persia, but the modern version is of Norwegian origin and is also popular in Denmark and Sweden. It is traditionally worked in white on white or natural fabric, but color on white or white on color is now being used for contemporary designs.

It is a type of drawn-thread embroidery and must be worked on even-weave fabric such as coarse linen or a special hardanger cloth. 20 to 26 threads to the inch is the best count on which to work, but in any case, accurate counting of threads as you work is essential.

The design is first outlined with blocks of satin stitch, each block consisting of five stitches taken over four threads of fabric, which is called a kloster block. The blocks are worked horizontally and vertically to form squares. Then threads are cut and drawn to form the open squares of the design. This must be done in both directions, alternately drawing four threads and leaving four threads. The threads that remain are worked with weaving or overcasting stitches to form bars. On elaborate pieces, the open squares are ornamented with lace made of loop stitches or twisted bars. Designs for this work should be kept to the block forms typical of Norwegian embroidery.

Kloster blocks of five stitches worked over four threads of fabric.

Kloster blocks worked in two directions to form a square, with center ready to be cut and drawn to form open squares and bars.

Designs are made up of combinations of these blocks worked both vertically and horizontally.

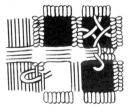

Typical Hardanger work showing drawn threads being worked with weaving stitches to form bars. Spider stitch is worked in one open square.

HUCK EMBROIDERY

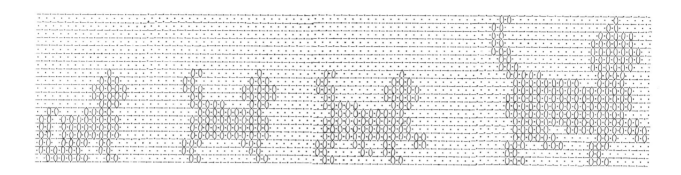

MATERIALS: Huck toweling with seven pairs of prominent threads to the inch, a piece 17" wide and 15" long. Six-strand embroidery floss in contrasting color, 2 skeins. Sewing thread. Grosgrain ribbon 1" wide, 1½ yards. Large-eyed, blunt needle.

DIRECTIONS: Place huck flat, with pairs of prominent threads vertical; cut off a 2"-wide piece across huck for waistband. Cut off end of waistband to make it 10½" long.

Using full six strands of embroidery floss in needle, weave six plain rows across waist-band, leaving ½" seam allowance above and below embroidery. Turn in ½" all around waistband and baste.

For skirt of apron, follow chart above. Embroider design across skirt, starting 2¼" from bottom.

If there are no selvages at sides of huck, make ¼" hems; make a ¼" hem across bottom. Gather top of skirt in to 9½". Baste waistband across gathers. Place grosgrain ribbon along back of waistband with even lengths at sides for ties. Stitch waistband to ribbon.

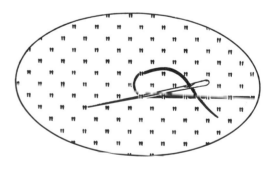

Cats on apron's band are worked entirely in a looping stitch, as shown in detail above. Straight rows of thread fill in background. Start at right of apron fabric and work to the left; embroider background and cats at the same time, following chart above. Apron is sized for a child.

Huck weaving is an embroidery technique done on huck toweling with a blunt-pointed (tapestry) needle. Huck toweling is a cotton fabric woven with pairs of prominent threads, around 7 or 8 to-the-inch. If the desired colors are not available, the toweling may be dyed. To weave, thread needle with embroidery floss, pearl cotton, heavy crochet cotton, or fine yarn, as specified in individual directions. Do not knot thread, but work over thread end at beginning of a strand and weave end of strand into finished embroidery. Working on wrong side of fabric, run needle under pairs of prominent threads, following a chart; do not go through the fabric itself. Work across the width of fabric with pairs of prominent threads in vertical position. Work repeat designs always from right to left, turning work upside down for the return row. To center a design, find center of fabric and start first row at center point. Work row to left edge, leaving sufficient thread at center to complete row to right. When left side of row is completed, rethread needle with other end of strand and work to right. Work succeeding rows from right to left, as for repeat designs.

Many articles not ordinarily thought of in connection with huck weaving can be made in attractive designs on huck fabric. The baby blanket and stole shown above combine a number of stitches and are worked to cover the huck completely. The outer portion of the baby blanket was worked in pink baby wool on pink huck fabric, while the center portion was done in white yarn. The stole, embroidered on white huck with green and gold metallic cotton thread, has long fringes at both ends.

OTHER FABRICS FOR HUCK EMBROIDERY

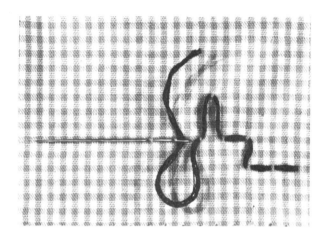

Detail shows huck weaving stitch goes through fabric, picking up the background check of the material as basis of pattern. It is interesting to note that the same design worked on two different fabrics produces different effects. On dotted Swiss fabric, the design is large and graceful. It is bolder and more striking on a fabric of small checks.

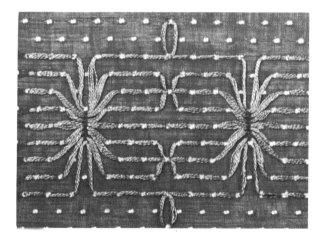

Huck-style weaving done on a variety of smooth-textured fabrics opens up possibilities for designing many new patterns. The basic huck weaving stitch is used, with stitches being taken through the material, picking up a few threads of the fabric pattern to form the design. A wide range of effects can be achieved by using different materials—checks, dots, tiny-patterned fabrics. All designs shown are worked in six-strand cotton.

The technique used here for embroidering designs on various fabrics is basically the same as huck weaving. However, since the fabrics are generally smooth and have no raised threads to work through, the stitches are taken through the material, picking up a few threads of a dot, check or pattern for each stitch. In huck weaving, the stitches are taken through raised threads and not through the huck fabric. The embroidery thread between these tiny stitches forms the design. Good fabrics to use are diagonal or square checks, dotted Swiss or other dotted cottons, fabric with very close patterns in even or alternating lines, waffle pique or monk's cloth.

Any huck weaving border chart can be used to embroider designs on checked fabrics, dotted Swiss, pique, or other tiny-patterned material. On checked fabric like gingham, for instance, every other check represents one stitch as shown on the chart. On fabric with a pattern of smaller checks, every fourth check would represent one stitch. To work on dotted Swiss, use each dot, just as on the charts, because the dots are placed in the same position as the pairs of prominent threads on huck. On waffle pique, the stitches go through the raised threads of the pique, but not through the fabric, just as in regular huck weaving.

The border with the corner is done on a fabric that

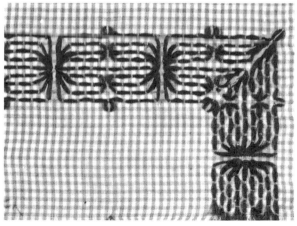

Fabric with a diagonal checked pattern can also be used. Here, as with regular checks, every other check, or more, would be skipped, depending upon the size of the checks. Small checks are shown right. A border with corner was worked on a small white fabric with a tiny all-over pattern, similar in appearance to huck. The same design looks quite different (below) when worked on a checked fabric.

looks like huck but has no raised threads. Therefore, each stitch goes through the fabric.

One advantage of using patterned fabrics, rather than huck, is that, because there are no vertical raised threads to work through, the stitches can be made in any direction. Therefore corners can be turned and designs worked both horizontally and vertically. Design your own corners to go with a straight huck weaving design.

The size of the finished design will vary depending on the size of the checks or dots of fabric used. When working on a two-colored check, the design can be made small and compact by working first row of stitches in each check of one color across and next row of stitches in alternate checks of other color in next row. To enlarge design, work stitches in alternating squares of one color for the first row and in alternating squares of other color in next row. On one-color checks, work first row of stitches in every other square and second row of stitches in alternate squares of next row. Dotted fabrics usually have rows of alternate dots, but the size of the design will vary with the spacing of the dots. When planning a definite size for an article such as a place mat, there will be more or less repeats of the border design around all sides depending on the size of checks or spacing of dots in the fabric. Work the repeats of design and corner as nearly as possible to size planned.

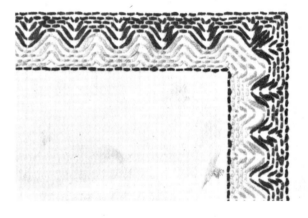

Since it is difficult to determine the exact size to cut fabric for finished article with corner motifs, it is best to leave the fabric uncut until the first row of weaving is done. Begin weaving at lower right-hand corner of fabric. Follow the bottom row of chart from corner repeating design along side to next corner, turn chart and work corner. Continue around all sides or as required.

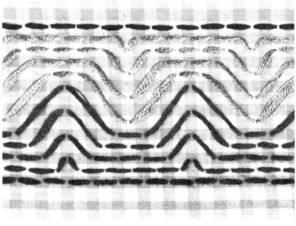

MACHINE EMBROIDERY

If you own a sewing machine, you can create beautiful embroideries in a fraction of the time it would take you by hand. The secret is in learning a special "free motion" technique, in which you move the fabric in any direction as the machine stitches. You needn't be a skilled seamstress or an expert at traditional embroidery to learn this exciting needle craft. All you need is a sewing machine in good running order, preferably one with the zigzag stitch built into most modern machines.

But whatever type of machine you have, explore its potential for "drawing" and "painting" with thread, while learning the few basics listed here. Then practice! In a short while, you will be ready for your first project.

MATERIALS TO USE

A firm, closely woven fabric will work best. Natural fabrics such as cotton will pucker less than synthetics, and if puckers do occur they are more easily ironed out. If working with a knit fabric or one that is too soft, reinforce it with a second layer, fusing Pellon® or basting organdy or strong tissue paper behind it.

Special cotton threads for machine embroidery are available in a wide range of colors. (Polyester is not recommended.) Thread size #50 will be suitable for most projects, although you might prefer size #30 for heavier fabrics. Experiment with various other threads, such as rayon imports; threads with a silky gloss will generally give the most attractive results.

TRANSFERRING DESIGNS TO FABRIC

If the pattern for your chosen design is shown actual size, just trace. If pattern is shown on squares, you must enlarge it to its actual size. Draw a grid on a sheet of paper with the same number of squares as our grid, but make each square of your grid the size directed (usually 1"). The grid can be easily drawn on graph paper. Then copy design onto your grid, square by square. (An easier procedure is to have the design enlarged by photostat, if such a service is available in your area.) Trace enlarged pattern or photostat. Transfer traced pattern to the fabric, using one of the following methods:

Carbon Paper: Place pattern on right side of fabric, with a piece of non-smudging dressmaker's carbon between. Carefully go over lines of design with a dry ball-point pen or a tracing wheel.

Colored Pencil: If embroidering on sheer fabric, lay fabric right side up over pattern; tape in place.

Trace pattern through the fabric, using a sharp, waterproof pencil in a color to blend with thread or fabric. Do not use lead pencil, which may smear.

Transfer Pencil: Go over lines of tracing on wrong side with a sharp hot-iron transfer pencil. Tape pattern wrong side down onto right side of fabric. Follow manufacturer's directions for transferring with a hot iron.

Stitch Outlining: Pin traced design to right side of fabric, design side up. Stitch around outlines of design, either by hand, using small running stitch, or by machine with the free-motion technique (see below). Use thread in a color to blend with either fabric or embroidery. When outlining is completed, tear away paper, leaving stitches.

PREPARING MACHINE FOR FREE-MOTION EMBROIDERY

1. Consult your machine manual for any specific instructions.
2. Be sure your machine is in good running condition and is clean and well-oiled.
3. Remove presser foot. For some purposes, you may want to replace it with a darning spring or embroidery foot (for especially thick or heavy fabrics) or a buttonhole foot (for built-up satin-stitch lines).
4. Lower feed dogs (or cover feed dogs with a plate or raise throat, depending on machine).
5. Use a fine needle, usually size #11 or #70.
6. Thread machine, using desired color in needle and white or any color in bobbin, unless otherwise directed.
7. Loosen tension of needle thread slightly so that thread and fabric will not pucker. Tension of bobbin thread will probably not need adjusting. Before you begin your design, practice with the fabric and thread you will be using to find correct

tension. Top thread should lie firmly but not tightly on the fabric. If tension is too tight, thread may break; if too loose, thread will loop and snarl.

8. Set stitch-width dial as directed; set stitch-length dial at 0.

9. Secure fabric in 8″ or 9″ embroidery hoop, with adjustable side screw: Place outer ring flat; place fabric over it, design side up; set inner ring inside to form a well. (For hand embroidery, the rings are placed in the opposite position.) Tighten hoop; fabric must be held taut while you stitch to avoid puckering. If necessary, wrap small ring with twill tape to hold fabric. Push inner ring a bit lower than outer ring, so that fabric will glide smoothly over bed of machine. If marked design is very close to edge of fabric, you may need to baste on an extra piece temporarily, to hold fabric in hoop.

10. Tilt hoop and slide under needle, design side up.

11. Lower presser bar, to engage tension of needle thread.

STITCHING

To begin, hold top thread and turn wheel by hand until bobbin thread appears on right side of fabric. Hold both thread ends until a few stitches have been taken, then clip. As machine stitches over marked design, move hoop toward or away from your body, to the right or left in any direction desired, depending on design effect you wish to create. Keep the movement slow and even; a too rapid or jerky movement could cause thread to break. To end a thread, turn stitch-width dial to 0 with needle in up position, then sew three stitches in place; clip thread.

The free-motion technique can be used for a wide variety of effects, duplicating many hand-embroidery stitches. Use either straight stitch or zigzag stitch, both to make lines and to fill in solid areas.

Lines: For very thin lines, use straight stitch. Set stitch-width dial at 0 (neutral). Lower needle into fabric. Start stitching along lines of design, moving hoop slowly and evenly in any direction required (Fig. 1). For a stronger or more textured effect, stitch back over lines two or three times (Fig. 2).

For heavier lines, use a wide or narrow zigzag stitch. To make a satin-stitch line, set stitch width at narrow (1 or 2). Move hoop very slowly as needle swings from side to side across the line, piling up stitches evenly and closely (Fig. 3). For contoured lines, do not rotate hoop as you go around a curve, but simply slide it sideways; the result will be a thick-and-thin curving line (Fig. 4).

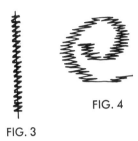

FIG. 3

FIG. 4

To make a line of outline stitching (also called side stitch in machine embroidery), set dial at any width, though wide (4-5) is most often used. Move hoop so that needle swings in a jogging pattern along, not across, line (Fig. 5). Move hoop a little faster than you would for satin stitch.

FIG. 5

Solid Areas: Solid-color shapes are usually filled with wide zigzag stitching. The stitch is the same as the outline stitch described above, though when used in this manner it resembles long and short stitch. Set the dial at 4-5 for large areas, narrowing it for smaller areas. Let the needle move freely in any direction desired; do not stitch in straight, even rows. For a naturalistic effect, you will want the stitching to follow the contour of the form you are making. To stitch a leaf, for example, turn the design so that you are stitching from base to tip. As you stitch, rotate the hoop slightly so that you are also curving outward from center of leaf toward its edges (Fig. 6). If shading a form with two or more colors, overlap edges of color areas in random fashion to blend. As you change colors, clip threads close.

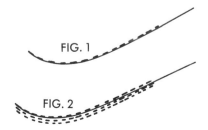

FIG. 1

FIG. 2

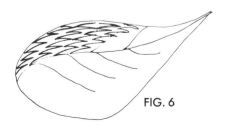

FIG. 6

continued on page 216

MACHINE EMBROIDERY — STRAIGHT STITCHING

These entrancing cats came to us from England, where their originator worked directly on the background fabric with a hand-operated sewing machine described as "by way of being an antique, so giving the interesting hoppity-hoppity line." However, you can duplicate these results without owning an antique machine.

This is an ideal type of embroidery for a sewing machine that does only straight stitching. The tension is loosened and a large stitch is used. A zigzag machine may be used, but a little ex-perimenting will have to be done to produce this stitch effect.

Using a purely inspirational approach, the cats can be stitched "freehand" on tailor's canvas or linen, adding detail and ornamentation ad lib. Or enlarge the drawings below to use as patterns. Creative readers will want to try original work in the same technique. For those who admire the whimsical results but lack their designer's light touch, we offer on the opposite page directions for embroidering and matting these pictures.

Detail shows wavy stitch line, which adds charm to the finished effect.
The chart below for the two cats and the stars is to be enlarged on ½" squares to make actual size. Enlarge patterns on tracing paper, which is used in the process of doing sewing machine embroidery.

MATERIALS: Pencils. Tracing paper. Ruler. Scissors. Sewing, beading, and embroidery needles. Sewing threads. Embroidery cottons. For fabric background, tailor's canvas or linen in white or eggshell; size specified below. Felt: dark gray or black for bodies, blue for eyes, contrasting color for flowers. Gauze or net in a contrasting color.

DIRECTIONS: Enlarge the patterns by copying on tracing paper ruled in ½″ squares. When working the machine-stitched portions, if your machine does only straight stitch, use loose tension and longest possible stitch; if your machine does zigzag stitch, experiment to find a point part way between a straight stitch and a narrow zigzag stitch which approximates line shown in stitch detail opposite.

To make cats and flowers, pin paper patterns for cats to 5″x9″ piece of felt; cut out the two cats. Pin or baste cats in position on 10″x14″ fabric background, and machine stitch twice around each. Hand-embroider noses, mouths, whiskers, and eye outlines, using black embroidery cotton and straight stitches. Define eyes by adding felt pupils, seed beads and a few stitches in white embroidery cotton between pupil and outline of eye.

Stitch star flowers ad lib to fabric background; three sample shapes are shown on pattern. For each flower, use a circle of felt as a center and a larger gauze circle in a contrasting color over it.

Backing Pictures: To back finished picture, cut white cardboard 3″ smaller around than background fabric. Turn 1½″ of background fabric over cardboard on all sides and glue.

Matting Picture: To mat picture, cut a mat-frame of desired size from mounting board. Cut an opening for picture ¼″ smaller all around than cardboard-backed picture. To support picture in cutout opening, glue narrow strips of mounting board around edge of opening on back of mat-frame; place picture in position face down on mat-frame to gauge exactly where to place these strips. Build up thickness of mat-frame at outer edge so it equals thickness of inner edge: cut four long strips of mounting board and paste completely around back edge of mat-frame.

From mounting board or heavy cardboard, cut a backing same size as mounting board mat-frame. Place picture in position face down on mounting board mat-frame. Apply glue to built up strips. Press the backing firmly in place and allow to dry.

MACHINE EMBROIDERY — ZIGZAG STITCHING

Enlarged detail of machine embroidery shows satin stitch outlines and appliques. Below are patterns for butterfly wings and bodies, to be enlarged on 1" squares.

1 RED   2 YELLOW   3 DARK YELLOW

4 GREEN   5 DARK GREEN   6 TURQUOISE

7 BLACK

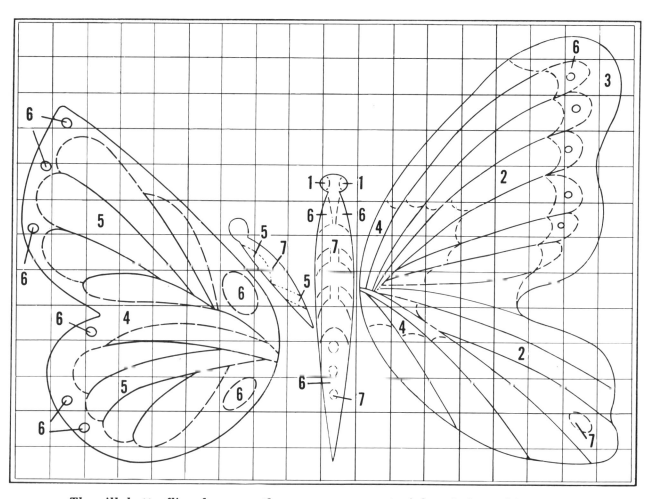

The silk butterflies shown on the opposite page can be done on a semi-automatic machine, a fully automatic one, or by using a zigzag attachment on a straight stitch machine. The zigzag stitch is worked very closely to produce satin stitch lines and dots to outline and accent the butterfly.

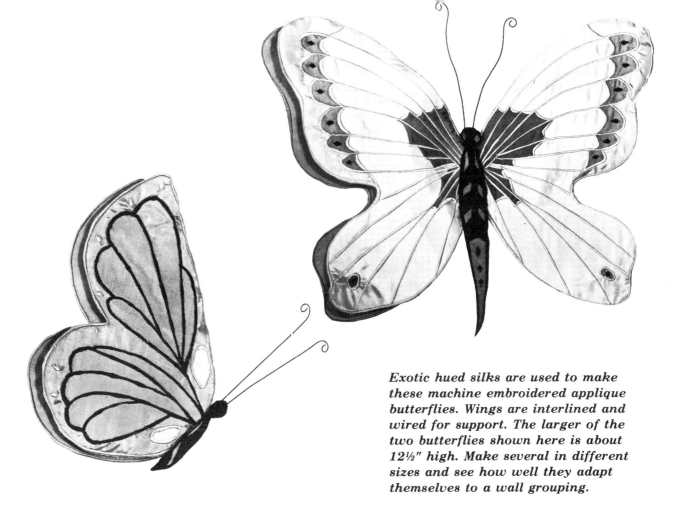

Exotic hued silks are used to make these machine embroidered applique butterflies. Wings are interlined and wired for support. The larger of the two butterflies shown here is about 12½" high. Make several in different sizes and see how well they adapt themselves to a wall grouping.

MATERIALS: Silk fabric, various colors. Matching sewing thread. Heavy Pellon. Medium wire. Tracing paper. Hard and soft pencils. Pins. Small, pointed scissors. Automatic zigzag sewing machine.

DIRECTIONS: Enlarge patterns on opposite page for wings and bodies by copying on tracing paper ruled in 1" squares.

With soft pencil, trace along lines of pattern on wrong side. Pin background silk on Pellon. Using pattern as a guide, pin pieces of different colors of silk as indicated on pattern to top of background silk (dash lines show outline of applique pieces, solid lines are stitching lines). Cut applique pieces a little larger than sizes on pattern. (If background color is darker than color of applique, place a piece of Pellon between them to insure true color of applique.) Now pin pattern securely, right side up, on silk, being sure pattern matches placement of applique pieces, and all edges of silk and Pellon are secure. With hard pencil, trace around pattern on applique outlines and stitching lines to transfer design to silk. Remove pattern, cut away excess fabric and Pellon around butterfly, leaving a 1" margin.

With a straight stitch, sew by machine around all solid lines and dash lines to hold silk in place. Trim off silk close to outside line of appliques (leave extra fabric around butterfly). Set machine for satin stitch and stitch along straight stitching lines, changing width of stitch as you go to form solid lines of varying thickness. Do not satin stitch around outside of butterfly. When all designs inside butterfly have been statin stitched, pull ends of threads through fabric to back and tie. Lay a contrasting color of silk on back of Pellon, pin in place. Following first straight stitching on front of butterfly (outline), satin stitch around outside. Trim away excess silk and Pellon close to stitching. Make bodies in same manner.

For each butterfly, make an extra plain wing in darker color for shadow effect. Sew appliqued wing to matching plain wing at body section; tack body to wings.

FINISHING: To stiffen wings, cut a tiny hole with small, pointed scissors at back of butterfly near inside edge of wing, about ¾ of the way from top, in silk only. Carefully insert wire in hole between silk and Pellon and push wire around top of wing and down other side to opposite point; bend wire to fit outline of wing. Bend a length of wire in half and shape into antenna; paint black. Tack antenna to back of butterfly body.

MACHINE EMBROIDERY continued from page 211

Small areas, such as a berry or a tiny leaf, can be filled in with satin stitch. Narrow or widen the stitch width as needed as you progress, moving the hoop with your left hand while adjusting dial with your right. (Fig. 7).

FIG. 7

Other interesting effects can be achieved by moving the hoop around in circles (Fig. 8) or in serpentine curves (Fig. 9), overlapping and filling in as lightly or as solidly as desired. Use either straight or zigzag stitch.

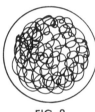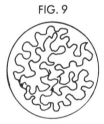

FIG. 9

FIG. 8

Bar Tacks: Set stitch dial for wide (4-5). Begin by lowering needle into fabric at one end of tack. Hold hoop in one position as needle swings back and forth several times to make bar. When bar is completed, change dial to 0 and stitch across ends to secure (Fig. 10).

FIG. 10

Dots: Set stitch width at 1 or 1½. Zigzag back and forth in place about 10 times as for bar tacks, to make a raised, smooth mound.

Cross-Stitch: Set stitch dial to narrow zigzag for satin stitch. Stitch down one line and up another to make a V shape, moving hoop to follow direction of lines; continue to stitch V's across row (Fig. 11). Stitch return row of crosslines in same manner, making a row of upside down V's and completing X's (Fig. 12).

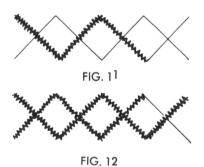

FIG. 11

FIG. 12

FABRICS	THREAD	NEEDLE
Fine fabrics or thin material	Six-strand embroidery thread (split for very fine work) Twisted cotton or fine mercerized thread Rayon, silk, or linen embroidery floss	Embroidery or crewel No. 1 to 10
Medium Textures such as linen, pique, or other cottons; or lightweight sweaters of wool, nylon, or angora	Pearl cotton No. 3, 5, and 8 Six-strand embroidery thread combining number of strands Rayon or linen embroidery floss Fine wool yarns or crewel yarn	Crewel No. 1 to 10 Tapestry No. 14 to 24 Darning No. 14 to 18
Heavyweight or Coarse Fabrics such as monk's cloth, burlap, felt, wool suitings, or heavy sweaters	Double-strand pearl cotton Metallic cord and thread Tapestry yarn or Persian yarn Sock and sweater yarn, nylon, angora, chenille, Germantown Rug yarn	Crewel No. 1 to 10 Tapestry No. 14 to 24 Chenille No. 18 to 22 Darning No. 14 to 18 Needles for rug yarn

MONOGRAMMING

A monogram is, of course, an arrangement of two or more initials used on personal and household articles as a mark of identification. (On small articles a single initial serves the same purpose.) A hand-embroidered monogram has also become something of a status symbol, as hand work of any kind becomes increasingly rare. In any case, a monogram should be very personal, with the style of lettering chosen to express one's taste and lifestyle. Several alphabets are given on the following pages; the cursive script letters are more formal than the cross-stitch ones or the still more casual lower-case letters. Whichever style you choose, the letters can be traced or enlarged or reduced by copying them on graph paper with larger or smaller squares. If initials of two different sizes are combined, the center and largest initial should be that of the last name. Before describing the method of embroidery, here is a brief outline of traditional monogram usage.

ON TABLE LINENS: A dinner cloth should be monogrammed at opposite ends or in opposite corners. A luncheon or tea cloth should be monogrammed only once, at the center of one end or in one corner. Monograms on place mats can be placed vertically or horizontally at the left-hand side, or centered above the plate position. The marking on a napkin can be a smaller version of that on the cloth or place mat, or a single initial. Place the initial or monogram on a dinner napkin in the lower left-hand corner so it is upright and parallel with the fork when the napkin is folded and in place.

ON TOWELS: The monogram is usually placed just above the hem or any decorative border, so that when the towel is folded in lengthwise thirds (before being folded over the towel bar) the monogram is still centered.

ON HANDKERCHIEFS: Handkerchiefs are always monogrammed, or simply initialled, in one corner. On lingerie and men's shirts as well as handkerchiefs, the monogram is usually quite small, and should be embroidered with fine thread or a single strand of six-strand embroidery floss.

ON HOPE-CHEST LINENS: Before marriage, linens are monogrammed with the initials of the maiden name, with that of the surname centered and largest if the letters are different sizes. After marriage, the three initials used are those of a woman's first name, maiden surname and married name, with the initial of the marriage surname the most dominant. If the three initials are the same size and placed either vertically or horizontally, the initial of the married surname comes last.

ON SHEETS: The monogram is placed in the center of the turnover, just above the hem. On a pillowcase, it is centered just inside the hem, with the bottoms of the letters parallel to the hem so the monogram can be used on either side of the bed.

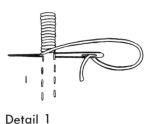

Detail 1

**SATIN STITCH WORKED OVER
RUNNING-STITCH OUTLINE**

Detail 2

**SATIN STITCH WORKED OVER
CHAIN-STITCH ''PADDING''**

Detail 3

**CURVED AND STRAIGHT
SATIN STITCH WORKED OVER
RUNNING-STITCH ''PADDING''**

EMBROIDERY THREAD: Two strands of six-strand embroidery floss make a suitable medium for most monogram embroidery. If a heavier or bolder effect is desired, or if the letters are unusually large, use additional strands. Persian-type acrylic yarns can also be used. Work with 18″ lengths of floss or yarn; longer lengths will knot. And keep the short end sharply cut; a frayed end will cause snags. Use the smallest-eyed needle that will hold the number of strands with which you want to work. Keep the floss from twisting so the strands will lie flat and parallel to each other as you stitch. Start with a knot if the article you are monogramming will be washed frequently.

STITCHING TIPS: It is important to cover all transferred markings with embroidery. Chain stitch, outline stitch, cross-stitch and many other stitches are used for monogramming, but satin stitch is the most popular and effective. Remember that some stitches have a tendency to pucker the fabric when used to fill in solid areas, so work loosely and also loosen the hoop from time to time to make sure this is not happening.

SATIN STITCH can be done by hand or machine. In either case, it is essential to use an embroidery hoop to hold the fabric taut while doing the embroidery. Fasten the hoop in place after the design for the monogram has been transferred to the fabric.

To give a hand-embroidered monogram the raised and rounded look that's so desirable, satin stitching should be "padded" with underlying stitches. The first step is to outline each letter with a simple running stitch, using slightly heavier embroidery thread than you plan to use for the satin stitching itself. Work the running stitch, with short stitches on the wrong side and longer stitches on the right side, just inside the marked outline. Satin stitching can then be worked over the two lines of running stitch, starting and ending each stitch on the original marked outline, just outside the running stitches. But a richer, more luxurious look is achieved by filling in the running-stitch outline with padding stitches—either chain stitch or solid running stitch. The covering satin stitching goes just beyond the filling stitches on each side. The satin stitches should be even in length or smoothly graduated, and as close together as possible for a smooth, solid effect. If a letter has a swirled end, a double-curved serif, or a graduated, shaped curve (such as in a C or an S), slant the stitches gradually to fill in the curve. In letters with corners (such as E and M), the stitches can change direction by spreading out like a fan, or the corner can be "mitered" by shortening the stitches in both directions as they meet each other.

The letters shown on these pages can be traced and used in the size drawn or they can be enlarged or decreased in size by copying on graph paper with larger or smaller squares.

Several ways of arranging monograms from the script letters are also shown below, incorporating decorative motifs as well. The open monograms are planned for satin stitch. However, if a very large monogram is desired, the letters may be filled in with rows of chain stitch. The monograms on page 220 are cross-stitch.

219

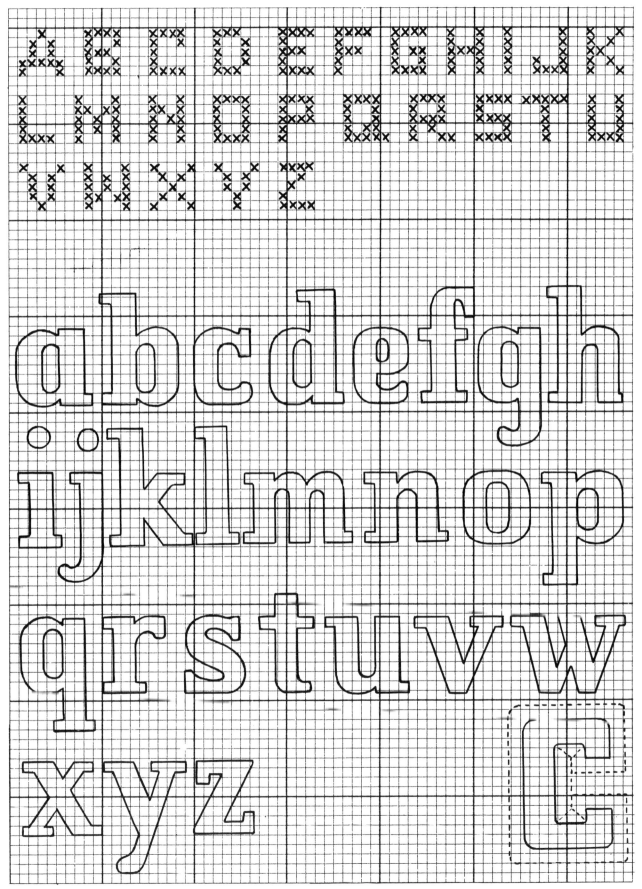

ABCDEFGHIJK
LMNOPQRSTU
VWXYZ

abcdefgh
ijklmnop
qrstuvw
xyz

A B C D E F G H I J K
L M N O P Q R S T U V
W X Y Z Mc

a b c d e f g h i j k
l mc n o p q r s t u
v w x y z

EMBROIDERY ON NET

Net or tulle with hexagonal meshes is used for the background of this embroidery and is worked in a manner so it resembles the fine old pillow laces. The embroidery may be done in a simple darning stitch or more elaborately by using a variety of stitches. Some stitch details are shown on these pages. Combine them to make your own designs on net. The embroidery can be done with a fine thread to make a dainty lace, or you may use heavier threads or yarn. The net should be of a good quality so that the meshes will not break while being embroidered. Use a needle with a blunt tip and darn in ends of threads to start and finish. Never make knots, because they show. You may draw your design on stiff paper and tack the net to the paper as a guide for embroidering. Or you may want to follow a pattern by counting the mesh of the net. You may find it easiest to outline your design first with a simple running stitch, then embroider in any stitches desired.

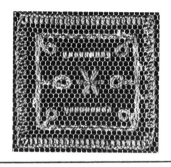

The sampler at left is a simple geometrical design, using many of the stitches shown.

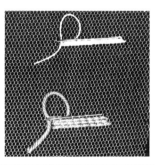

DARNING   This is worked in rows back and forth, going over and under one mesh for each stitch, or more, depending on embroidery thread being used. The top detail shows a fine yarn being darned. In this detail three rows of darning are put alternately over and under each mesh. The second detail shows a heavy yarn being used with just one row through each mesh of the net.

OUTLINING   This is merely a running stitch worked over and under each mesh to outline a design. To fasten the embroidery thread, fold it over on back of work and embroider over it. Run the end back into the embroidery to finish off a thread.

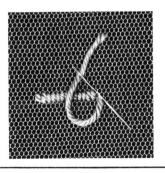

OVERCASTING   To overcast, the embroidery thread is worked over two or more meshes of net solidly. When using a fine thread at least two stitches should be made over each mesh to fill; for a heavier yarn, make just one stitch over each mesh.

OPEN BUTTONHOLE STITCH This is worked just the same as buttonhole stitch on any fabric. Make one buttonhole stitch in each mesh of the net. Can be worked horizontally, vertically or diagonally and in fine or coarse thread.

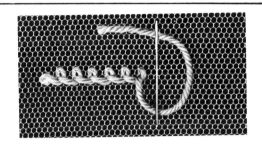

CLOSED BUTTONHOLE STITCH This is the same as open buttonhole stitch except that a number of stitches are worked over each mesh to fill solidly. This stitch is normally used when working with a fine thread.

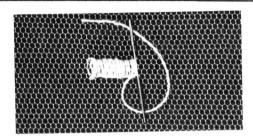

COUCHED BUTTONHOLE If a design is first outlined, this is the way buttonholing would be done. When working by the counting method, first run a single thread in and out of the meshes to the desired outline. Then work buttonholing over the outline.

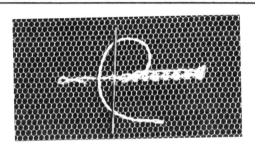

EYELET ROW This is worked in two rows back and forth. Work in and out of each mesh of net, going below and around one side of first mesh, then above and around one side of next mesh. Continue across row in this manner, then work back around the same meshes to complete the eyelets.

STEM AND EYELET First darn a single line for the stem, then work completely around one mesh for eyelet. Alternating the darning, work around eyelet again and down stem.

STAR When using a fine embroidery thread, two stitches should be taken for each arm of star; with a heavier yarn, make one stitch for each. Take stitches over two meshes or more, down through center mesh and out at next diagonal, horizontal, or vertical row of meshes. Continue around in this manner to make a star with six evenly spaced arms.

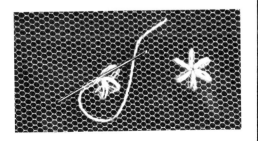

OPENWORK

Openwork, also called punch stitch, is sometimes mistakenly called drawn work, although no threads are drawn from the fabric. The reason for the name punch stitch is that a large three sided punch needle is sometimes used when working on coarse fabric. This needle separates the threads of the fabric, making an open space. A punch needle is not necessary, however. A regular needle may be used, but a much thicker one than for ordinary embroidery.

Openwork is used mainly for backgrounds and filling spaces. It can be done as shown in the samples below in oblong or square spaces, or used as borders. Designs can be worked out in bold geometric fashion, working diagonally and straight. Since the threads are not drawn, it can also be worked in circles and curved lines, as in intricate fruit, flower and leaf shapes. This work often is used in combination with other embroidery to fill open areas of a design.

Loosely woven linen is best to use, as the threads must be counted and each stitch taken over the same number of threads, usually four. However, fine linen or lawn, or even satin may be used. Thread should be strong, a little finer than the material, and usually the same color.

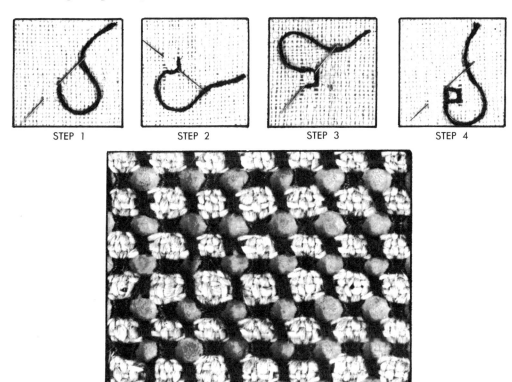

STEP 1   STEP 2   STEP 3   STEP 4

The four-sided square is made in four steps and worked horizontally. On the back of the work, cross-stitches are formed in the process of making the blocks. For a diagonal row, work the top and one side stitch for length desired; then work back with the bottom and other side stitch to complete the squares. As each stitch is taken, the thread is pulled tightly, thus accenting the holes.

Because the needles used are large and have big eyes, you may find it easier to tie the end of the thread to the needle eye when working. Pull thread tight after each stitch. Bring thread to front of fabric, count up four threads; insert needle at this point and bring out again at beginning point. Insert needle again at top of stitch and bring out four threads to left and four threads down, Step 1. Insert needle in beginning hole and bring out in hole four threads to left. Insert again at beginning stitch and bring out four threads up and four threads to left, Step 2. Insert needle four threads to right in hole of first stitch, bring out in hole to left. Insert again in hole to right and bring out four threads to left and four threads below, Step 3. Complete square with two stitches in same manner as before, as shown in Step 4. Continue making squares for length desired. Turn work to make next row, and work in holes of previous row.

RAISED WOOL EMBROIDERY

SATIN STITCH PETALS
FRENCH KNOT CENTER

FLORAL SPRAY MADE BEFORE CIVIL WAR.
COURTESY SMITHSONIAN INSTITUTION

You can create your own lovely flower picture like the museum piece, left, which is an example of shaded wool embroidery in a raised effect. If you hesitate to use your own design, choose a flower picture and sketch it on a dark colored fabric with chalk or dressmaker crayon. Place the fabric in an embroidery frame and work in crewel yarns of leftover wools. In this embroidered piece, the multicolored flowers and leaves are worked mostly in satin stitch, with some petals and leaves stitched on top of others. Other stitches used are stem stitch, French knots and lazy daisy stitch. See detail, above, of satin stitch petals and French knot center. Add seed beads and details in embroidery floss.

TUFTED WOOL EMBROIDERY

TURKEY WORK LOOPS

DETAIL, DECORATED TABLE COVER.
COURTESY SMITHSONIAN INSTITUTION

Start with unknotted yarn end on front of work and make a small anchoring stitch. Loop yarn above needle and take another small stitch as shown, holding the loop; then with yarn below needle take another small stitch to anchor the loop. Continue placing each stitch close to preceding stitch. Shade the colorings as you work. Complete the tufting of a petal or the whole flower, then shear off the loops, cutting parts shorter than others to give a rounded, realistic form to the pile.

Wool embroidery above is also from an original museum design. The detail is part of a black broadcloth table cover.

To embroider a similar tufted design, outline the flower pattern on dark fabric with chalk or crayon. Embroider the stems first in outline or stem stitch. Then start with the larger flower at the center. Tuft the area by sewing with turkey work loops as shown in drawings.

TENERIFFE EMBROIDERY

This type of embroidery involves the same technique as for needleweaving. However, no threads are drawn from the fabric for Teneriffe. Long straight stitches make the web or spoke, and then you work over and under these long stitches to weave the design.

It is a simple matter to use checked gingham as the background to form an even outline for your design. Form designs of squares, triangles, diamonds and circles, using the checks of the gingham as a guide for placing the long straight stitches.

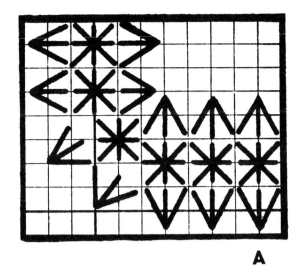

A

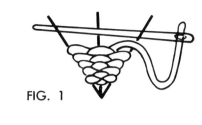

FIG. 1

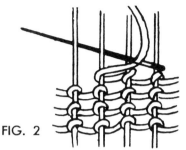

FIG. 2

Chart for working design shown on apron. Each square represents one check of gingham fabric.

MATERIALS: Gold-and-white checked gingham with 4 checks to the inch, 1⅛ yards, 36" wide. White sewing thread. Pearl cotton No. 5: two balls each hunter green and steel blue. Tapestry needle No. 20. Bone ring, 1". Terry cloth, 6¾" square.

DIRECTIONS: Apron: Keeping selvages at sides, make skirt 36" wide and 22½" long. Turn up a 4" hem; press, but do not sew. Make Teneriffe border following directions right. Gather top edge of skirt to measure 16¾". Cut waistband 17¼" long and 5" wide. Fold in half lengthwise. Turn in long edges and ends. Insert gathered top edge of skirt between halves of waistband and stitch across. Cut two ties, each 27" long and 5" wide. Stitch ¼" hems on both long edges and one end of ties; fold end over to adjacent side and stitch together, forming triangle. Repeat for other tie end. Make a tuck in raw end of each tie and insert in ends of waistband; stitch across.

Cut pocket 8" wide and 9" deep. Make design across top, following directions below. Press sides under ½" and bottom edge ¼". Make 2" hem along top. Stitch pocket to skirt 5" below bottom edge of waistband and 3¾" in from right side.

Pot Holder: Cut two pieces of gingham, each 9" square. Follow weaving directions right for border. With right sides together and squares matching, stitch along three sides, making 1" seams. Turn to right side and insert terry cloth padding. Fold in remaining edges and stitch together. Make a few small stitches through all thicknesses to secure.

With blue, single crochet closely around bone ring and sew to one corner of pot holder.

To Weave Teneriffe Design: For apron, start design at right corner of third square in from right edge and 4½" up from pressed hem. With green, make three straight stitches for bottom triangle web as shown at point A on chart. Each square on chart represents a check on gingham. Bring thread to front of gingham at bottom of triangle and weave design as shown in Fig. 1; run needle over and under spokes of web, working back and forth to fill spokes. Do not pull thread too tightly; push rows of threads down toward point to fill closely. At top, bring needle to back of work and fasten. Work top triangle in same way. With blue, make center web on four squares of gingham, starting each of eight stitches from center, between the two triangles as illustrated in chart. Starting at center of web, loop around each spoke of web as shown in Fig. 2; work around web twice. Work next triangles and center wheel reversing colors. Repeat straight across apron to complete border, ending with green triangles and blue web.

For pocket begin design 4½" up from 9" edge and ½" from 8" edge. Work design across as for apron until it measures about 7" across, beginning and ending with blue triangles.

For pot holder, make design on one piece only. Begin in right corner of 13th square in from left edge and 6th square up from lower edge. Starting at point A on chart, work with green as for apron. Then reverse colors, moving to the left. For corners, follow chart and work the two outside corner points with green and the center web with blue; work the two inside corner points with blue. Repeat design, alternating colors, except for corners, around entire pot holder; make corners all the same.

GENERAL EMBROIDERY DIRECTIONS

The final effect of an embroidered piece depends, to a great extent, upon the materials you choose to execute it. You can create a delicate effect by using fine threads on a fragile fabric, or translate the identical design into a bolder, more dramatic piece by using heavier threads on a coarser fabric. The thickness of the yarn or thread determines the size needle to use; the eye should be no larger than needed to accommodate the specific yarn or floss.

Embroidery needles, which are rather short and have long, slender eyes, are available in sizes from 1 to 10; the higher the number, the finer the needle. Some types of embroidery are traditionally done with a certain yarn or floss; others technically require a particular kind. The chart opposite lists the most appropriate needles and threads for different types of fabrics.

Keep a good selection of needles on hand for the types of embroidery you do, and protect them by storing them in a needle case. You can keep them clean and sharp by running them through an emery strawberry occasionally.

You will also need the right kind of scissors. Embroidery scissors should be small and have slender, pointed blades, which must be sharp. Protect the points by keeping the scissors in a sheath.

Embroidery is usually worked while held in a frame, to keep the fabric taut and even. It's much easier to make neat and accurate stitches if the fabric is held taut than if it's held by hand while working. Many embroidery hoops and frames are equipped with a stand or clamps to hold the work in position and leave both hands free.

Before beginning to work on a piece of embroidery, set up a system for keeping yarn or floss conveniently at hand and neatly separated by color. Cut the strands into 18" to 20" lengths, which are less likely to become frayed or tangled than longer lengths. Then loosely braid all colors together so it's easy to grasp an end and pull out a strand of whatever color is needed.

Six-strand embroidery floss can be separated into one, two or more strands for working fine stitches. To separate strands after cutting them into usable lengths, count the number of strands needed and carefully pull them out together, holding the remaining strands apart

to prevent tangling and knotting. Plies of wool yarn can also be separated in this manner when finer thread is desired.

To thread yarn or floss through the eye of a needle, double it over the end of the needle and slip it off, holding the doubled thread tightly as close as possible to the fold. Push the eye of the needle down over the folded end and pull the yarn through.

To begin a stitch, take two or three tiny running stitches toward the starting point, then take a tiny backstitch and begin. It is never adviseable to have knots on the back of embroidery; when finishing, run the needle through several stitches on the wrong side of the piece and cut yarn off close to the fabric. Fasten off the thread in this manner when finishing each motif, rather than carrying it to another motif.

To remove embroidery when a mistake has been made, run a needle, eye first, under the stitches to be removed. Pull the embroidery away from the fabric with the needle and carefully clip the stitches with your embroidery scissors, pressing the scissors against the needle. Pick out the cut threads of the embroidery; catch the loose ends of the remaining stitches on the back of the work by pulling the ends under the stitches with a crochet hook.

To help keep embroidery neat and clean, keep it in a plastic bag when not actually working on it. If wool embroidery is not really soiled but needs a little freshening after it is finished, just brushing over the surface with a clean cloth dipped in a good cleaning fluid may do the trick. This should freshen the fabric and brighten the yarns, restoring both to their original look. If the piece has become really soiled while being worked on, it must be laundered with care.

After blocking or pressing, mount embroidered picture immediately to prevent creasing. If storing embroidery, place blue tissue paper on front and roll smoothly, face in, onto cardboard tube. Then wrap outside in tissue.

Pressing: An embroidered piece for a picture or a hanging should be blocked rather than simply pressed after embroidery is completed. But hemmed articles, such as tablecloths or runners, should be pressed, because blocking would damage the finished edge of the fabric. To press an embroidered piece of this type, use a steam iron on a well-padded surface, or use a damp press cloth instead of steam. If the piece was worked while in a frame, it should need very little pressing. But if it was held by hand while being embroidered, it may be quite wrinkled and require dampening. If this is the case, sprinkle it with water and roll it loosely in a clean towel; press after it has become evenly damp.

Embroidery should always be pressed lightly so the stitching will not be flattened against the fabric. Place the piece, embroidery side down, on the padded surface and press from the center outward. If the embroidery is raised above the background, use extra-thick, soft padding, such as a heavy blanket. If beads or sequins have been added to the embroidery, be careful not to use too hot an iron, since decorations of this type may melt. They must also be pressed face down; the padding below will protect them from breaking.

Washing: Embroidered pieces worked in colorfast yarn or floss on washable fabric can be laundered safely. Wash with mild soap or detergent in warm water, swishing the piece through the water gently; do not rub. Rinse in clear water without wringing or squeezing. When thoroughly rinsed, lift the piece from the water and place on a clean towel; place another towel on top and roll up loosely. When the piece is dry enough to press, proceed as described above.

Blocking: Following the thread of linen and using needle and colorfast thread, make $\frac{1}{4}''$ stitches to mark guidelines where picture will fit into the frame rabbet. The plain linen border around embroidery extends approximately $1\frac{1}{4}''$ at sides and top and $1\frac{1}{2}''$ at bottom. Allow $3''$ to $4''$ excess linen all around embroidery to have enough linen for this border and blocking. Now, matching corners, find and mark with a few stitches the exact center of each side.

If the picture is soiled, wash in a mild detergent and warm water and block immediately. To prepare blocking surface, cover a drawing board or other softwood surface with brown wrapping paper held in place with thumbtacks. Mark original size of linen on paper. As you block be certain not to pull linen beyond original size. (Embroidery sometimes pulls slightly out of shape.) Check that corners of drawn rectangle are square.

If the embroidery is not soiled, rinse and let drip a minute. Place embroidery right side up on paper inside guidelines and tack down four corners. Tack centers of each side. Continue to stretch the linen to original size by tacking all around sides, dividing and sub-dividing the spaces between the tacks already placed until you have a solid border of tacks. In cross-stitch pictures, if stitches were not stamped exactly even on linen thread, it may be necessary to remove some tacks and pull part of embroidery into a straight line. Use ruler as a guide for straightening lines of stitches. Hammer in tacks or they will pop out as embroidery dries. Allow embroidery to dry thoroughly.

Mounting: Cut a piece of heavy white cardboard about $\frac{1}{8}''$ smaller all around than size of rabbeted frame to be used. Stretch embroidery over cardboard, following the procedure for blocking described above. Following thread guidelines, use pins to attach the four corners of embroidery to mounting board. Place pins in center of each side and gradually begin to stretch embroidery into position until you have a complete border of pins around picture about $\frac{1}{4}''$ apart. When satisfied that design is even, drive pins into cardboard edge with a hammer. If a pin does not go straight in, remove and reinsert it. Wrap and tape or glue raw edges of linen to wrong side of mounting board. Frame picture, using glass, if desired.

TO FRAME IN AN OVAL: Cut out of thick cardboard an oval $\frac{1}{8}''$ smaller than the rabbet of your frame. Copy the oval on tracing paper; fold the tracing in half lengthwise and crosswise to find the top, bottom, and side center points of the traced oval. Replace the cardboard oval on the tracing; lay a ruler over the cardboard along the fold lines of the tracing paper and mark four center points at the edge of the cardboard oval with lines about $\frac{1}{4}''$ long. Find the four center points of the embroidered design and mark on edges of fabric in the same way. Place the embroidered fabric on the cardboard oval. Position the embroidery pleasingly. The markings on the cardboard should be visible through the fabric; if not, lift the fabric to check. The center-point markings on the fabric and the oval need not match but must be parallel, so that the fabric threads will be parallel with the axes of the oval. Push pins through the fabric into the edge of the cardboard at center of top, bottom, and sides. Continue pushing in pins on opposite sides as described above. Trim the edges of the fabric to an oval and tape to the back of the cardboard. Place the oval in the frame. To hold the picture, hammer brads about $\frac{1}{8}''$ into the rabbet, bracing the frame against a heavy object to prevent its coming apart. Cover the back with heavy brown wrapping paper.

EMBROIDERY

can be as simple or as intricate as the needleworker cares to make it. Many of the basic stitches are the heritage of assorted cultures and are centuries old. To these have been added variations and new techniques that enrich the art with today's sense of color and design. The embroideries in this book have been selected for their beauty and versatility. It is our hope that they will also serve as inspiration for new and innovative ways with stitchery. The abstract sampler at right is a vibrant example of such innovation—mixing a traditional idea (the sampler) with contemporary color combinations and modern geometrics. For directions, see page 250.

VICTORIAN AFGHAN *was lavishly embroidered with flowers, animals, a religious symbol and the date it was completed. Work the separate sections in afghan crochet, embroider with cross-stitch, then join the sections. Substitute a third dog's head for the symbol, if you prefer, and insert your own date. Directions and charts begin on Page 276.*

WOOLWORK WREATH *of dimensional posies is puffed and padded in the Victorian manner, after making petals and leaves by sewing strands of yarn together. Stems and smaller flowers are made with embroidery stitches, the cherries from ball fringe! Directions, Page 280.*

CRAZY QUILT *from the Victorian era was made from a colorful melange of elegant patches—satin, velvet and grosgrain ribbons, pieces of hand-painted silk, printed fabrics with picture motifs. After the pieces were basted together, the embroidered artistry began–the greater the variety of stitches, the richer the quilt. For stitches and general directions, see Page 258.*

DOG LOVER'S PILLOW *portrays a pampered spaniel taken from the center of a Victorian child's carriage robe. Design is cross-stitched in true-to-life colors on afghan-crocheted background. Directions, with chart, begin on Page 259.*

ROSE IN BLOOM

is a gigantic cross-stitched blossom, with a center of nubby French knots giving it texture and dimension. Worked in heavy yarn on even-weave fabric, the 44" x 30" picture makes an impressive wall hanging. Directions, with chart, begin on Page 272.

TABLECLOTH *with a sumptuous Della Robbia look can be richly embroidered on a sewing machine! Start with a purchased round cloth and follow the actual size quarter-pattern on Pages 274–275 to embroider the festive 23"-diameter wreath of colorful fruits and nuts. Ideal for the holidays—and a dazzling gift!*

ABCDEFGHIK
LMNOPQRSTUV

ABCDEFGHIK.LcM
NOPQRSTUVWE

CDEFGHK
LMNOPQRSTU
VWXYZ

ABCDEFGHIKLMNOPQRS
TUVWXYZ1234567890

Ye proud, ye selfish, ye severe
How vain your mask of state
The good alone have Joy sincere
The good alone are great
Finished by x x Nora Bell Pickent
The 6th of April, 1970, in New York

GARDEN FLOWERS *bloom in bright profusion on a lighthearted pillow, while butterflies, attracted by their fresh Spring colors, flit among them. All the embroidery is done in four easy stitches, using lustrous pearl cotton. Directions for 10″ x 16″ pillow, with full-size pattern, begin on Page 263.*

ALPHABET SAMPLER *is a wall-size adaptation of an 18th century original, complete with the same alphabets, motifs and morality verse. Even the antique letter formations are the same; thus, the reversed P for a Q and the missing J's and U's, omitted because they were not likely to be needed. Worked on burlap, the framed version opposite is 41″ x 62″: the counted-thread center panel is done in tapestry yarn; border is worked over a tissue pattern. Directions, Page 252.*

EMBROIDERED SWEATER

is ablaze with vibrant tulips that bloom all year—making it a bright and fashionable top layer for any season. Easy-to-knit long cardigan is embroidered in duplicate stitch. Directions for small, medium and large sizes, Page 259.

FLORAL BOUQUET *is a stunning arrangement of stylized roses and delphinium, worked in over twenty glowing shades of floss over Penelope canvas. Design is 13½" x 18½", ideal for a picture or a pillow.*
Directions with chart, Page 263.

PILLOW CASES

become decorative assets via the quick-change magic of sewing-machine embroidery. Edges can be scalloped and finished with satin stitching or crochet. Directions for designs seen opposite start on Page 266.

PLACE MATS *that look good enough to eat can also be embroidered on a sewing machine, shading delectable-looking fruit by changing thread colors as you stitch. Shaded grapes center the tray-shaped mat above, easily trimmed to its curvaceous shape after embroidery is completed. Strawberries-in-a-basket make the ingenious motif of the place mat below, with each matching napkin trimmed with a single ripe berry. Directions for making both mats: Pages 269—270.*

PATCHWORK PILLOW is a brilliant accent piece—

and also a sampler of embroidery stitches. Cut patches in two uniform sizes from any fabrics that suit your color scheme; stitch them together and emblazon the seams with a variety of stitches in contrasting color. Directions for 12" x 12" pillow are on Page 266.

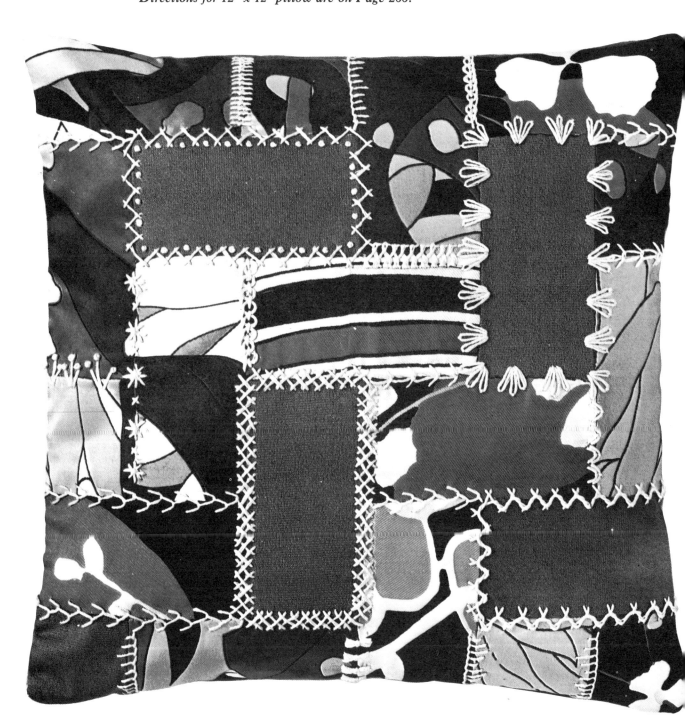

BUTTERFLY PILLOW *in sun-bright colors is cross-stitched over Penelope canvas on crisp white fabric. When embroidery is complete, canvas is removed, strand by strand. Twisted cord and tassels add a jaunty flourish to the 14" x 15" pillow. Chart and directions are on Page 257.*

YARN PICTURES

have a whimsical, spontaneous charm born of quickly worked embroidery stitches done with knitting yarn scraps on hopsacking or similar rustic fabric. The little girl with a garland, opposite, standing in a daisy-spattered field of straight-stitched mohair grass, wears a fashionable "crocheted" dress of blanket stitches. And the bouquet, below, textured and colorful in its lace-trimmed felt bowl, is done with a few basic embroidery stitches. Directions for both are on Page 284.

ABSTRACT SAMPLER

ON PAGE 233

SIZE: 16½" x 12½"

EQUIPMENT: Sharp, hard-lead pencil. Ruler. Compass. Large and medium-size embroidery needles. Straight pins. Sewing needle. Stapler.

MATERIALS: Even-weave embroidery fabric in natural or white, 24" x 20", with the same thread count to the inch vertically and horizontally. Canvas stretchers, two 24" and two 20", or frame approximately 24" x 20". Pearl cotton, six-strand embroidery floss, heavy embroidery cotton, crewel wool, knitting worsted and cotton rug yarn in a related color scheme such as the one shown in photograph on page 233. Dressmakers' tracing paper.

DIRECTIONS: Enlarge pattern for embroidery onto paper ruled in 1" squares. Using dressmakers' tracing paper, transfer pattern to embroidery fabric, centering it on right side of fabric. Using ruler, go over outlines of blocks with sharp, hard-lead pencil, making sure all lines are straight and perpendicular. Use compass to mark perfect circles. Divide and mark the blocks with symmetrical designs inside (H, I, P, O, N, T and X) into four equal parts by drawing a center vertical and horizontal line through each. This will mark the center point, usually a dot or a circle, from which to work the design outward, and make it easier to keep the design symmetrical. The rectangles with smaller rectangles or squares inside can be divided lengthwise to aid in marking the placement of the interior blocks.

Stretch fabric over assembled canvas stretchers or frame and staple in place. To duplicate stitches shown in photograph, embroider each block in stitches listed below — or select your own stitches; stitch diagrams and descriptions start on page 286. On blocks with center designs, work the center motif first, then proceed outward. Work the smaller blocks within blocks first, in satin stitch with a French knot center unless otherwise indicated; then fill in remainder of block and outline it where indicated.

The seven smaller circles outside of blocks are all worked in straight stitches radiating from the center point, with a French knot at the end of each stitch. The larger circle at the top has a satin stitch center with two straight stitches across it and four French knots worked over the straight stitches; the border is done in buttonhole stitch and French knots circle the border.

When embroidery is complete, block if necessary and mount the embroidered piece on heavy cardboard, following directions, page 231. Frame if desired, or hang without framing.

BLOCKS A: Center stripe is fishbone stitch; sides are fagot filling.

BLOCKS B: Rows of chain stitch.

BLOCK C: Couching worked in a "maze" around satin stitch square.

BLOCK D: Rows of interlacing stitch with backstitch outline.

BLOCK E: Roumanian stitch fills both sections of rectangle.

BLOCK F: Rows of slanted satin stitch worked in alternating directions and outlined with backstitch. Small block is horizontal satin stitch outlined with running stitch.

BLOCK G: Diagonal filling stitch with backstitch outline.

BLOCK H: Circle is couching with a cluster of French knots in the center; background is rows of running stitch. Working outward, border is couching, clusters of straight stitch, and backstitch outline, with double cross-stitches in corners.

BLOCK I: Satin stitch circle with couching outline, straight stitch triangles. Squares are satin stitch; border is rows of chain stitch, couching, coral stitch, threaded running stitch and backstitch.

BLOCK J: Triple rows of threaded running stitch with backstitch outline.

BLOCK K: Pekinese stitch with backstitch outline.

BLOCK L: Three rows of satin stitch with outline stitch between and around them.

BLOCK M: Rows of buttonhole stitch with thread running through.

BLOCK N: Circles are couching with French knot centers; background is running stitch; border is couching and chain stitch.

BLOCK O: Sunburst in center is straight stitches tipped with French knots, and star filling stitch worked over the center; wide border, working outward, is backstitch, couching, outline stitch, double lazy daisy stitch, couching, whipped running stitch.

BLOCK P: Circle is couching with French knot center surrounded by outline stitch; triangles are satin stitch; long straight stitches end with cross-stitches and French knots. Border is backstitch and buttonhole stitch over a heavy thread.

BLOCK Q: Flat stitch outlined with backstitch.

BLOCK R: Long and short stitch with backstitch outline. Small block is satin stitch with seeding stitch and backstitch outline.

BLOCK S: Rows of horizontal running stitch with vertical rows of cross-stitch between them and whipped running stitch outline.

BLOCK T: Satin stitch circles are surrounded by outline stitch, then buttonhole stitch circles. Background is filled in with running stitch; outline is couching.

BLOCK U: Diagonal filling with backstitch outline.

BLOCK V: Backstitch squares filled in with straight stitches.

BLOCK W: Couching, with small satin stitch block outlined with backstitch.

BLOCK X: Central motif is done in satin stitch and couching, with lazy daisy stitch and straight stitches over center; working outward, border is couching, cross-stitches, chain stitch, couching outline.

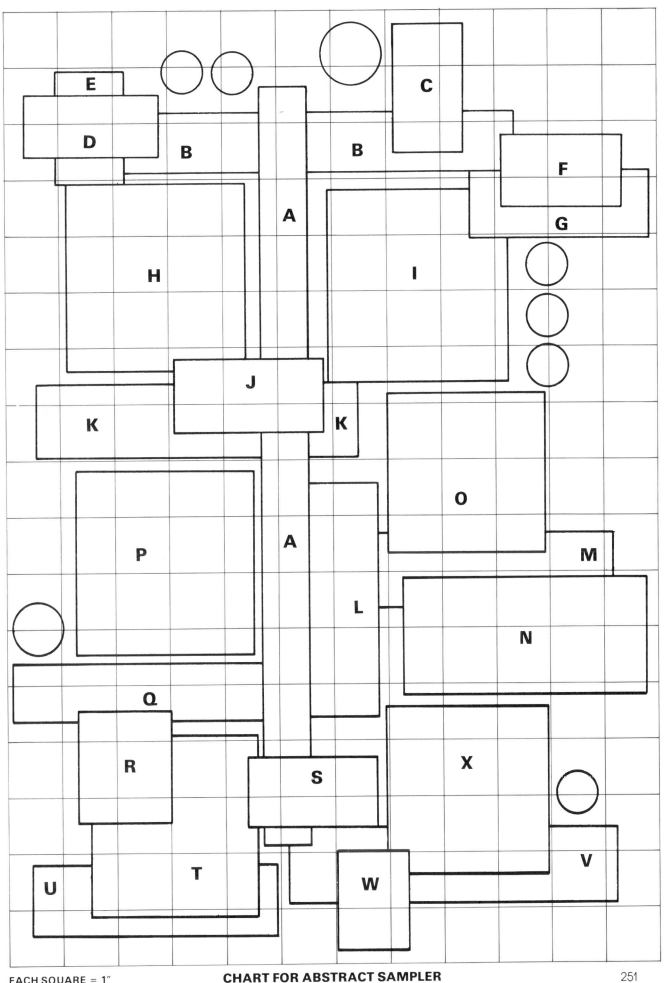

CHART FOR ABSTRACT SAMPLER

ALPHABET SAMPLER

ON PAGE 240

SIZE: 62" x 41", framed.

EQUIPMENT: Paper for patterns. Large sheets of tissue paper. Pencil. Scissors. Tapestry and sewing needles. Small and large straight pins. Tape measure.

MATERIALS: Green burlap 52" wide, 2 yards. Tapestry yarn in 8-yard skeins: 10 skeins pink, 12 skeins medium coral, 7 skeins dark coral, 3 skeins red, 19 skeins yellow, 9 skeins gold, 7 skeins rust-brown, 9 skeins pale blue, 9 skeins medium blue, 5 skeins orange, 4 skeins black, 14 skeins white, 34 skeins yellow-green. White sewing thread. Fiberboard 62" x 41". Masking tape.

DIRECTIONS: Before doing embroidered borders, work all the lettering in center panel, following Large Chart on Pages 254 and 255. See page 193 for how to cross-stitch. All crosses are worked over two horizontal and two vertical threads of burlap. Crosses are indicated on charts by symbols that represent different colors; see Color Key. Each square of chart represents two horizontal and two vertical threads of burlap. Other stitches are worked as shown on chart.

To do the star-stitch squares that make up the letters at top of chart, work each stitch from center point out over two threads of burlap, making eight stitches to complete each square. Use single strands of yarn in tapestry needle throughout.

To start, measure 10" in from top left corner of burlap, then measure 10" down; this is top left corner of Large Chart. Following chart, work border of pink cross-stitches across top and down both sides for some distance; continue cross-stitch border as work progresses. Starting two threads down and four threads in from top left corner of border, work star-stitch letters in pink yarn, following chart. Make first three letters pink, next three medium coral, next three dark coral, last letter red. Skip two horizontal threads of burlap and work row of cross-stitch in pale blue. Skip one thread of burlap and make next row of letters: first three medium blue, next three pale blue, next three yellow-green, last two yellow.

Work band of cross-stitch diamonds following chart. Make row of cross-stitch letters, another row of cross-stitch in pink, and next row of cross-stitch letters following chart and Color Key. On band of pointed motifs, first make outlines of stars in rust-brown. Then make straight stitches within outline, making first three motifs yellow, next three yellow-green, next three pink, next three medium coral, next two dark coral, next three yellow-green, last three yellow.

On next row make letters with straight stitches, each over four threads of burlap. Make first two letters medium coral, next two white, next two yellow-green, next two pale blue, last two yellow. Make row of pink cross-stitches. On next row of straight-stitch letters, make first two pale blue, next letter pink, next letter medium coral, next two yellow, next letter gold, last three letters orange. Work band of two-color cross-stitch motifs. On next row of straight-stitch letters, make first three pale blue, last two white.

Following chart and Color Key, work remainder of chart in cross-stitch to bottom row of triangles. Work cross-stitch outlines of triangles first. Fill in with straight vertical stitches, making first two motifs medium coral, next motif dark coral, next two motifs medium coral, next motif white, next medium blue, next medium coral, next medium blue, next white, next two medium coral, next motif dark coral, last two medium coral.

Using letters already worked as a guide, plan name, date, and place to give sampler your personal signature.

Following Tree Chart, work tree panel below row of cross-stitch triangles. Start at bottom center of panel and work tree chart out to right. Work complete half chart; then work chart in reverse to left to finish tree design. Make all trees and flowers in cross-stitch, all mounds along bottom in a combination of cross-stitch and straight vertical stitches. Where indicated on chart, work a tiny bird in half crosses over one thread of burlap, following chart for Tiny Birds.

Work basket at top center of cross-stitch panel on Large Chart; then work basket from Tree Chart on each side at bottom of panel (bottom of basket aligns with last stitch of border on Large Chart).

Embroidered Border: The remainder of sampler is worked in various embroidery stitches. See stitch diagrams starting on page 286. Enlarge patterns on page 256 on paper ruled in 1" squares. Trace patterns on tissue paper.

Starting at top of panel above right side of basket, pin tissue paper Pattern A in place, matching short dash lines to edges of basket. With long white thread in sewing needle, make running stitches along all pattern lines through tissue and burlap. Carefully pull away tissue, leaving running stitches as embroidery guide. Pin Pattern B around right top corner of panel and down side. Match dot-dash lines on Pattern C to dot-dash lines on B and pin C in place down side of panel to bottom basket. Make running stitches along all lines on patterns as before and pull away tissue.

Trace all patterns in reverse by turning each pattern over and retracing on tissue for left side of panel. Place tissue patterns on left side and outline as before with white thread.

Trace Pattern D four times. Pin one Pattern D at center top of each mound across bottom of panel and outline with white thread. Trace Birds E and F as given and make a reverse tracing of each one. At points indicated by letters E and F on Tree Chart, pin the four birds in position, all facing toward center; outline with white thread as for other patterns.

Embroider all stems in green, using single strand of yarn in needle. Embroider continuous stems down sides in chain stitch; make offshooting stems in split stitch. Following numbers for stitches and letters for colors, embroider flowers and leaves, using single strand of yarn in needle. Work straight stitches of flowers radiating out from center point. Where outline stitch, split stitch, or chain stitch is indicated to fill an area, make rows of stitches close together, conforming to shape of area.

On birds, work satin stitch with shortest stitches possible to fill in areas. Solid black areas are done with black yarn.

FINISHING: When embroidery is complete, stretch burlap over fiberboard, placing bottom of mounds along bottom edge of fiberboard. Push pins through burlap into edges of board, starting at center of each side and working toward corners. Stretch burlap smoothly and be sure threads of burlap are straight. Turn excess burlap to back of fiberboard and tape in place.

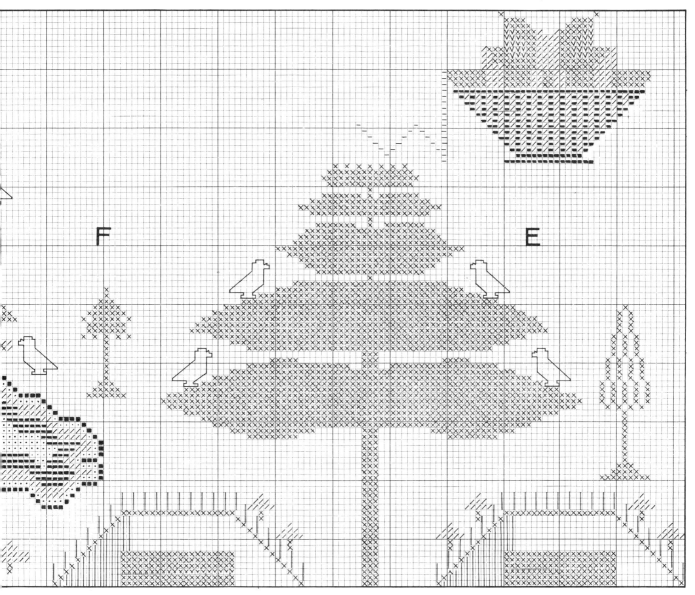

TREE CHART

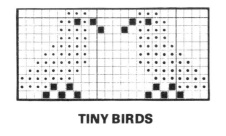

TINY BIRDS

CROSS-STITCH COLOR KEY

⊟ PINK	⊠ YELLOW-GREEN
◫ MEDIUM CORAL	⊡ WHITE
◩ DARK CORAL	▱ RUST-BROWN
■ BLACK	

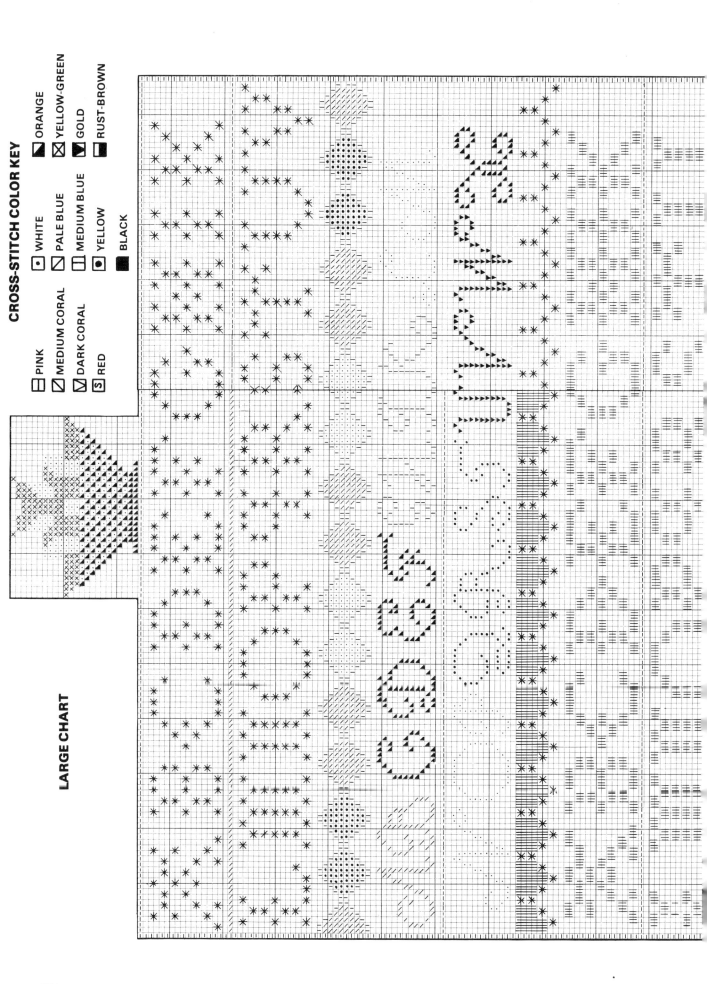

CROSS-STITCH COLOR KEY

PINK
MEDIUM CORAL
DARK CORAL
S RED

WHITE
PALE BLUE
MEDIUM BLUE
YELLOW

ORANGE
YELLOW-GREEN
GOLD
RUST-BROWN

BLACK

LARGE CHART

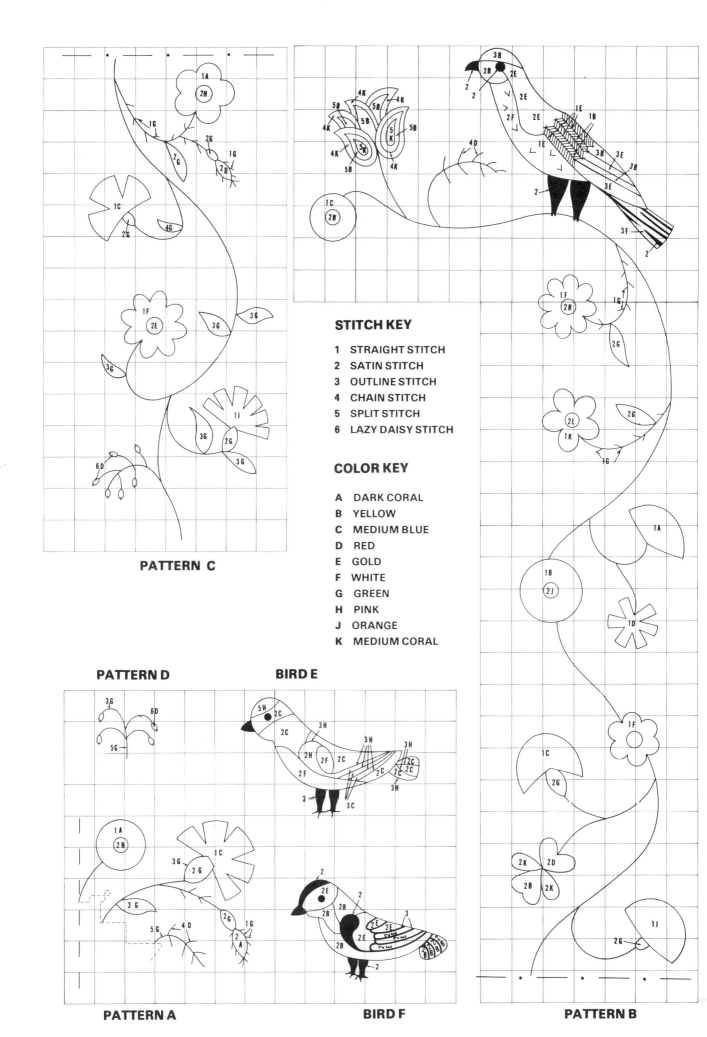

PATTERN C

STITCH KEY

1 STRAIGHT STITCH
2 SATIN STITCH
3 OUTLINE STITCH
4 CHAIN STITCH
5 SPLIT STITCH
6 LAZY DAISY STITCH

COLOR KEY

A DARK CORAL
B YELLOW
C MEDIUM BLUE
D RED
E GOLD
F WHITE
G GREEN
H PINK
J ORANGE
K MEDIUM CORAL

PATTERN D

BIRD E

PATTERN A

BIRD F

PATTERN B

BUTTERFLY PILLOW

ON PAGE 247

SIZE: 14" x 15"

EQUIPMENT: Embroidery needle. Scissors. Piece of cardboard, 2" wide.

MATERIALS: White linen-like fabric, 15" x 32". Penelope cross-stitch canvas, 7-mesh-to-the-inch, 14" x 15". White and pastel sewing thread. Six-strand embroidery floss: Green, 13 skeins; orange, 3 skeins; yellow, 1 skein. Knife-edged pillow form, 15" x 16".

DIRECTIONS: See page 193 for how to cross-stitch and how to work over Penelope canvas. Cut two pieces of white fabric, 15" x 16". On one piece, mark vertical center line (at center of 16" edges) as a guide for placing butterfly design. Center Penelope canvas over fabric and baste in place.

Follow chart and Color Key to work embroidery, using full six strands of floss in needle. Each square of chart represents one cross-stitch. Start 5" down from center top and work center top stitch of butterfly head (between antennae) with green floss. Continue center line of crosses down to bottom of body. Following chart, work right half of design, completing half of body, antenna and right wing. Starting at left of center line, work left side. When design is completed, remove basting and threads of Penelope canvas.

Place back and front sections of pillow cover together, right sides facing; stitch together ½" from raw edges, leaving one side open. Turn cover to right side and insert pillow form. Turn raw edges in ½"; slip-stitch opening closed.

Using three skeins of green floss, make twisted cord; see page 302 for directions. Stitch cord around edge of pillow, covering seam.

Read directions for making tassels on page 302. Make four tassels, using one skein of green floss for each one and winding it around 2"-wide piece of cardboard. Sew a tassel to each corner of pillow.

COLOR KEY   ◨ GREEN   ⊟ ORANGE   ⊡ YELLOW

CRAZY QUILT

ON PAGE 236

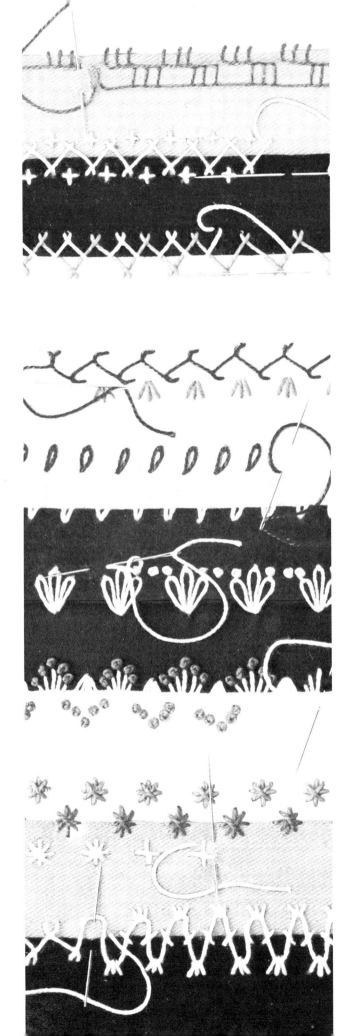

This type of quilt traditionally utilizes scraps of luxurious fabrics such as satin, velvet, taffeta and brocade in rich colors. Scraps are cut into squares, rectangles, triangles and other shapes to fit together to make the desired quilt size.

It's a good idea to make the quilt in sections, sewing the patches to 12" x 18" foundation pieces of muslin or old sheeting. First, pin the patches to the foundation, overlapping the edges by ½". Arrange adjoining colors and textures for a pleasing effect, cutting the patches where necessary to fit them together. Turn under each overlapping edge and baste to the foundation. Then baste the foundation pieces together to form the desired quilt size. The seams are then reinforced and decorated with embroidery stitches, using silk thread, pearl cotton or embroidery floss. The patches can also be stitched together by machine by beginning in one corner and alternately pinning the patches in place and seaming the edges together.

The photograph at the right shows some of the stitches used in the quilt on page 236. Descriptions of these and other stitches start on page 286. Embroidery can be done in one or more colors, and different stitches can be combined, but at least part of the stitching must go over the seam. The stitches shown here are listed from top to bottom:

TOP SEAM: Two rows of buttonhole stitch worked in groups of three. The first row crosses the seam; the groups of stitches in the second row alternate with those of the first row. Buttonhole stitch is usually worked from right to left, but can be worked in the opposite direction. Bring needle up through fabric; holding thread under thumb, form a loop and take a vertical stitch downward and over the looped thread.

SECOND SEAM: Herringbone stitch with upright crosses. Work herringbone stitch from left to right. Bring needle up on lower side of seam, insert on opposite side above and to the right; take a short horizontal stitch to the left and then a diagonal stitch downward to the right, then another short horizontal stitch to the left.

THIRD SEAM: Two rows of herringbone stitch. Work the second row on top of first row, making the short backstitches between stitches of the first row.

FOURTH SEAM: Straight featherstitch with clusters of straight stitches between the featherstitches. Work featherstitch from right to left; loop thread above seam and take a short horizontal stitch to the left with needle over the loop, then loop thread below seam and take another short horizontal stitch to the left.

FIFTH SEAM: Three alternating rows of lazy daisy stitches. To make lazy daisy, bring thread up at base of petal, bring thread around in a loop and take a stitch the length of petal desired with needle over loop. Insert needle at base of petal, holding loop in place with thumb, and then anchor loop with a small stitch over top of loop (or petal).

SIXTH SEAM: Lazy daisy clusters with French knots between them. To make French knot, bring thread up through

258

fabric, wrap thread over and under needle, crossing beginning thread; insert needle in fabric close to where it came up and pull to tighten knot.

SEVENTH SEAM: Fan-like clusters of straight stitches tipped with French knots, alternating direction as they span the seam.

EIGHTH SEAM: Three rows of double cross-stitch upright crosses topped with diagonal crosses to form stars. The center row goes over the seam.

NINTH SEAM: A row of herringbone stitch couched above, below and over the seam with straight stitches.

It is not necessary to interline this type of quilt, but it does require a lining. If edges of joined sections are not straight and true when embroidery is completed, trim evenly. Cut a piece of lining fabric, such as satin or taffeta, to same size as patchwork. To make a 4" ruffle, cut strips of lining fabric on the bias or partial bias; join strips diagonally until piece is twice as long as perimeter of quilt; join ends to make a complete circle and press seams open. Fold strip in half lengthwise, wrong sides together, and press fold. Run two rows of gathering stitches ¼" and ½" from raw edges; pull up bobbin threads and pin ruffle to right side of quilt with all raw edges even; adjust gathers evenly, allowing extra fullness at corners. Stitch ruffle to quilt ½" from edges. Turn ruffle outward and press seam allowances toward center. Turn edges of lining ½" to wrong side and slip-stitch to wrong side of quilt along seam line, enclosing all raw edges.

SPANIEL CUSHION
ON PAGE 237

SIZE: 10½" x 13".

EQUIPMENT: Afghan hook size H. Large-eyed tapestry needle. Sewing needle. Tape measure. Scissors. Cardboard, 2¾" wide.

MATERIALS: Knitting worsted, 2-oz. skeins: One off-white; one medium gold. Tapestry yarn, small skeins: One each of black, white, beige, tan, medium brown, dark brown, light rust, dark copper, dark green, medium green, light green, light yellow-green, deep red, bright red, deep blue, medium blue, light blue, deep yellow, light yellow, magenta, lilac, and pale pink. Heavy cotton fabric 48" wide, off-white, ½ yard. Polyester fiberfill for stuffing.

DIRECTIONS: For afghan-stitch background the gauge is: 4 sts = 1"; 4 rows = 1". Using off-white knitting worsted and afghan hook, crochet background for cushion top in afghan stitch; see Victorian Afghan, Page 276. To begin, ch 53 to measure 13¼" long. Repeat Row 2 for 10¼" (about 42 rows).

Work design in cross-stitch, following chart and Color Key on page 260. On each square of afghan-stitch background, work four cross-stitches: two cross-stitches cover vertical bar and one cross-stitch is worked over each horizontal bar. Mark exact center of chart and find center of afghan-stitch

background. Work first row of cross-stitches on background from center to left, following chart; complete row from center to right. Finish design following each row of chart.

Cut two pieces of fabric 11½" x 14". Center embroidered afghan-stitch piece on right side of one of them and baste to fabric. Fabric should extend ½" on all sides. Place the fabric-backed embroidered piece face down on right side of remaining fabric piece, with raw edges even. Stitch together ½" from edges, immediately next to crochet, leaving one short side open. Stuff with fiberfill to desired plumpness. Turn raw edges in ½" and slip-stitch opening closed.

Using four strands of gold knitting worsted, make twisted cord following directions on page 302. Slip-stitch cord around edge of pillow, covering seam.

To make each of four tassels, wrap gold knitting worsted around 2¾"-wide piece of cardboard 16 times. Tie strands tightly together at one edge of cardboard, leaving ends of ties 3" long. Cut strands at opposite edge. Wrap another piece of worsted around all strands several times, ½" to 1" below tie, and knot. Trim ends evenly and sew a tassel to cord at each corner of pillow.

EMBROIDERED SWEATER
ON PAGE 242

SIZES: Directions given first for small size, 8-10 (31½" to 32½" bust). Changes for medium size, 12-14 (34" to 36" bust), and large size, 16-18 (38" to 40" bust) are in parenthesis. Blocked bust measurement: 34" (38"; 42").

MATERIALS: Yarn of knitting worsted weight, 5 (5; 6) 4-ounce skeins off-white; 1 skein each pink, rose, wine, green, light blue, medium blue and gold. Knitting needles No. 6 and No. 8. Large-eyed embroidery needle.

GAUGE: 5 sts = 1"; 6 rows = 1" (No. 8 needles).

Cut and join colors as needed. Embroidered design is worked in duplicate stitch when sweater is completed.

BACK OF SWEATER: Begin at lower edge; with off-white yarn and No. 8 needles, cast on 81 (91; 101) stitches.

Ribbing: Row 1 (right side): Knit 1, * purl 1, knit 1, repeat from * across.

Row 2: Purl 1, * knit 1, purl 1, repeat from * across, increase 0 (0; 1) stitch at end of row — 81 (91; 102) stitches.

Stripes: * Working in stockinette stitch (knit 1 row, purl 1 row), work 4 rows medium blue, two rows off-white, 8 rows wine, 2 rows medium blue, 38 rows off-white, 2 rows medium blue, 4 rows light blue, 2 rows medium blue, 2 rows off-white, 6 rows wine *. Working with off-white only, work even until piece measures 21" from start, or desired length to underarm. Mark each side of last row for underarm. Check gauge; piece should measure 16" (18"; 20") wide. Work even until piece measures 7½" (8"; 8½") above marked row.

To shape shoulders: Bind off 6 (7; 8) stitches at beginning of next 8 rows. Bind off remaining 33 (35; 38) stitches.

CHART FOR SPANIEL CUSHION

COLOR KEY

◣	DARK GREEN
◪	MEDIUM GREEN
⊞	LIGHT GREEN
⊔	YELLOW-GREEN
⫴	RED
■	BLACK
⊡	WHITE
⊓	PALE PINK
⊞	DEEP YELLOW
⊞	LIGHT YELLOW
s	TAN
◿	MEDIUM BLUE
◹	DEEP BLUE
◎	LIGHT BLUE
●	MAGENTA
▷	LILAC
⋰	BEIGE
▮	DARK BROWN
⊠	MEDIUM BROWN
▶	DARK COPPER
⫼	LIGHT RUST
⊠	DARK RED

LEFT FRONT: Using No. 8 needles and off-white yarn, cast on 37 (43; 49) stitches. Work in ribbing same as for back for 2 rows, increase 1 (0; 0) stitches on last row — 38 (43; 49) stitches. Work same as for back until piece measures same as back to marked underarm, end with purl row. Mark end of last row for arm side. (On right front, mark beginning of last row for arm side.) Check gauge; piece should measure 7½" (8½"; 10") wide.

To shape neckline: Decrease 1 stitch at center edge of next row, then decrease 1 stitch at same edge every 4th row 2 (3; 4) times, then every other row 11 (11; 12) times — 24 (28; 32) stitches. Work even until armhole measures same as back.

To shape shoulder: Bind off 6 (7; 8) stitches at beginning of arm side 4 times.

RIGHT FRONT: Work same as for left front, reversing shaping.

SLEEVES: Beginning at lower edge, with off-white yarn and using No. 8 needles, cast on 65 (71; 77) stitches. Work in ribbing same as for back. Work stripes from first * to second *; *at the same time,* increase 1 stitch each side every 1½" five times — 75 (81; 87) stitches. Check gauge; piece above last increase row should measure 15" (16"; 17½") wide. Work 2 rows off-white, 2 rows green, 28 rows off-white, 2 rows green, 4 rows pink, 2 rows green. Work with off-white only until piece measures 18" from start, or desired sleeve length. Bind off loosely.

CENTER BAND: Band is worked separately. Using off-white yarn and No. 6 needles, cast on 9 stitches. Work in ribbing, same as for back, until band is same length, when slightly stretched, as measurement from bottom of left front, around neckline and down right front of sweater. Bind off in ribbing.

EMBROIDERY ON BACK: Skip 4 rows at lower edge of first wide off-white stripe. Skip first 5 (10; 8) stitches at side edge; * following Chart 1, embroider tulip over next 11 stitches in duplicate stitch, skip next 4 stitches, repeat from * across, leaving 5 (10; 8) stitches at outer edge — 5 (5; 6) tulips.

EMBROIDERY ON RIGHT FRONT: Skip 4 rows at lower edge of first wide off-white stripe. Skip first 6 (1; 4) stitches at center edge, * embroider tulip over next 11 stitches in duplicate stitch, skip next 4 stitches, repeat from * 1 (2; 2) times, leaving 6 (1; 4) stitches at side edge — 2 (3; 3) tulips. Work left front same way.

EMBROIDERY ON SLEEVES: Run a basting line down center of each wide off-white stripe on sleeve. Skip 4 rows at lower edge of first stripe. Following Chart 1, embroider tulip over center 11 stitches, * skip 4 stitches on each side of tulip; embroider tulip on next 11 stitches, repeat from * to outer edges. Skip 2 rows at lower edge of second wide off-white stripe. Following Chart 2, begin at center stitch, then repeat from A to B to right side edge, from C to D to left side edge. Embroider second sleeve in same manner.

Block pieces. Stitch fronts and back together at shoulder seams. With sides of sleeves at markers, stitch bound-off edges of sleeves to armholes. Stitch side and sleeve seams. Sew center band to front and neckline edges. Steam seams.

● ● ● ● ● ● ● ● ● ● ● ● ● ● ● ● ● ● ● ●

To block: Smooth pieces flat, wrong side up, on a padded surface. Using rustproof pins, place pins at top and bottom of each piece, measuring to insure correct length. Pin sides of pieces to correct width. Place pins all around outer edges about ½" apart. Do not pin ribbings. For acrylic yarns, cover with damp cloth. Let dry. Do not press. For flat pressing of wool yarns, cover with damp cloth and lower iron gently, allowing steam to penetrate knitted fabric. Do not press down hard or hold iron in one place long enough to dry out pressing cloth. Do not slide iron over surface.

Duplicate stitch: This embroidery stitch looks the same as knitted-in designs and is worked on the finished garment. Thread tapestry needle; draw yarn from wrong side of work to right side, through center of lower point of stitch. Insert needle at top right-hand side of same stitch. Then, holding needle in horizontal position, draw through top left-hand side of stitch and insert again into base of stitch to left of where needle came out at start of stitch. Keep yarn loose enough to lie on top of work and cover knitted stitch.

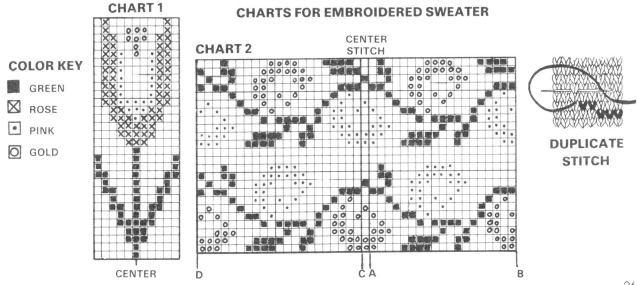

CHART 1

CHARTS FOR EMBROIDERED SWEATER

CHART 2

CENTER STITCH

COLOR KEY

■ GREEN
☒ ROSE
⊡ PINK
▣ GOLD

DUPLICATE STITCH

CENTER   D   C A   B

CHART FOR FLORAL BOUQUET

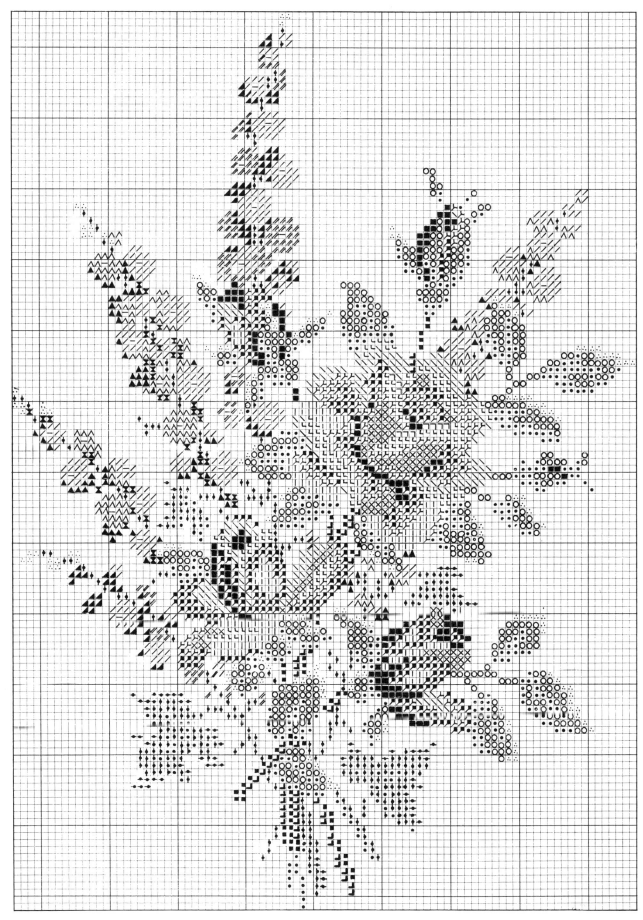

FLORAL BOUQUET

ON PAGE 243

SIZE: Design area, approximately 13 ½" x 18 ½".

EQUIPMENT: Pencil. Ruler. Embroidery scissors. Embroidery and sewing needles. Tweezers. Penelope cross-stitch canvas, 7-mesh-to-the-inch, approximately 15" x 20". Embroidery hoop. For blocking: Sewing thread. Soft wooden surface. Brown wrapping paper. Square. Rustproof thumbtacks.

MATERIALS: White or cream linen, at least 21" x 26". Six-strand embroidery floss: 1 skein each of white, light coral, medium coral, light rose, medium rose, deep rose, dark rose, deep red, medium blue, deep blue, light hyacinth blue, deep hyacinth blue, violet, light yellow-green, light emerald green, dark emerald green, yellow, light brown, dark brown; 2 skeins each of forget-me-not blue, medium yellow-green, dark green. For mounting: Stiff mounting cardboard (size of picture). Small straight pins. Masking tape.

DIRECTIONS: See page 193 for how to cross-stitch and how to work over Penelope cross-stitch canvas. Center canvas on linen and baste in place.

Following chart opposite and Color Key , work cross-stitch design over canvas mesh and through linen. Work all cross-stitches using six strands of floss in needle. Each filled-in square on chart represents one cross-stitch.

When embroidery is complete, cut and remove canvas threads carefully, strand by strand. Block and mount picture, following directions, page 231. Frame as desired. Embroidered piece could also be used to top a pillow or cushion.

COLOR KEY

⊟ WHITE		◹ LIGHT HYACINTH BLUE	
⊔ LIGHT CORAL		◣ DEEP HYACINTH BLUE	
◪ MEDIUM CORAL		⊠ VIOLET	
⊠ LIGHT ROSE		⊡ LIGHT YELLOW-GREEN	
⊞ MEDIUM ROSE		◙ MEDIUM YELLOW-GREEN	
⊿ DEEP ROSE		⊡ DARK GREEN	
◩ DARK ROSE		⊟ LIGHT EMERALD	
■ DEEP RED		⊕ DARK EMERALD	
◪ FORGET-ME-NOT BLUE		⊟ YELLOW	
◪ MEDIUM BLUE		◱ LIGHT BROWN	
◤ DEEP BLUE		■ DARK BROWN	

GARDEN PILLOW

ON PAGE 241

SIZE: 10" x 16"

EQUIPMENT: Tracing paper. Hard-lead pencil. Dressmakers' tracing or carbon paper. Masking tape. Ruler. Scissors. Embroidery hoop. Sewing and large-eyed embroidery needles. Straight pins. For blocking: Soft wooden surface. Brown paper. Square. Rustproof thumbtacks.

MATERIALS: Sturdy white fabric, 11" x 17". Red fabric for backing, 11" x 17". Red flat braid, ¾" to 1" wide, 1 ½ yards. Pearl cotton No. 5: one ball each of colors listed in Color Key. Red sewing thread. Muslin for inner pillow, 36" wide, ⅝ yard. Polyester fiberfill.

DIRECTIONS: Read general directions for embroidery starting on page 230. Trace full-size pattern on pages 264–265 onto tracing paper. Mark 12" x 7¾" design area in center of white fabric with pins. Using red thread, outline this area with running stitches. Tape edges of fabric to keep them from raveling.

Center tracing on outlined area on right side of fabric; place carbon paper between tracing and fabric. Go over design with hard-lead pencil to transfer it to fabric. Remove tracing and carbon; go over any lines that need clarifying.

Place fabric in hoop. To work embroidery, follow Stitch and Color Keys next to pattern, referring to stitch diagrams and descriptions starting on page 286. Work solid black dots on pattern in French knots. Fill in petals of red poppies with couching, following contours of the individual petals.

When embroidery is completed, block the piece following directions on page 231. Then remove running-stitch outline.

To make pillow cover, pin embroidered piece and red fabric together, right sides facing. Insert flat braid between the two layers, with all outside edges even, folding the braid diagonally on itself to go around three corners; overcast ends and conceal joining in fourth mitered corner. Stitch embroidered piece, braid and backing together ½" from edges, leaving opening in center of one side for turning. Trim seam allowances of fabrics and clip into braid at corners. Turn cover to right side and push out corners.

To make inner pillow, cut two pieces of muslin 12" x 18". Stitch together ½" from edges, leaving opening in center of one side for turning. Turn to right side and stuff plumply with fiberfill. Turn raw edges to inside and slip-stitch opening closed. Insert inner pillow into embroidered cover. Turn raw edges of cover to inside and slip-stitch opening closed.

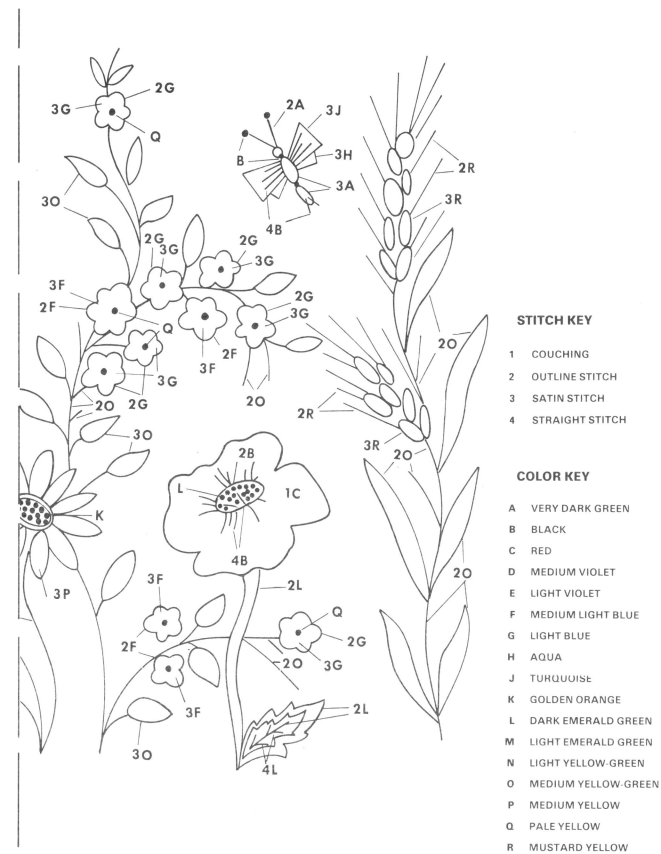

STITCH KEY

1   COUCHING

2   OUTLINE STITCH

3   SATIN STITCH

4   STRAIGHT STITCH

COLOR KEY

A   VERY DARK GREEN

B   BLACK

C   RED

D   MEDIUM VIOLET

E   LIGHT VIOLET

F   MEDIUM LIGHT BLUE

G   LIGHT BLUE

H   AQUA

J   TURQUOISE

K   GOLDEN ORANGE

L   DARK EMERALD GREEN

M   LIGHT EMERALD GREEN

N   LIGHT YELLOW-GREEN

O   MEDIUM YELLOW-GREEN

P   MEDIUM YELLOW

Q   PALE YELLOW

R   MUSTARD YELLOW

WHEN TRACING PATTERN

PATCHWORK PILLOW

ON PAGE 246

SIZE: 12" square.

EQUIPMENT: Pencil. Ruler. Embroidery needle. Stiff cardboard. Scissors. Sewing needle. Steam iron.

MATERIALS: Scraps of any rich-looking fabrics such as satin, faille, velveteen and brocade in prints and solid colors. Unbleached muslin, 12½" square. Solid-color fabric for back of cover, 12½" square. Matching thread. Six-strand embroidery floss in color desired, three skeins. Knife-edged pillow form, 12" square.

DIRECTIONS: Cut two pieces of cardboard for patterns, 2" x 2" and 2" x 4". Using patterns, mark outlines of squares and rectangles on wrong sides of fabrics. Cut seven 2" x 2" squares and fourteen 2" x 4" rectangles, adding ½" all around each one for seam allowance. Arrange pieces as shown in photograph to form a 12" square after they have been seamed together. With right sides facing, machine- or hand-stitch pieces together along marked seam lines. Trim seam allowances (of firmly-woven fabrics only) and lightly steam-press allowances open. Center patchwork on muslin and baste in place. Work decorative stitching over each seam, using six strands of floss in needle and working through both layers of fabric and seam allowances. Steam-press lightly on wrong side on a padded surface.

With right sides of embroidered piece and backing together, stitch around three sides ½" from raw edges. Turn cover right side out and insert pillow form. Turn raw edges in and slip-stitch opening closed.

Starting at upper left of photograph and reading across and down, stitches shown are: Roumanian, buttonhole, Pekinese, feather, herringbone with French knots, lazy daisy, interlacing, wheat-ear, straight stitch with French knots, star filling with cross-stitch, double herringbone, threaded herringbone, and fagot filling. Diagrams and descriptions of these and other stitches start on page 286. Any stitches you prefer that can be worked across a seam can be substituted for those shown.

PILLOW CASES

ON PAGE 244

EQUIPMENT: Zigzag sewing machine. Adjustable embroidery hoop, 8" to 9". Hard-lead pencil.

MATERIALS: Purchased pillow cases. Paper for patterns. Tracing paper. Dressmakers' tracing or carbon paper. Machine embroidery thread, #30 or #50, in colors desired.

DIRECTIONS: Read general directions for sewing machine embroidery on page 210. Enlarge patterns shown opposite or on page 268 by copying on paper ruled in 1" squares. Trace enlarged patterns; complete pattern for butterflies by reversing half-pattern along dash line indicating center of design. Trace actual-size pattern for cross-stitch design. Using carbon paper and hard-lead pencil, transfer traced designs to pillow cases. If using cross-stitch design, place the

basic six-sided motif in the center, repeat three times on each side, and end with additional double-scroll motif and diamond shapes included in pattern.

EMBROIDERY: Prepare machine for free-motion embroidery. Place top of pillow case in hoop, and work with length of case away from you.

To embroider the top design shown in photograph, begin with flower centers. Set zigzag dial at wide (4-5) when filling in solid areas such as flower centers and wider leaves. To outline flower petals, set zigzag dial at 3; satin stitch along line for each petal without rotating hoop, for thick-and-thin contouring. For accent lines within petals, set dial at 1. Outline and accent larger leaves in same manner. Work narrow solid leaves with satin stitch. Work tiny leaves with bar tacks. For stems, set stitch for wide and zigzag between and over marked lines.

Work remaining flower and butterfly designs in same manner, widening or narrowing the zigzag stitch as necessary. For pink dogwood design, fill in centers of flowers with wide stitch (4-5) in green, if using colors shown, then set zigzag dial at 2 and add yellow dots (hard to see in photograph, but clearly indicated on pattern). Fill in leaves, adding darker green center areas.

For bottom flower design shown in purple, embroider only dots in centers of flowers. If desired, inner areas of petals and leaves which are simply outlined in satin stitch can be cut away; use small scissors and cut close to stitching without clipping into stitches.

For cross-stitch design, set machine for narrow zigzag stitch and make lines of fine, even satin stitch; see general directions.

FINISHING: When embroidery is complete, steam-press lightly on wrong side. To make scalloped edge shown in purple, complete half-pattern at bottom of opposite page and transfer to both open edges of pillow case. Satin stitch along marked lines and trim away excess fabric close to stitching.

For a crocheted edge, as shown with orange flower design at top of photograph, first cut edge of pillow case into shallow scallops. Then make a narrow hemstitched edge by machine and follow directions for crocheted edging below. You'll need one large ball of mercerized crochet cotton, size 30, in color desired (variegated thread was used for edging shown), and a steel crochet hook, No. 12.

CROCHETED EDGING: Rnd 1: Make lp on hook; sc in each hemstitched hole around edge, being sure not to pull in edge of pillowcase; sl st in first sc.

Rnd 2: Ch 1, * sc in each of 4 sc, 2 sc in next sc, repeat from * around. Sl st in first sc.

Rnd 3: Ch 3, dc in same sc with sl st, 2 dc in next sc, * ch 2, sk 2 sc, 2 dc in each of next 2 sc, repeat from * around, end ch 2, sl st in top of ch 3.

Rnd 4: Sl st in each dc to next ch-2 sp, ch 3, 3 dc in ch-2 sp, * ch 2, 4 dc in next ch-2 sp, repeat from * around, end ch 2, sl st in top of ch 3.

Rnd 5: * (Ch 2, sc in next dc) 3 times, 2 sc in ch-2 sp, sc in next dc, repeat from * around, end sl st in first ch. End off.

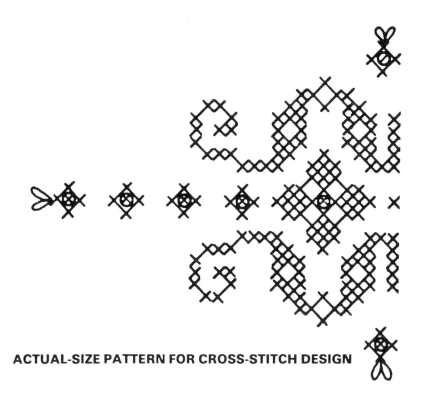

ACTUAL-SIZE PATTERN FOR CROSS-STITCH DESIGN

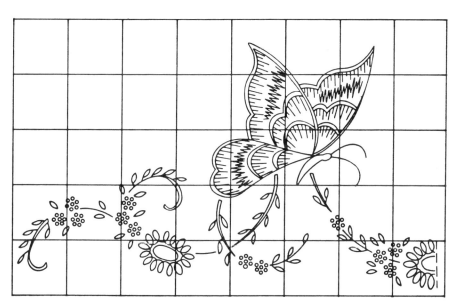

HALF-PATTERN FOR BUTTERFLY DESIGN

EACH SQUARE = 1"

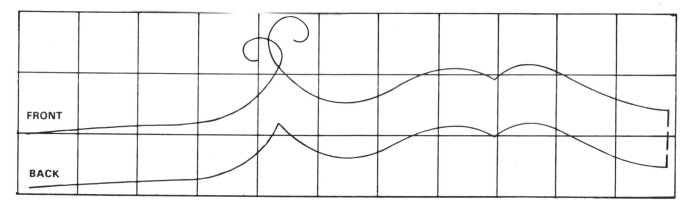

FRONT

BACK

HALF-PATTERN FOR SCALLOPED EDGING

EACH SQUARE = 1"

TRAY-SHAPED PLACE MAT

ON PAGE 245

SIZE: 15½" x 12¾"

EQUIPMENT: Zigzag sewing machine. Embroidery hoop, preferably plastic, 8" to 9". Ruler. Blue pencil. Scissors.

MATERIALS: White organdy, 36" wide, 1 yard for four place mats. Machine embroidery thread #50: Dark purple, medium purple, fuchsia, peach, lavender, dark olive green, bright green, yellow-green, dark brown, medium brown, tan, royal blue, cornflower blue, medium grey-blue. Paper for pattern. Tracing paper.

DIRECTIONS: Enlarge pattern by copying on paper ruled in 1" squares. For each mat, cut a piece of organdy 14" x 17". Center organdy right side up over pattern and lightly trace all outlines with blue pencil, omitting the fine interior lines that indicate darkest shadings of color. Do not cut tray shape out. Read general directions for machine embroidery on page 210. Prepare machine for free-motion embroidery.

Grapes: Set stitch-width dial at 4-5. Place center of fabric in hoop. Shading is done by changing thread color as you work, stitching partially over the previous color. Start each grape in center, using peach thread. Change to fuchsia and stitch partially over and around peach area. Using medium purple, stitch partially over fuchsia and slightly over peach in spots. Using dark purple, work partially over medium purple and out to edge of grape, stitching in direction indicated by fine lines. Change to a narrow stitch and outline each grape

with a line of lavender stitching. Work leaves in same manner, starting with dark olive green along fine lines that indicate veins, changing to yellow-green, then working bright green lightly over yellow-green. Refer to color photograph as you work. Fill in most of stem with tan thread, shading with medium brown and then dark brown where indicated by fine lines on pattern. Work bright green lightly over tan thread in spots, continuing into bright green tendril.

Shaded areas of tray: Set stitch at 0. Using grey-blue thread, work inner and outer shaded areas indicated by solid black on pattern. Graduate direction of stitches as you go around tray, so stitches radiate from center of mat.

Latticed areas: Stitch a bright green flower in each diamond-shaped space by moving hoop to form four small loops, beginning and ending each loop at the same point in center of diamond. Using cornflower blue, stitch along each line of lattice three times.

Defining lines: Remove fabric from hoop, replace presser foot, and work remainder of embroidery in a close zigzag stitch, with tracing paper under organdy for firmness. Using cornflower blue with stitch set at 1/16" wide, stitch along outer edge of inner shaded area. Change stitch width to ⅛"; stitch along lower and right edges of tray and along broken lines. Change thread to royal blue and stitch around latticed areas; stitch around outline of place mat at left and top, continuing onto inner edge of outer shading at right and bottom of tray.

Carefully trim away organdy around tray shape close to stitching; steam-press on wrong side on a padded surface.

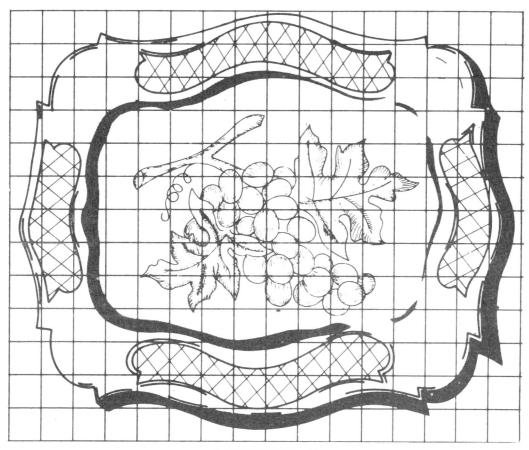

EACH SQUARE – 1"

STRAWBERRY PLACE MAT

ON PAGE 245

SIZE: Approximately 11 ½ " x 17 ½ "

EQUIPMENT: Hard-lead pencil. Ruler. Straight pins. Scissors. Zigzag sewing machine. Adjustable embroidery hoop, 8" to 9". Steam iron. Two terrycloth towels for pressing.

MATERIALS: White fabric, 45" wide, 1 yard for two sets of place mat and napkin, or ½ yard for two place mats. Lightweight Pellon, 36" wide, ½ yard for two place mats. Paper for pattern. Tracing paper. Dressmakers' tracing or carbon paper. White sewing thread. Machine embroidery thread #50 in following colors (amounts vary, but a set can be done with less than one spool each): Bright red, dark red, black, white, bright yellow, light green, medium green, beige, medium brown.

DIRECTIONS: Read general directions for machine embroidery on page 210. Enlarge half-pattern for mat by copying on paper ruled in 1" squares; trace and complete pattern by reversing strawberry-and-flower design along dash line, but continue basket weave border design in same direction all around mat. Enlarge and trace corner strawberry design if making matching napkins. You need not trace seed marks on strawberries nor the fine lines which indicate shading.

Cut 22 ½ " x 16 ½ " piece of fabric for each place mat. Using dressmakers' carbon paper and hard-lead pencil, transfer design onto right side of fabric, leaving 2 ½ " margin all around. Do not cut out. Cut piece of Pellon the same size as fabric and pin to wrong side; machine-stitch together ½ " beyond outline of place mat.

For each napkin, cut a piece of fabric 19" x 20 ½ ". On tracing paper, mark a 14" x 14" square. Matching heavy, straight lines of pattern with lower right corner of ruled square, trace the single strawberry and three leaves onto the tracing paper. Using dressmakers' carbon paper and hard-lead pencil, transfer the complete napkin design to fabric, placing it so 2 ½ " of fabric extends beyond any marking.

Embroidery: Prepare sewing machine for free-motion embroidery. Set zigzag stitch dial to wide (4-5) unless otherwise instructed. Place fabric in hoop. To shade embroidery, change thread color and zigzag over the edge of previously embroidered area. Fine lines on pattern indicate approximate placement of shaded areas and need not be followed precisely.

Begin embroidery by filling in the strawberries, using bright red thread for outer areas and shading inner areas with dark red. Using black thread, make small bar tacks for seeds. Fill in petals of flowers with white, then the centers with bright yellow. Change stitch dial to fine or 0 and stitch around petals with bright yellow. Fill in strawberry caps with medium green and stems with light green. Fill in leaves with light green, then use medium green for shading around outer edges. Satin stitch over the edges of leaves which extend beyond outline of place mat or napkin.

For basketwork border on place mat, work fill-in embroidery with beige thread, turning hoop so stitches follow basket outline. Work the fine lines indicating shading in brown, with the stitch dial set at fine or 0. Embroider the crisscrossing outlines that make the border look like basketwork in brown also, in a narrow satin stitch.

Finishing: To finish edge of mat, raise feed dogs, replace presser foot, set zigzag dial for medium width and slowly stitch around mat while moving fabric to follow outline. Finish edges of napkin with matching satin stitch worked over ruled outline. When all embroidery is complete, trim excess fabric away close to outer stitching. Turn mat to wrong side and carefully trim away excess Pellon from center of mat, close to inner stitching. Place embroidery face down between two terry towels and steam-press on wrong side.

EMBROIDERY PATTERN FOR CORNER OF NAPKIN

EACH SQUARE = 1"

HALF-PATTERN FOR STRAWBERRY PLACE MAT

EACH SQUARE = 1"

ROSE-IN-BLOOM WALL HANGING

ON PAGE 238

SIZE: About 28¾" x 41¾"

EQUIPMENT: Large-eyed tapestry needle. Scissors. Ruler. Pencil. Large straight pins. For blocking and mounting: Large, soft wooden surface. Large piece of brown paper. Square. Hammer. Thumbtacks.

MATERIALS: White evenweave fabric, 4-threads-to-the-inch, 33" x 47". Bulky or 4-ply knitting yarn, 2-ounce skeins (60 yards): 3 skeins each of beige, deep rose, mauve pink; 1 skein each of medium teal blue, loden green, bright turquoise, dark green, lime, chartreuse, dark lime, wine, shamrock green, orange, saffron. For mounting: Fiberboard, 28¾" x 41¾". Masking tape.

Note: Evenweave fabrics and yarns may vary slightly; we recommend testing the yarn by working cross-stitch over four threads of the fabric you select to make certain it covers the background completely.

DIRECTIONS: Tape edges of fabric to prevent raveling. Using pencil, mark 28¾" x 41¾" design area centered on fabric. Then determine center of design area by folding fabric in half horizontally and vertically. Mark center point with pins.

EMBROIDERY: The picture is worked in cross-stitch with French knots around center of large flower; use one strand of yarn in needle. Work each stitch over four threads; each square on chart represents one cross-stitch worked over four vertical and four horizontal threads.

Do not make knots on back of work. When beginning, leave an end of yarn on back and work over it; begin and end successive strands by running end of yarn through stitches on back. When working cross-stitch, be sure that all crosses are made in the same direction. Work all underneath stitches in one direction and all top stitches in the opposite direction; see stitch diagram on page 193. Be sure ends of all crosses touch; begin and end adjacent stitches in the same hole. Keep all stitches smooth, even and flat.

To begin embroidery, find center square on chart by following center rows until they meet; center rows are marked by arrows. Following chart and Color Key, work cross-stitch embroidery from center out. After completing large rose, embroider leaves and buds; then fill in the background to marked edges of design area. When cross-stitch is completed, work saffron-colored French knots around chartreuse center of flower; work short, straight saffron stitches radiating from center point over center circle of cross-stitches. Refer to photograph on Page 238 when working this area.

BLOCKING: Follow directions on page 231.

MOUNTING: After embroidered piece has been blocked, center and stretch fabric over fiberboard, wrapping it around edges of board. Starting at center of each side and working toward corners, push pins through fabric and partially into edge of board, spacing them about ¼" apart. Check to see that the rows of stitches are straight and perpendicular, both horizontally and vertically, then carefully hammer pins in the rest of the way. Turn excess fabric to back of board, folding it miter-fashion at the corners, and tape in place. Glue narrow braid or a twisted cord around edge of fiberboard if desired.

COLOR KEY

☐	BEIGE
Ⓢ	MEDIUM TEAL BLUE
◫	LODEN GREEN
⊠	BRIGHT TURQUOISE
◪	DARK GREEN
◩	LIME
⊟	CHARTREUSE
⊞	DARK LIME
⊡	WINE
⊘	DEEP ROSE
⊡	MAUVE PINK
◨	SHAMROCK
⋈	ORANGE
⊟	SAFFRON

COLOR KEY

A	DEEP RED*	**N**	LIGHT YELLOW
B	CHINESE RED	**O**	DARK YELLOW-GREEN*
C	DARK CORAL*	**P**	MEDIUM YELLOW-GREEN
D	MEDIUM CORAL*	**Q**	LIGHT YELLOW-GREEN
E	LIGHT CORAL*	**R**	LIGHT OLIVE GREEN*
F	ECRU*	**S**	LIGHT APPLE GREEN
G	BURGUNDY	**T**	MEDIUM APPLE GREEN
H	DARK MAUVE	**U**	KELLY GREEN*
I	MEDIUM MAUVE	**V**	CHOCOLATE BROWN
J	LIGHT MAUVE*	**W**	MEDIUM BROWN
K	EGGPLANT PURPLE*	**X**	LIGHT BROWN
L	LIGHT YELLOW-ORANGE*	**Y**	BRIGHT MUSTARD GOLD
M	DEEP YELLOW-ORANGE*	**Z**	PEACOCK BLUE

274

"DELLA ROBBIA" TABLECLOTH

ON PAGE 239

SIZE: Design area, 23"-diameter circle.

EQUIPMENT: Zigzag sewing machine. Adjustable embroidery hoop, 8" to 9". Hard-lead pencil.

MATERIALS: Round tablecloth. Tracing paper. Dressmakers' tracing or carbon paper. Machine embroidery thread #50, in colors listed in Color Key.

Note: Colors marked with star are used in small amounts; you may prefer to use other types of thread available in small spools.

DIRECTIONS: Read general directions for machine embroidery on page 210. Pattern is for one-quarter of embroidered circle and is repeated four times. Diagram at left shows how the four sections fit together.

Trace actual-size quarter-pattern, omitting key letters (and lines leading to them). Divide tablecloth into four equal sections by folding and creasing it into halves, then into quarters. Trace pattern; using dressmakers' carbon paper, transfer it to tablecloth by placing it on one quarter section so that ends of pattern are along creased folds. Move pattern to next section and retrace so circle continues as indicated in diagram. Complete remaining half of circle in same manner. Or make a string compass and lightly mark a 14"-diameter circle in center of cloth, using point where quarter-sections of cloth meet as the center point. Quarter-pattern can then be moved around this inner circle for tracing.

EMBROIDERY: Prepare machine for free-motion embroidery and place area of cloth to be worked first in hoop. Refer to Color Key, key letters on pattern, and color photograph to work embroidery. Shading is accomplished by changing thread color as you work and stitching over part of the previously-embroidered area. Set zigzag stitch dial to wide (4-5) for filling in interior areas of fruits, nuts and leaves; start with highlight areas and change colors as indicated, shading to darkest areas while contouring stitches to conform to individual outlines. Change to narrower zigzag stitch to work grape tendrils, wheat sprays and veins of leaves. Use very narrow stitch for contour lines on nuts and other fine lines. Satin stitch small solid areas such as pomegranate seeds.

When embroidery is complete, steam-press lightly on wrong side on a padded surface.

275

VICTORIAN AFGHAN

ON PAGE 234

SIZE: 58" x 71", plus fringe.

EQUIPMENT: 14" aluminum afghan hook, size 9 or J. Large-eyed tapestry and rug needles. Tape measure. Scissors. Cardboard, 3" piece.

MATERIALS: Knitting worsted, 16 4-oz. skeins black for background: 1 skein each of the following colors for embroidery (or use tapestry wool, crewel wool, or leftover yarns):

Four reds: pale red, light red, medium red, cardinal.

Three purples: lavender, light purple, dark purple.

Three old-rose tones: light old rose, medium old rose, dark old rose.

Four greens: pale almond green, light almond green, medium almond green, dark almond green.

Four beige tones (white rose): oyster white, natural heather, celery, camel.

Five tans (horse and dogs): parchment, pale russet brown, light russet brown, medium russet brown, dark russet brown.

Four yellow-browns: tobacco gold, copper, wood brown, dark wood brown.

Two rusts: dark apricot, rustone.

Yellow.

GAUGE: 7 sts = 2"; 7 rows = 2".

AFGHAN STITCH: Make a chain with same number of chs as desired number of sts.

Row 1: Pull up a lp in 2nd ch from hook and in each ch across, keeping all lps on hook.

To work lps off: Yo hook, pull through first lp, * yo hook, pull through next 2 lps, repeat from * across until 1 lp remains. Lp that remains on hook always counts as first st of next row.

Row 2: Keeping all lps on hook, pull up a lp under 2nd vertical bar and under each vertical bar across. Work lps off as before. Repeat row 2 for desired number of rows.

CENTER SECTION: Ch 155. Work in afghan st on 155 sts for 112 rows. Piece should measure 44¼" wide, 32" long.

Next row: Sl st loosely under 2nd vertical bar and in each vertical bar across. End off.

Mark between 17th and 18th sts from right edge for right edge of cross-stitch design. Mark between 11th and 12th rows from bottom for bottom edge of design. Following chart on **Page 279**, embroider horse in cross-stitch; see diagram.

SIDE ROSE BORDERS; make two: Ch 112. Work in afghan st on 112 sts for 46 rows. Piece should measure 32" wide, 13" deep.

Next row: Sl st loosely under 2nd vertical bar and in each bar across. End off.

Mark between 3rd and 4th sts from right edge for right edge of design. Mark between 3rd and 4th rows for bottom of design. Following Chart 1 on Page 278, embroider rose border.

TOP AND BOTTOM ROSE BORDERS; make 2: Ch 155. Work in afghan st on 155 sts for 46 rows. Piece should measure 44¼" wide, 13" deep.

Next row: Sl st loosely under 2nd vertical bar and in each bar across. End off.

Mark between 4th and 5th sts from right edge for right edge of design. Mark between 3rd and 4th rows for bottom of design. Following Chart 2, embroider rose border from A to B, then repeat end rose only from C to D.

CORNERS; make four: Ch 46. Work in afghan st on 46 sts for 46 rows. Piece should be 13" square.

Next row: Sl st loosely under 2nd vertical bar and in each bar across. End off.

Dog Heads: Mark between 8th and 9th sts from right edge for right edge of design. Starting in 4th row and following chart, embroider head in cross-stitch. For second corner (top right), follow first corner, reversing design.

Monogram of Jesus: Mark between 6th and 7th sts from right edge for right edge of design. Starting in first row and following chart, embroider monogram in cross-stitch.

Date: Using illustration of afghan as guide and chart on opposite page, plan date to fit space. Use graph paper, if necessary, to work out most pleasing arrangement of letters and numbers.

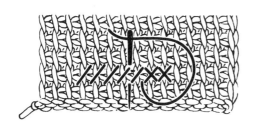

CROSS-STITCH ON AFGHAN STITCH

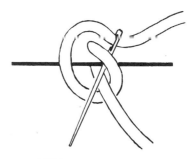

KNOTTING FRINGE

FINISHING: Weave in yarn ends on wrong side. Pin out pieces to correct measurements; steam-press. When pieces are dry, sew them together with black yarn. Cover joinings with cross-stitch in palest tone of horse. With same color yarn, work 1 row of sc around edge, making sc in each st or row, 3 sc in each corner. Join in first sc, end off.

FRINGE: Row 1: Use 4 strands of black yarn, cut 24" long, in large-eyed rug needle. Hold afghan right side up with edge of afghan toward you. Bring needle up from wrong side through a st on edge. Pull yarn through, leaving 2" end in back. Hold this 2" end in left hand.

Slip needle from right to left under end in left hand; bring it up, forming loop at right. Insert needle from top to bottom through loop; pull tight, forming knot on edge. Drop 2" end. * Skip 3 sc to left on edge, bring needle up from wrong side through next st on edge. Pull yarn through, forming scallop of yarn on edge. Insert needle from front to back through scallop. Pull yarn through, forming loop. Insert needle from top to bottom through loop; see diagram; pull tight, forming knot on edge. Repeat from * around edge. Weave in ends on wrong side.

Row 2: Thread 4 strands of black yarn in large-eyed needle. Tie yarn in center of any scallop, leaving 3" end. Working from right to left as before, * bring yarn up through next scallop and down through scallop just formed, forming a loop. Insert needle from top to bottom through loop; pull tight, forming knot. Repeat from * around, alternating one deep scallop with one scallop straight across. Finish off strands by tying knot and leaving 3" of yarn hanging. Start new strands with a knot on next scallop, leaving 3" of yarn hanging. Tie these ends together in a deep scallop and cut ends close.

Tassels: Finish each deep scallop with a tassel of yarn tied to center of scallop. To make tassel, wind several strands of yarn of different colors around a 3" piece of cardboard 4 or 5 times. Slide a strand of yarn under one edge and knot it as tightly as possible to hold strands together. Cut through yarn on opposite edge. Wrap and tie a strand of yarn around tassel 1" from top. Tie tassel to scallop by inserting threaded needle up through tassel, over scallop, then back through tassel. Knot yarn close to wound part of tassel; clip even with bottom of tassel.

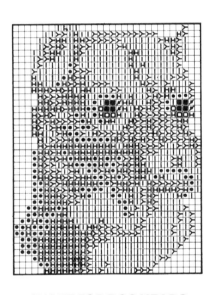

CHART FOR DOG HEADS

COLOR KEY

- ⊞ PARCHMENT
- ⋁ PALE RUSSET BROWN
- ⋈ LIGHT RUSSET BROWN
- ⊞ MEDIUM RUSSET BROWN
- ◨ DARK RUSSET BROWN
- ■ DARK ALMOND GREEN
- ⧄ DARK APRICOT
- ▭ YELLOW

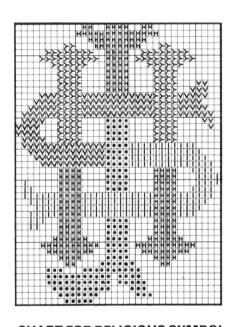

CHART FOR RELIGIOUS SYMBOL

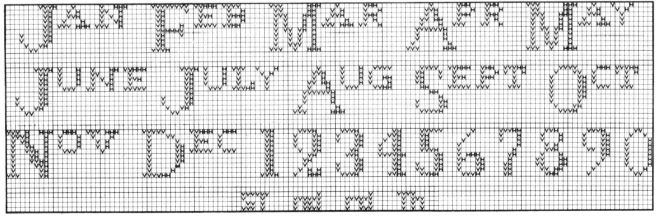

CHART FOR PERSONALIZED DATE

CHART 1: SIDE ROSE BORDERS ON VICTORIAN AFGHAN

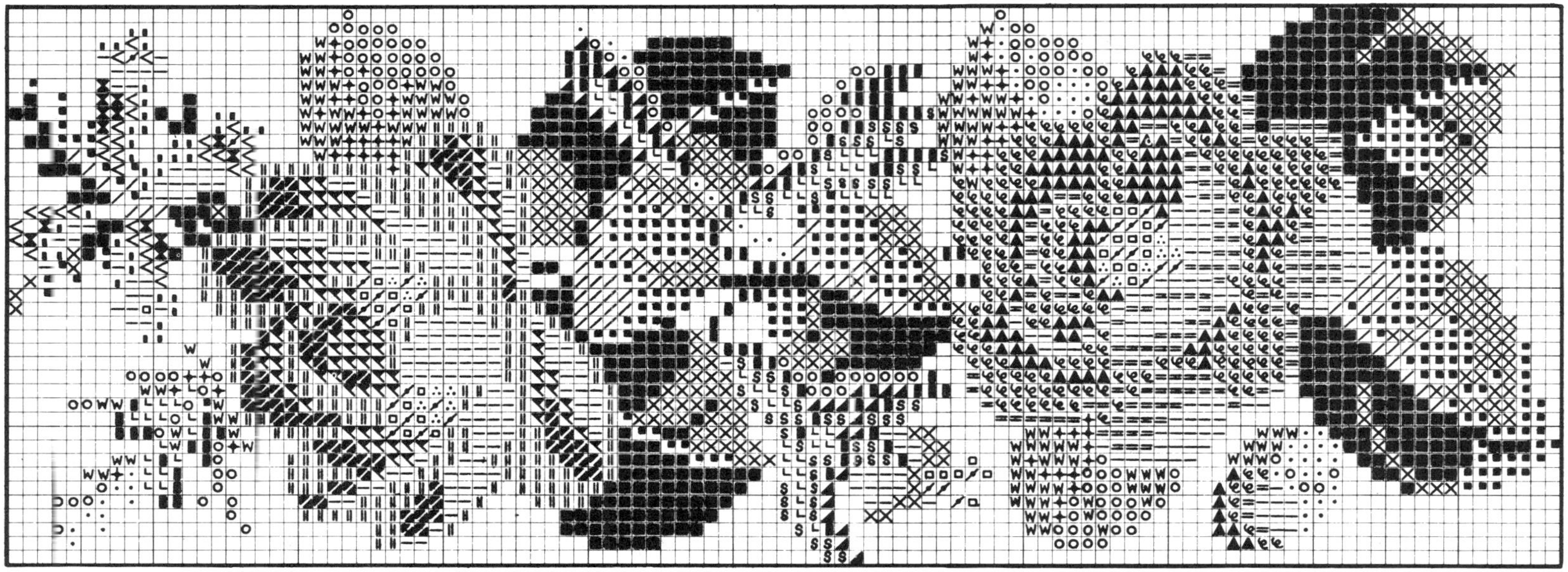

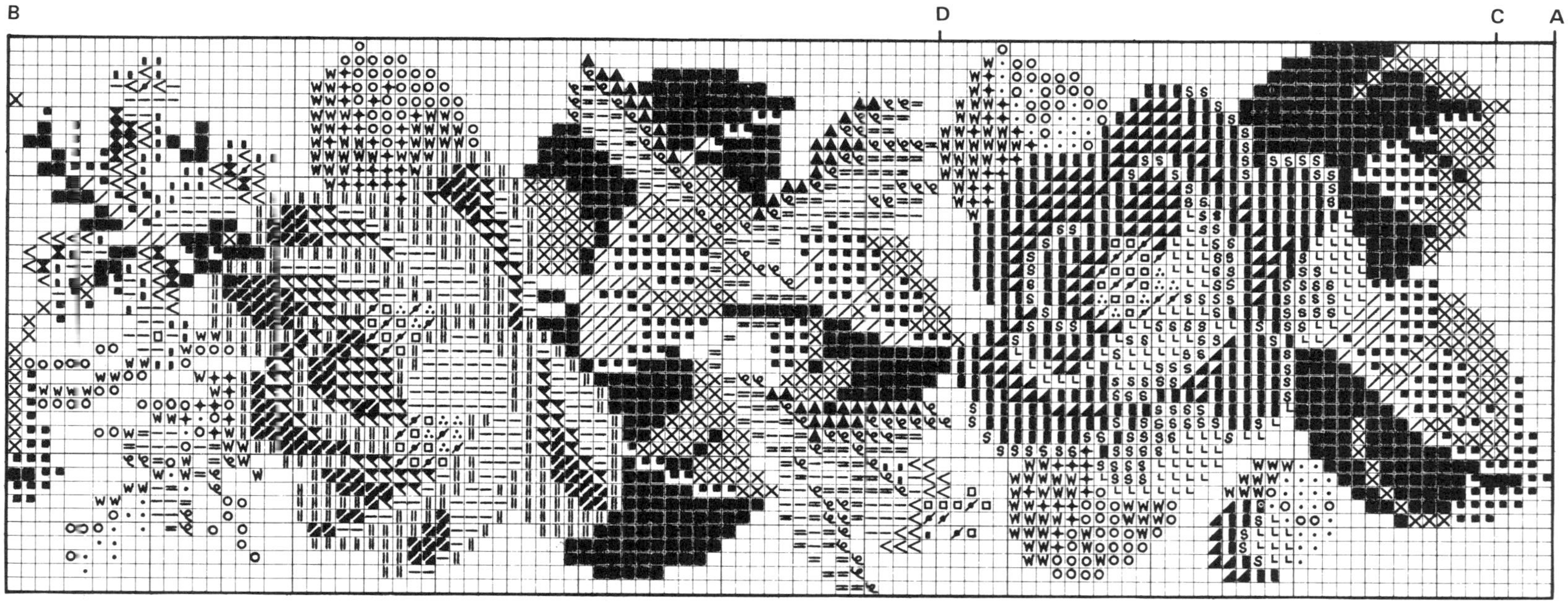

CHART 2: TOP AND BOTTOM ROSE BORDERS ON VICTORIAN AFGHAN

COLOR KEY

⌐	PALE RED
S	LIGHT RED
◼	MEDIUM RED
◢	CARDINAL
◼	LAVENDER
∨	LIGHT PURPLE
✕	DARK PURPLE
‖	LIGHT OLD ROSE
◢	MEDIUM OLD ROSE
◀	DARK OLD ROSE
◿	PALE ALMOND GREEN
◻	LIGHT ALMOND GREEN
⌧	MEDIUM ALMOND GREEN
◼	DARK ALMOND GREEN
—	OYSTER WHITE
‖	NATURAL HEATHER
◿	CELERY
◤	CAMEL
·	TOBACCO GOLD
○	COPPER
W	WOOD BROWN
✚	DARK WOOD BROWN
◸	DARK APRICOT
⬡	RUSTONE
⊘	YELLOW
‖	PARCHMENT
▽	PALE RUSSET BROWN
◿	LIGHT RUSSET BROWN
⊞	MEDIUM RUSSET BROWN
●	DARK RUSSET BROWN

278

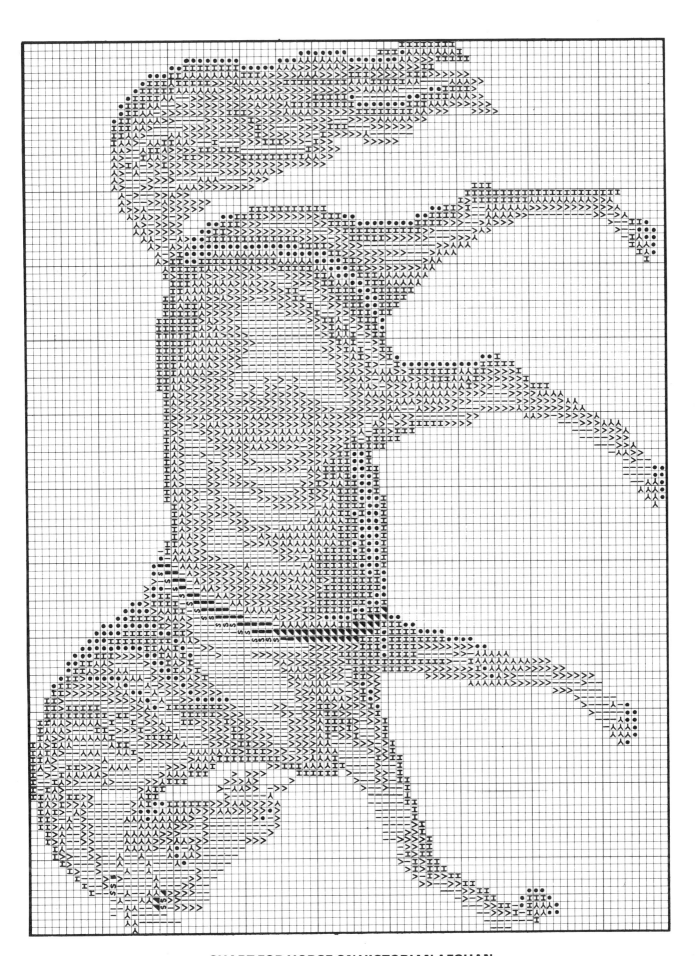

CHART FOR HORSE ON VICTORIAN AFGHAN

WOOLWORK WREATH

ON PAGE 235

SIZE: Design area, 16" square.

EQUIPMENT: Hard-lead pencil or dry ball-point pen. Scissors. Ruler. Sewing needle. Large-eyed embroidery needle. Tack hammer for framing.

MATERIALS: Black suede cloth or good-quality felt, 24" square. Paper for patterns. Tracing paper. White dressmakers' tracing paper. Tapestry yarn, 8-yard skeins: 2 skeins each of white, olive green, light olive, deep green, dark green; 1 skein each of dark blue-green, dark gold, pale olive, medium green, pale green, light green, dark brick red, medium brick red, pale brick red, burnt orange, light orange, yellow, scarlet, coral, salmon, maroon, pink, deep blue, royal blue, light blue, pale blue, deep red. Sewing thread to blend with yarns in each color group listed under Color Key. Six red pompons from ball fringe. White cotton flannel for stuffing. Carpet thread. Gold-colored silk or metallic thread. Small piece of stiff cardboard. For framing: Heavy mounting cardboard, 20" square. Wide shadow-box frame with glass, rabbet size same size as mounting board. Masking tape. Brown wrapping paper.

DIRECTIONS: The three-dimensional effect of this woolwork is achieved by making individual flowers, petals and leaves from strands of yarn which have been sewn together and then sewing them to the background fabric. Stems and some flowers are embroidered directly on the background.

Enlarge pattern by copying on paper ruled in 1" squares. Trace pattern. Place white dressmakers' tracing paper between fabric and pattern; using pencil or dry ball-point pen, go over outlines of flowers, leaves and stems.

Typical flowers, petals and leaves are identified by a letter from A to H on the pattern; all leaves on the same stem and similar petals on a flower which are not lettered are made the same way. The letters refer to the Identification Key, which indicates the type of flower, petal or leaf. The numbers on the pattern refer to the Color Key, which indicates the color combination to be used. When assembling the strands of yarn listed in the Color Key, arrange the strands from the lightest color to the darkest; when the strands are folded, either the lightest or darkest color will be in the center. Change the colors and combinations if you like, trying different combinations as you practice making the petals and leaves.

Refer to Identification and Color Keys to make each three-dimensional piece. Each petal and leaf is made from strands of yarn which have been stitched together. Cut strands to lengths indicated and work over a small piece of cardboard. Wrap strands around cardboard, holding them taut and flat. Using sewing needle and thread that blends with the color combination being used, carefully insert needle through strands from right to left, then from left to right, as shown in first illustration. Make rows of stitching about ⅛" apart; do not pull thread tight, but keep it taut enough to hold the strands of yarn close together and flat. Continue stitching through strands along complete length on front and back of cardboard. Then make individual pieces as follows.

A; STRAIGHT FOLDED STRIP: Cut strands of yarn as indicated in Color Key (No. 3 color combination), long enough to form complete folded arrangement on pattern plus 2". Stitch strands together as shown in first illustration. Turn ends of strands under and tack. Place strip over outline on black fabric, folding and tacking to conform to zigzag shape; tack to fabric wherever necessary to hold in place.

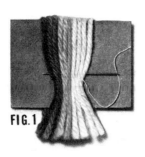

FIG. 1

THE BASIC STEP:
STITCH STRANDS OF
YARN TOGETHER

FIG. 2

FOR STUFFED PETALS:
SEW CENTER STRANDS TOGETHER

FIG3

FLANNEL ROLL
FOR STUFFING
STUFFED PETALS

B; STUFFED PETALS: For each petal, cut strands of yarn as indicated in Color Key, twice the length of petal on pattern plus 2". Wrap around cardboard and stitch together as before. Remove cardboard and fold strip in half, making a U-turn at top and keeping strands flat. Using one finger and thumb to hold strands in flat curve at top so rest of strands lie flat in a row, stitch the two center strands together, catching just the adjoining edges of the yarn.

To stuff petals, measure the length of each petal on pattern; cut strip of flannel to that width and roll tightly until roll is about ½" in diameter. Wrap white thread around roll and knot thread. Whip edges of flannel together at one end to make rounded shape; see illustration. Place stitched-together strands of yarn over flannel roll, with U-turn at top over rounded end of roll, and strands covering front and sides of roll. Tack strands of yarn to roll, then tack stuffed petal in place on background. Fold ends of yarn under bottom of roll and tack to background; see illustration.

C; UNSTUFFED PETALS: Make the same way as stuffed petals, but omit the roll of flannel stuffing; turn ends of yarn under and tack to strands on top. Three unstuffed petals are placed over and around one or two stuffed petals to make tulip-shaped flowers.

D; POINTED LEAVES: Cut strands of yarn as indicated in Color Key, about 2½" long; stitch together. Fold strip in half, making a U-turn at top and keeping strands flat, so ends of strands form a point. Stitch ends of strands tightly together. Turn leaf over and tack to black background at tip and base; turn ends under leaf and embroider a straight stem stitch with yarn.

E; LEAVES WITH STITCHED TIPS: Make the same way as pointed leaves, but stitch across strands ⅛" from pointed tip; pull thread tight and knot. Stitch to black background at tip and base.

F; FLOWERS WITH SMALL PETALS: For each petal, cut strands of yarn as indicated in Color Key, 2" long. Make 54 small petals in the same manner as pointed leaves, but do not tack to background. Cut a cardboard circle slightly smaller than circles F on pattern; pad with a few layers of flannel to make a slight mound. Cut a larger flannel circle and cover padded mound; gather edge of circle and draw taut on back of cardboard so padded mound is covered smoothly. Starting around outer edge of circle, tack a round of petals to mound with points outward. Tack another round of petals inside and overlapping the first, with points of petals between those of previous round. Continue in to center, attaching five more rounds of petals. Sew a small pompon in center of petals and tack flower in place on black background.

G; PADDED ROSES: Cut long strands of yarn in quantities and colors indicated in Color Key; stitch together as for other flowers. For padding, cut a circle of flannel about 4" in diameter; gather the edge with small running stitches and stuff with small pieces of flannel, making a plump mound slightly smaller in diameter than pattern circles G. Draw gathering stitches up and knot thread. Starting in the center, stitch end of sewn-together strands to mound; winding strands around center, tack to flannel about every ½", overlapping each round slightly until top and sides of mound are covered. If first strip is not long enough to completely cover mound, stitch another strip together, tack to end of first strip and continue winding. Stitch finished rose to background around outside edge. Make a small yarn pompon and stitch to center of rose.

EMBROIDERY: After all separate pieces have been sewn to background, embroider remaining parts of the design in colors indicated on pattern. Split tapestry yarn into four single-ply pieces and use a single-ply in needle or use other fine yarn. Embroider stems in outline stitch, loop petals in lazy daisy stitch; work straight lines in straight stitch.

FIG. 4

COMPLETED
STUFFED PETAL

FIG. 5

FLOWER FORMED BY
UNSTUFFED PETALS
OVER STUFFED PETAL

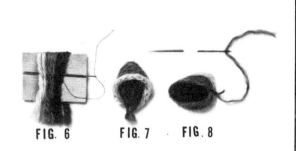

FIG. 6   **FIG. 7**   **FIG. 8**

MAKING POINTED LEAF

COLOR KEY

NO. 1 LEAVES
1 STRAND DARK BLUE-GREEN
2 STRANDS OLIVE GREEN
2 STRANDS LIGHT OLIVE
2 STRANDS DARK GOLD

NO. 2 LEAVES
1 STRAND DARK BLUE-GREEN
2 STRANDS DARK GREEN
2 STRANDS MEDIUM GREEN
2 STRANDS PALE OLIVE

NO. 3 LEAVES
2 STRANDS DEEP GREEN
2 STRANDS OLIVE GREEN
2 STRANDS LIGHT OLIVE
1 STRAND PALE GREEN

NO. 4 LEAVES
2 STRANDS DEEP GREEN
3 STRANDS DARK GREEN
2 STRANDS LIGHT GREEN

NO. 5 FLOWER
1 STRAND DARK BRICK RED
1 STRAND MEDIUM BRICK RED
2 STRANDS LIGHT BRICK RED
1 STRAND PALE BRICK RED
1 STRAND WHITE

NO. 6 FLOWER
1 STRAND BURNT ORANGE
2 STRANDS LIGHT ORANGE
3 STRANDS YELLOW
3 STRANDS WHITE

NO. 7 FLOWER
1 STRAND DARK BRICK RED
1 STRAND SCARLET
1 STRAND CORAL
2 STRANDS SALMON
1 STRAND PALE BRICK RED

NO. 8 FLOWER
2 STRANDS WHITE
4 STRANDS PALE BRICK RED
1 STRAND SALMON

NO. 9 FLOWER
2 STRANDS MAROON
2 STRANDS PINK
3 STRANDS WHITE

NO. 10 FLOWER
1 STRAND DEEP BLUE
1 STRAND ROYAL BLUE
1 STRAND LIGHT BLUE
3 STRANDS PALE BLUE

NO. 11 FLOWER
1 STRAND DEEP RED
1 STRAND DARK BRICK RED
3 STRANDS BURNT ORANGE
1 STRAND LIGHT ORANGE

NO. 12 FLOWER
8 STRANDS WHITE
1 STRAND LIGHT BLUE

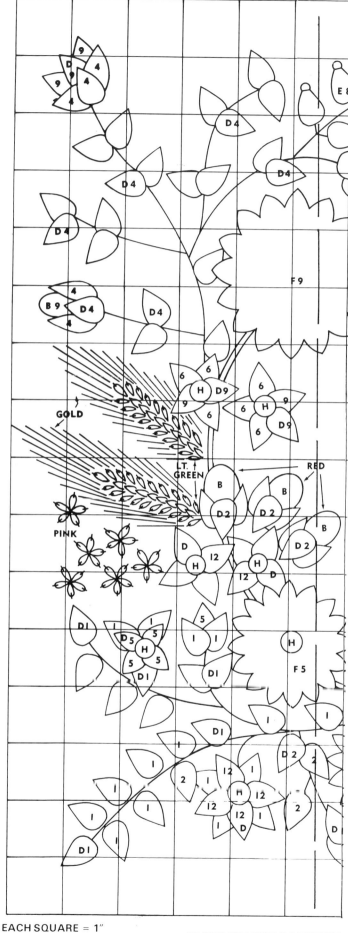

EACH SQUARE = 1"

EMBROIDERY PATTERN

282

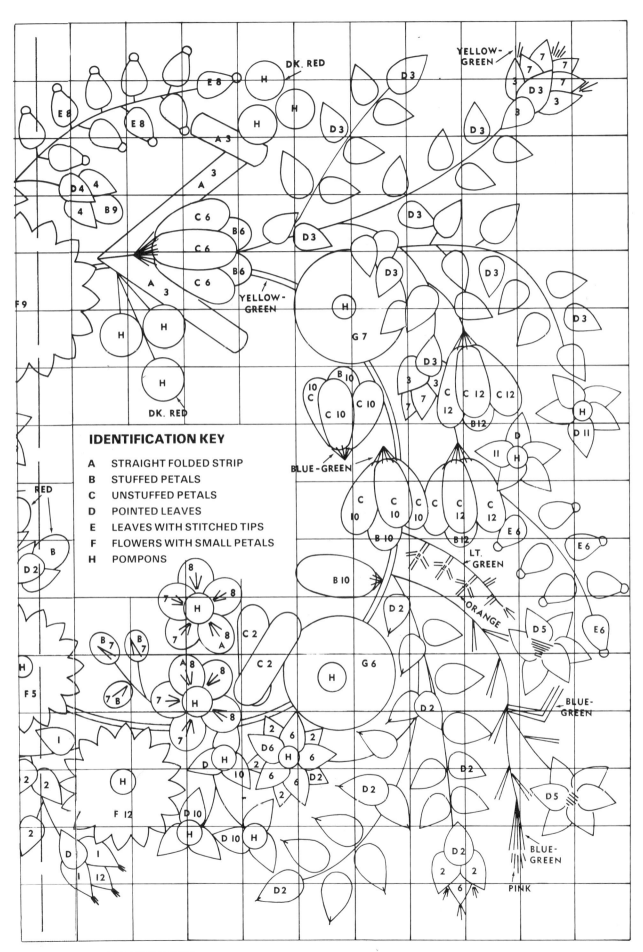

IDENTIFICATION KEY

A   STRAIGHT FOLDED STRIP
B   STUFFED PETALS
C   UNSTUFFED PETALS
D   POINTED LEAVES
E   LEAVES WITH STITCHED TIPS
F   FLOWERS WITH SMALL PETALS
H   POMPONS

FOR WOOLWORK WREATH   OVERLAP BROKEN LINES WHEN COPYING PATTERN

GIRL WITH GARLAND

ON PAGE 248

SIZE: 9" x 12"

EQUIPMENT: Scissors. Hard-lead pencil. Ruler. Large-eyed needle. Staple gun. For framing, if desired: Handsaw. Small, flat paintbrush. Hammer.

MATERIALS: Olive green hopsacking or other rustic fabric, 13" x 16". Scrap of smooth, tightly-woven white fabric for face. Tracing paper. Dressmakers' tracing or carbon paper. Turquoise and yellow sport yarn; black, white, and royal blue crochet cotton; yellow-green mohair; chartreuse pearl cotton. White sewing thread. Canvas stretchers, two 9" and two 12". Staples. For framing, if desired: Pine wood stripping, ¼" thick, ¾" wide, 4' long. Small finishing nails. Brown wrapping paper.

DIRECTIONS: Trace embroidered design from photograph on page 248 for actual size pattern. Center pattern on background fabric over carbon paper and go over all lines with hard-lead pencil. In same manner, transfer outline of head to white fabric; machine-stitch around outline. Cut out ¼" beyond stitching. Turn edge under along stitching and press. Baste in place on background fabric; slip-stitch to background along turned edge.

Assemble stretchers to make 9" x 12" frame. Stretch fabric over canvas stretchers and staple to back.

Referring to color photograph, embroider design on background fabric. Work turquoise dress in buttonhole stitch, outlining inner edges of sleeves with one row of chain stitch. Work black eyes in double cross-stitch. Work yellow bangs in long and short stitch; make braids by working cross-stitch over two strands of yarn. Embroider left hand in white satin stitch, black stockings and shoes in chain stitch. Work yellow-green garland in outline stitch and yellow-green blades of grass in straight stitch. Highlighted blades of grass in chartreuse pearl cotton are also worked in straight stitch. Work white flowers in straight stitch, royal blue buds in satin stitch. Yarn and thread of weights other than those specified may be substituted; just be sure to use a variety of weights and textures.

When embroidery is completed, re-stretch fabric if necessary so it is taut on frame; staple fabric to edges of stretchers. Cut wood stripping to fit around stretchers; stain, then nail to stretchers. Cut brown paper to fit and glue to back of frame.

YARN BOUQUET

ON PAGE 249

Note: The flowers in the yarn picture shown on page 249 were done in related shades of pink, mauve, lavender, violet, raspberry, plum, and white, the leaves in three shades of green, from bright yellow-green to dark olive; the shocking pink felt bowl was glued to the background of pale yellow-green hopsacking. Since only small amounts of twelve to fifteen different colors are required, this could be an attractive and satisfying way to utilize left-over yarns in fine and medium weights. If you choose a group of colors that look well together, it doesn't matter which you use for any particular flower, but it's easy to tell from the photograph which flowers were done in white; these should be scattered throughout the bouquet.

SIZE: 12" x 16"

EQUIPMENT: Hard-lead pencil. Ruler. Scissors. Large-eyed embroidery needles. Staple gun. For framing, if desired: Handsaw. Hammer. Small, flat paintbrush.

MATERIALS: Paper for pattern. Dressmakers' tracing or carbon paper. Homespun-type fabric, 17" x 21", in desired background color. Canvas stretchers, two 12" and two 16". Fine and medium-weight yarns in a variety of colors for flowers, three shades of green for leaves. Piece of felt, 5½" x 9", in desired color. Piece of white Venice lace edging, 1¼" to 1¾" wide, 8" long. For framing, if desired: Pine stripping, ¼" thick, 1¼" wide, 5' long. Small finishing nails. Wood stain in color to blend with background fabric. Brown wrapping paper. All-purpose glue.

DIRECTIONS: Enlarge pattern by copying on paper ruled in 1" squares. Center pattern on background fabric. Using dressmakers' carbon paper, transfer pattern to fabric.

Assemble canvas stretchers to make 12" x 16" frame. Stretch fabric over frame, making sure threads are straight and perpendicular; wrap edges around stretchers and staple to back. Transfer shape of bowl to piece of felt and cut out. (Top of bowl is straight; overhanging flowers and leaves are embroidered through felt and fabric.) Glue strip of Venice lace across bowl, 1" down from top. Glue bowl to background.

Use single strand of yarn in needle to embroider flowers, stems and leaves, following stitch diagrams and descriptions that start on page 286. Embroider solid lines in outline stitch, loops for leaves in lazy-daisy stitch, straight lines in straight stitch, pointed V-shapes in fly stitch, dots in French knots; fill in large areas of flowers between outlines in satin stitch.

When embroidery is completed, re-stretch fabric if necessary so it is taut on frame; fold excess fabric at corners miter-fashion and staple to back of stretchers. Measure and cut four pieces of pine stripping to fit around stretchers; stain according to manufacturer's directions and let dry. Nail stripping to stretchers at corners and in center of each side with finishing nails. Cut brown paper to fit and glue to back of frame.

EMBROIDERY PATTERN FOR YARN BOUQUET

EACH SQUARE - 1″

EMBROIDERY STITCHES

All basic embroidery stitches are easy. What may appear to be a difficult, complicated work is often the result of a well thought-out combination of several basic stitches to produce a richly-embroidered piece.

Practice the basic long and short, satin, outline, chain and lazy daisy stitches, then try some of the more complicated and decorative stitches. The more familiar you become with these stitches, the greater the excitement you can derive from developing your own combinations.

To practice the stitches, you need embroidery wools or thread, a linen or linen-like textured fabric and embroidery needles, which are available in sizes 1 to 6. Although an embroidery frame is optional, it is often preferable so that you can keep your stitches even and smooth.

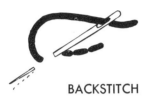

BACKSTITCH

BACKSTITCH Short stitches are placed end to end for a slim outline. This may be used alone for stems or borders, or to outline solid areas. The stitches just meet in the row, but the thread is carried under the fabric for twice the distance. Work from right to left, and carry the thread along the outline.

THREADED BACKSTITCH

THREADED BACKSTITCH Made in the same way as the threaded running stitch. A second color is worked in and out of the stitches of the backstitch without piercing the fabric. A third color may thread through to make loops on the opposite side as well. See dotted lines in illustration.

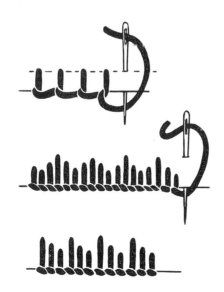

BLANKET STITCH

BLANKET STITCH A quicker stitch made in the same way as buttonhole stitch, but more widely spaced. This may be used on a raw edge of material that will not ravel, or on a turned edge of other fabric. The hem turn should be basted in place first, then the stitches placed over the width of the hem, and close enough together to hold it firmly in place. These two stitches are often used in applique work. For a most decorative effect vary the depth of the stitches of either buttonhole stitch or blanket stitch. These edgings may be done in varied colors, or a single color. See diagram of two variations, one a pyramid border, and one a sawtooth border.

CLOSED BLANKET STITCH Forms tiny inverted V's all along the edge. The needle is slanted to the left as shown in the diagram for the first stitch. The next stitch starts at the top of the same stitch and slants toward the right, taking up a bit of the lower edge to hold it firmly in place. Alternate stitches 1 and 2 all across the edge.

CLOSED BLANKET STITCH

CROSSED BLANKET STITCH Worked on the same premise of alternating angled stitches but the tops of the stitches cross instead of joining at the top.

CROSSED BLANKET STITCH

KNOTTED BLANKET STITCH Worked in two steps. First a loosely worked blanket stitch is formed. Then with the stitch still free from the fabric the needle is passed through the loop again to form a knot. This stitch or any of the above edge stitches may be used on knitted garments to form an edge finish, and may be substituted for a crocheted edge finish. In delicate yarns or embroidery thread it is very useful for baby garments.

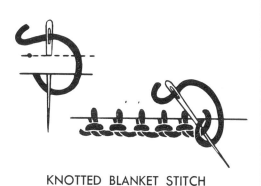

KNOTTED BLANKET STITCH

BOKHARA STITCH. One thread is laid across the area at a time, and couched in place as shown with small stitches, using the same thread. Good for filling large spaces.

BOKHARA STITCH

BRAID STITCH. This stitch should be worked closely and kept rather small. Wrap thread around needle once as shown to make an inverted loop; insert needle in fabric from top to bottom, thus twisting thread. Bring thread under needle tip. Pull needle through and tighten stitch carefully. Do not pull too tightly, or braid effect will be lost.

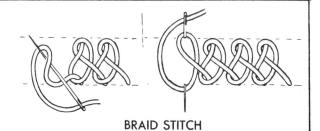

BRAID STITCH

EMBROIDERY STITCHES

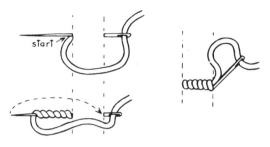

BULLION STITCH

BULLION STITCH. Insert point of needle in and out of fabric for length of stitch desired, do not pull needle through. Wrap thread around needle a number of times as shown, enough to fill space of stitch. Hold wrapped needle and fabric firmly with thumb and finger of left hand and pull needle through, drawing the thread up; this will reverse direction of the stitch, so that it lies in the space of first stitch. Insert needle in fabric at end of stitch.

BUTTONHOLE STITCH

BUTTONHOLE STITCH Worked from left to right. Bring needle up through fabric. Holding thread under left thumb, form a loop; then pass needle through fabric and over the looped thread; repeat.

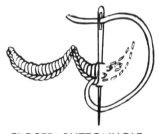

CLOSED BUTTONHOLE

CLOSED BUTTONHOLE STITCH Made in same manner as above, but with stitches close together. May be used to make scalloped edges as shown, or to fill an area by working several touching rows.

CHAIN STITCH

CHAIN STITCH Worked from top down. Bring needle up through fabric; hold loop with thumb and insert needle again at same place. Bring needle up a short distance away with thread looped under needle; repeat. Use for heavy outlines or as a filling, making rows of chains follow the outline of shape being filled.

WITH BACKSTITCH

CHAIN WITH BACKSTITCH, WITH COUCHING
Make backstitch down center of chain; or couch down on one side of chain as shown, using another color of yarn.

WITH COUCHING

HEAVY CHAIN Start with a small vertical stitch; then make a small loop through stitch, without picking up the fabric. Continue making loops under the second one above.

ROMAN CHAIN Made in a similar manner to regular chain, except that the loop ends are wide apart. Keep the width of the loops even and make them close together.

HEAVY CHAIN   ROMAN CHAIN

DOUBLE CHAIN Use when a broader border decoration is desired. This is done in same way as regular chain stitch except that the needle is angled from right to left, then from left to right as shown.

DOUBLE CHAIN

CHEVRON STITCH Involves herringbone stitch with a second step at each diagonal end. This consists of a perpendicular stitch marking each end.

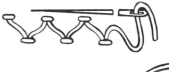

CHEVRON STITCH

CHEVRON PATTERN Is an allover area of chevron stitch simply consisting of repeated rows of the stitch. Each end stitch can be elaborated with repetition, or it may be worked out with a contrasting color stitch to resemble smocking.

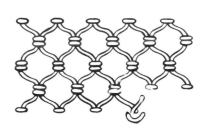

CHEVRON PATTERN

EMBROIDERY STITCHES

CORAL STITCH

CORAL STITCH Work from right to left. Bring thread up through fabric and hold with thumb. Take a small stitch across line, under and over thread. Pull up thread to form a small knot; repeat. May be used for fine stems.

COUCHING

COUCHING Lay thread to be couched across fabric. Use an embroidery frame. With the same color or a contrasting color of thread, take small stitches at even intervals over the laid thread. Couching can be used solidly for special effects on small areas.

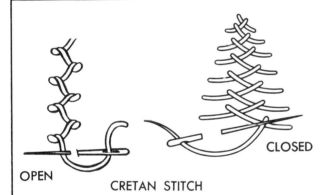

OPEN   **CLOSED**

CRETAN STITCH

CRETAN STITCH Made with the needle turned toward the center of the row, and the zigzags worked back and forth from right to left alternately as in catch stitch. *Closed Cretan Stitch* simply involves setting the stitches closer together. They may be closed up tight if desired in the same way as in closed chain stitch.

CROWN STITCH

CROWN STITCH. Make center straight stitch with two slightly shorter stitches at either side as shown; bring needle to front of fabric above and to left of three stitches. Then pass needle under the three stitches, but not through fabric. Insert needle in fabric again above and to right.

DIAGONAL FILLING

DIAGONAL FILLING Take stitches diagonally across area to be filled, in opposite directions. With contrasting color of thread, take short stitches across diagonal stitches where they cross, proceeding diagonally from top left to bottom right as shown.

DIAMOND STITCH. A good border decoration. Take a horizontal stitch from left to right and bring needle out just below as shown; pass needle under the stitch, under and over the thread and pull to make knot. Bring thread across and knot on opposite end of first stitch. Insert needle through fabric under knot and bring out a short distance below. Knot again at center of last stitch as shown; insert needle at opposite side and bring out just below.

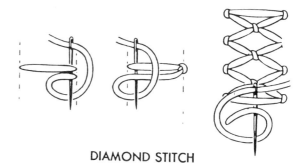

DIAMOND STITCH

ERMINE FILLING   Take an upright stitch. Bring up needle to right of upright, nearly at bottom; insert needle near top at left of upright. Bring needle out at left near bottom and insert at dot on right, near top. Use in rows, alternating spacing to fill area.

ERMINE FILLING

FAGOT FILLING   Take four or five stitches close together across fabric. Tie the stitches together at middle with two small stitches through fabric and around stitches to make a bundle.

FAGOT FILLING

FEATHERSTITCH   Worked along a single line outline with the needle slanted to touch the line. Placed first to the right, then to the left and so on alternately each time, the thread is passed under the needle for a buttonhole loop. This is similar to the chain stitch, but the loop is open, not closed. The branches may be kept all even with each stitch the same length, or they may be varied in length.

FEATHERSTITCH

EMBROIDERY STITCHES

CLOSED FEATHERSTITCH

CLOSED FEATHERSTITCH Worked along a double outline, with the needle kept erect along that line instead of being pointed toward the center. The same method of alternating the stitches from right to left is used as in plain featherstitching, but each stitch is taken at bottom of the stitch above.

STRAIGHT FEATHERSTITCH

STRAIGHT FEATHERSTITCH Formed in the same way with a double guideline and perpendicular stitches, but the ends of the thread do not meet the stitch above.

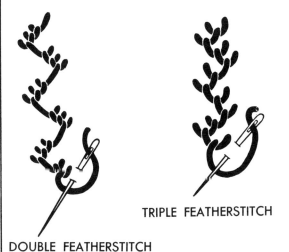

TRIPLE FEATHERSTITCH

DOUBLE FEATHERSTITCH

DOUBLE AND TRIPLE FEATHERSTITCH
There are many fancy variations of featherstitching. Two stitches may be taken at each side before alternating the side. This forms Double Featherstitch. Or three stitches may be taken to form Treble or Triple Featherstitching. A definite scallop or zigzag may be used as a guide in featherstitching.

FISHBONE STITCH

FISHBONE STITCH Starting at point, work as shown, slanting each succeeding stitch more until correct angle is obtained. Try with two needles and two shades of the same color.

FLAT STITCH   Work in similar manner as shown for small leaves and petals. For larger areas, work bands of stitch side by side, interlocking bands at sides to resemble braid effect at center.

FLAT STITCH

FLY STITCH   Similar to lazy daisy stitch, but the ends of the loop stitch are widely separated. Make a small backstitch to anchor the center in place, bringing needle up in position for next stitch. Can be used as a scattered space filler where a simple, textured background is desired.

FLY STITCH

FRENCH KNOT   Bring thread up through fabric. Wrap thread over and under needle, crossing beginning thread; insert needle in fabric close to where it came up. Thread may be used double to produce larger knots if desired.

FRENCH KNOT

HERRINGBONE STITCH   Worked between two lines. Bring thread up through lower line, insert needle in upper line a little to the right and take a short stitch to the left. Insert needle on lower line a little to the right and take a short stitch to the left. May be used for thick stems, or to connect two solid areas for softening effect.

HERRINGBONE

EMBROIDERY STITCHES

COUCHED HERRINGBONE

COUCHED HERRINGBONE   First make herringbone stitch. Then couch down with separate thread in contrasting color, if desired, where stitches cross.

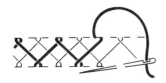

DOUBLE HERRINGBONE

DOUBLE HERRINGBONE STITCH   First make a row of herringbone stitch. Then make a second row over the first, placing the upper loops of the second row opposite the bottom loops of the first row and vice versa. Use same or a contrasting thread.

THREADED HERRINGBONE STITCH

THREADED HERRINGBONE STITCH   Created by running contrasting thread through the zigzags of the herringbone stitch without going through the fabric beneath. Diagram shows method of looping the thread around the crossed ends of the stitch.

INTERLACING STITCH

INTERLACING STITCH Make two rows of back stitch the distance apart desired, with stitches alternately spaced as shown. With a different color thread, loop stitches under back stitches and over thread as shown, alternating on top and bottom rows.

LAID STITCH

LAID STITCH Take stitches across the area to be filled, allowing a space between each, the size of another stitch. Fill these spaces with another series of stitches. This method conserves yarn and produces smooth, flat stitches, which may also be couched at intervals.

LAZY DAISY STITCH A popular stitch for making flower petals. Bring thread up at base of petal, hold loop with thumb and anchor it with a small stitch. Work lazy daisy petals in a ring with base of each close, for a round flower. May also be used as a filling stitch by scattering lazy daisies at random.

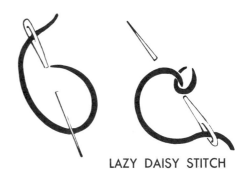

LAZY DAISY STITCH

LOCK STITCH This stitch may be worked in one or two colors and is a good banding design. Take a number of vertical stitches spaced as desired, either close or wide apart. With another thread, work from left to right as shown, along bottom section of stitches. Repeat across top in same manner.

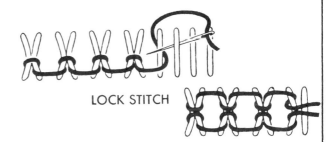

LOCK STITCH

LONG AND SHORT (KENSINGTON) STITCH Used to fill areas solidly, and shade colors. The first row is alternating long and short stitches, as shown. Following rows are stitches of equal length, worked at ends of short and long stitches. Regularity of the following rows depends on shape to be filled. Start at outer edge and work toward center or downward, keeping stitches generally in the same direction. Plan the stitches in an area so they fill it naturally and gracefully; it is helpful to mark with pencil the direction of some of the stitches. Shade colors into each other in rows.

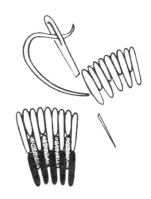

LONG AND SHORT STITCH

OPEN LEAF STITCH Start at base, left of center. Insert needle on opposite margin part way up, bring out at base, right of center. Continue as shown, alternating from side to side.

OPEN LEAF STITCH

EMBROIDERY STITCHES

OUTLINE STITCH

OUTLINE STITCH Bring needle up through fabric. With thread to left of needle, insert needle a short distance away and on the line and bring needle out again on the line. This stitch makes a fine line and is used around edge, for veining and detail lines.

ORIENTAL STITCH

ORIENTAL STITCH Since satin stitch is very popular in Oriental embroideries it is natural that one variation should be so named. This stitch is used to cover a fairly large area. Long floating threads of satin stitch are first placed vertically over the area. Another thread is then laid across them and held in place with short anchoring stitches spaced equally, as in couching. These anchoring stitches may match or contrast in color. The couched threads may also be laid across the background threads diagonally.

PALESTRINA STITCH

PALESTRINA STITCH To start, take a short diagonal stitch, bringing needle out below. Draw needle under stitch from top down and over thread as shown; pull up thread gently and repeat. For next stitch, insert needle to right from top to bottom, making a diagonal stitch and repeat. Keep stitches short and close together.

PEKINESE STITCH

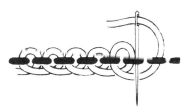

PEKINESE STITCH This is most effective when two colors or two different kinds of thread are used. First make a line of fairly large backstitches. Then make looped stitches through the backstitches.

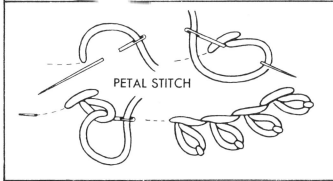

PETAL STITCH

PETAL STITCH This is actually a combination of outline stitch and lazy daisy stitch, worked simultaneously. Take one stitch of outline, bringing needle back to middle of stitch; make lazy daisy to one side, then continue with another stitch of outline.

ROUMANIAN STITCH May be used as a solid filling by making rows of stitches close together; or for borders or spot decorations. It is made in two steps. One long stitch is fastened in the center with a short couching stitch as shown in the diagrams.

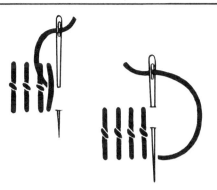

ROUMANIAN STITCH

RUNNING STITCH Worked along a line that is either straight or curved. It consists of evenly spaced stitches even in size. It may have variations with one stitch longer than the others placed at even intervals. It may be used for a flower stem, or to form veins in leaves. It may fill in an open area with an allover design of many rows.

RUNNING STITCH

THREADED RUNNING STITCH Another variation. The running stitch has a second thread worked through in a wave by passing the blunt pointed needle first through the right of one stitch then through from the left of the next stitch. This differs from the twisted stitch in which the second thread is always passed through from the right to the left.

THREADED RUNNING STITCH

WHIPPED RUNNING STITCH A combination of two stitches. First the running stitch is completed with evenly spaced stitches. Then the blunt pointed needle is threaded with contrasting color and worked through the stitches without going through the fabric. This gives the effect of a twisted cord.

WHIPPED RUNNING STITCH

EMBROIDERY STITCHES

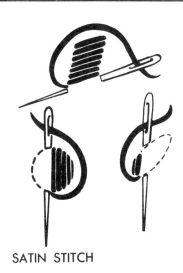

SATIN STITCH

SATIN STITCH Straight stitches worked side by side, usually slantwise, to fill small areas. For straight areas, work slantwise from top to bottom; for small circles, work center long stitch vertically first, then fill each side; for leaf shapes, work diagonally, starting at left edge.

SATIN STITCH LEAF

SATIN STITCH LEAF When area is large, divide into sections; work separately, changing direction of stitches for each section. Keep neat, firm outline and smooth, parallel stitches.

SCROLL STITCH

SCROLL STITCH. Working from left to right, loop thread around as shown; take a tiny stitch to the right with needle over both top and bottom of loop. Pull up thread to make knot. Space the tiny stitches far enough apart so scroll effect is clearly defined.

SEEDING STITCH

SEEDING STITCH Take two small stitches side by side, or one small single stitch. Scatter over area to be filled, alone or combined with other stitches.

SHADOW EMBROIDERY STITCH or CROSSED BACK-STITCH   On the right side of the work this stitch resembles two rows of backstitch and on the wrong side it looks like a closed herringbone stitch. Slant the needle and take a backstitch, bring it out above and to the left; then work the line above in same manner. Work on sheer materials for shadow effect.

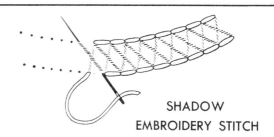

SHADOW EMBROIDERY STITCH

SIENESE STITCH. When worked closely, this stitch makes a good border. Make first vertical stitch, bring needle out at bottom and to right. Loop thread around vertical stitch as shown; insert needle at top to the right and bring out at bottom, ready for next vertical stitch.

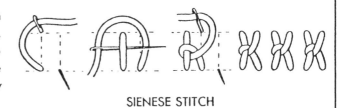

SIENESE STITCH

SORBELLO STITCH. First take a horizontal stitch and bring needle out below and left. Loop thread around horizontal stitch twice as shown; insert needle below and right; bring out to right even with horizontal stitch for beginning of another stitch.

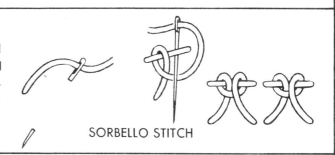

SORBELLO STITCH

SPLIT STITCH. When a fine line is desired, this stitch may be used. Work as for outline stitch, bring needle out through thread as shown, thus splitting it in half.

SPLIT STITCH

STAR FILLING   Work an upright cross, then a diagonal cross. They all are held together with a small cross worked over center of large crosses. May be used in combination with other stitches as filling.

STAR FILLING

STEM OR CREWEL STITCH   This differs from outline stitch in that the thread is held on the opposite side of the line; the needle is inserted to the right of the line and brought up to the left of the line, making a thick outline. This stitch may be used as a filling by working rows along side of each other.

STEM STITCH

EMBROIDERY STITCHES

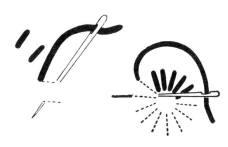

STRAIGHT STITCH

STRAIGHT STITCH   May be made as single stitches here and there in a design, or separated straight stitches in a ring or semicircle to form a flower. It may be made in various lengths and in clusters, but each stitch is always separated from the others.

THORN STITCH

THORN STITCH   Work in an embroidery frame. First lay a long thread across area. Take diagonal stitches from side to side to hold long thread in position as shown. Used for some stems to produce a special effect.

TRELLIS AND CROSS

TRELLIS AND CROSS   Take long stitches across area to be filled in, horizontally and vertically. Where stitches cross, work a small cross in same or contrasting color of thread. French knots are sometimes worked in center of squares.

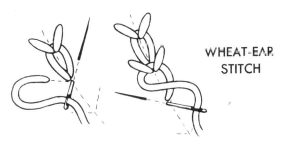

WHEAT-EAR STITCH

WHEAT-EAR STITCH. First make two straight stitches forming a V; bring needle out below at center. Pass needle under the two stitches and insert needle in fabric again at center below, making a chain loop.

HOW TO . . .

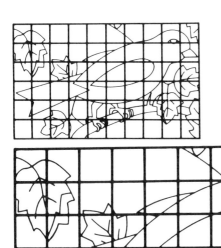

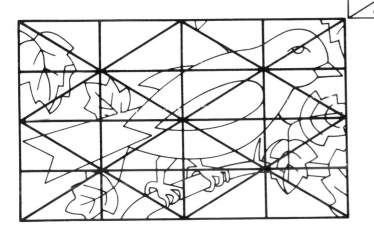

ENLARGE OR REDUCE A DESIGN

There are several ways to enlarge or reduce a design so that all parts remain in proportion.

SQUARE METHOD: If the design you want to use is not already marked off in squares, make a tracing of it. Mark tracing off in squares of ½″ to 2″, depending on size of the design—small squares for small designs, larger ones for larger designs. Mark a piece of paper with the same number of squares, similarly placed, in the space to be occupied by the enlarged design. For instance, if you want to make the design twice as high and twice as wide as the original, make the squares twice as large. Copy each part of design from smaller squares into corresponding large squares. Reverse procedure to reduce design to smaller size.

DIAGONAL METHOD: Make tracing of original design. Draw square or rectangle to fit around it. Draw second square or rectangle of same proportions to fit desired size of design. Draw diagonal lines from corners to opposite corners of both outlines, as shown. Draw horizontal and vertical lines to divide each outline equally. Copy design from divisions of original into corresponding larger or smaller divisions.

TRIMMINGS

Method requires two people. Tie one end of yarn around a pencil. Loop yarn over center of second pencil, then back to first, around first pencil and back to second, making as many strands between pencils as desired for thickness of cord. Length of yarn between pencils should be three times length of cord desired. Each person holds end of yarn just below pencil with one hand and twists pencil with other hand, keeping the yarn taut. When yarn begins to kink, catch it over a doorknob; keep yarn taut. One person now holds both pencils together while other grasps center of yarn, sliding hand down yarn and releasing yarn at short intervals, letting it twist.

Wind yarn around a cardboard cut to size of tassel desired, winding it 25 to 40 times around, depending on thickness of yarn and plumpness of tassel required. Tie strands tightly together around top as shown, leaving at least 3″ ends on ties; clip other end of strands. Wrap a piece of yarn lightly around strands a few times about ½″ or 1″ below top tie and knot. Trim ends of tassel evenly.

Cut strands of yarn double the length of fringe desired. Fold strands in half. Insert a crochet hook from front to back of edge where fringe is being made; pull through the folded end of yarn strand as shown in Fig. 1. Insert the two ends through loop as shown in Fig. 2 and pull ends to tighten fringe. Repeat across edge with each doubled strand, placing strands close together, or distance apart desired. For a fuller fringe, group a few strands together, and work as for one strand fringe.

The fringe may be knotted after all strands are in place along edge. To knot, separate the ends of two adjacent fringes (or divide grouped fringes in half); hold together the adjacent ends and knot 1″ or more below edge as shown in Fig. 3. Hold second end with one end of next fringe and knot together the same distance below edge as first knot. Continue across in this manner. A second row of knots may be made by separating the knotted ends again and knotting to gether the ends from two adjacent fringes in the same manner as for the first row of knots.

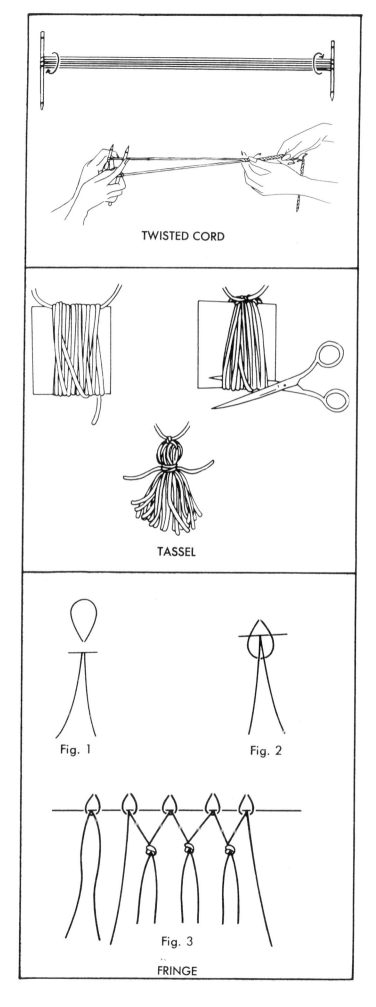

TWISTED CORD

TASSEL

Fig. 1   Fig. 2

Fig. 3

FRINGE

INDEX

Page numbers in bold indicate illustrations.